Underworld & Archetypes
Fully Illustrated

Dedication

For my wife Judy: without your love and encouragement this would not have been possible, and for our daughter Rachel: your creativity and imagination are inspirational, and for all those family, friends and teachers, both living and dead, who have accompanied me on and assisted my life journey whether they are aware of it or not.

Underworld & Archetypes Fully Illustrated

James Bennett

GOLDENAER

First published in 2015 by Goldenaer

Chapter 1, Out There, was previously published as "Beings From Outer Space" in Spring Journal by Lost Souls, Vol. 65, Spring 1999.

Chapter 2, Archetypal Underworld, was previously published as "The Earth's Dark Underbelly, The Archetypal Underworld and the Psychogeography of Descent" in Stella Maris, a Journal of Jungian Psychology Healing and Education Vol. 2, 2002—03; and also in Transitions, A Journal of Crossings Sept. 2011 by Pavement Pounders CIC.

Chapter 3, The Space Between, was previously published as "An Archetypal Background to Liminality: the Space Between" in Transitions 2A Journal of Crossings Nov. 2012 by Pavement Founders CIC.

Front cover: *The Return of Persephone* by Frederic Leighton 1891. Modified.

Goldenaer books are available in various formats,
go to Goldenaer.com to compare all media and prices. These include:
Printed books from Goldenaer.com/ Amazon.com/books/ and other outlets
Ebooks from Amazon.com/Kindle-eBooks/ and other outlets
iBooks from Apple.com/ibooks/

BISAC: REL114000 Religion / Ancient
BISAC: OCC000000 Body, Mind and Spirit / General
BISAC: SOC011000 Social Scince / Folklore & Mythology

Library of Congress Publisher's number 9907031
LOC: BL300-325 The myth. Comparative mythology
LOC: RC475-489 Therapeutics. Psychotherapy

1. Mythology 2. Psychotherapy 3. Underworld 4. Jungian Psychology

ISBN 978-0-9907031-3-6

Published by GOLDENAER, P.O. Box 14644, Portland, Oregon 97293, U.S.A.

Contents

Lycurgus reformed Spartan society in accordance with the Oracle at Delphi.

Lycurgus Consulting the Pythia by Eugène Delacroix ca1840

See page 79 *et seq* for full detail all the images in this book

Introduction

What on earth is an archetype you may well ask? The word is not found in the English language till the Mid 16th century and is derived from two Greek words *arche* (beginning, origin) and *tupos* (type, pattern, model). This notion was then taken up by Archetypal Psychologist C.G. Jung during the development of his ideas about the Collective Unconscious and expanded upon during his subsequent writings and by the many writers and psychologists influenced by and further developing his ideas. However, the idea remains elusive and difficult to clarify with any certainty. Looking at ourselves and our world through an archetypal lens involves immersing ourselves in images and stories. Archetypes are not things like the chair I'm sitting on as I write this, or those white hydrangeas I picked yesterday sitting in a vase on my dining room table, although it's possible that the chair and the flowers may become imbued with archetypal significance to the person witnessing them: the chair is a throne for kings and queens, the flowers emblematic of the earthly paradise for example. Archetypes are more like dynamic patterns accessible through experiencing the power of images to move us deeply and the ability to look at ourselves, our lives and our world metaphorically and imaginally. We witness the presence and action of archetypes in our nightly journeys to the dream world and in the myths and tales of different cultures and times, as well as in the developments and events of the world around us. Archetypes influence and act upon us whether we know it or not, since they emerge from the deepest structures of self and world.

The following pages written over a period of twelve years were originally published in three separate journals and are published here for the first time in an integrated format with illustrations. Although their subject matter is distinct, they are thematically linked and complement and enrich each other.

Out There looks at what is perhaps a tendency in all of us to want to fly away from the experience and tensions involved in our physical, biological existence here and its implied transience, and the dangers of acting out archetypal dramas through over identification with a one sided perspective (spiritual versus physical).

Underworld Archetypes explores the ancient traditions of descent and attempts to imagina-

Although some strive to rise above the earth it is often the earth gods who bring healing and wisdom.

Photos: *left, Attis*, Pergamon Museum. *right Naga couple*, Halebidu. wikimedia cc

tively restore the pathway down as a vital and necessary part of human and cultural experience that is encountered by all of us at some point in our lives. This journey is often feared and denied in the wider culture (up versus down).

The Space Between examines the image of the threshold and its attendant resonances in our individual lives, as well as in different times and cultures. It is a perspective that imaginatively addresses the territory of change, loss and transience as we navigate life's journey (here versus there).

My hope is that as you read these pages, you allow the stories, pictures and images to sit with you and speak to you. Perhaps this will spark your own connections and associations and open doors for you in unexpected and meaningful ways.

James Bennett

Cybele, Ceres, Flora, corybantes and cherubs, surrounded by natural abundance

Engraving by A. Tempesta, after himself, 1592. Wellcome Library, London, creative commons

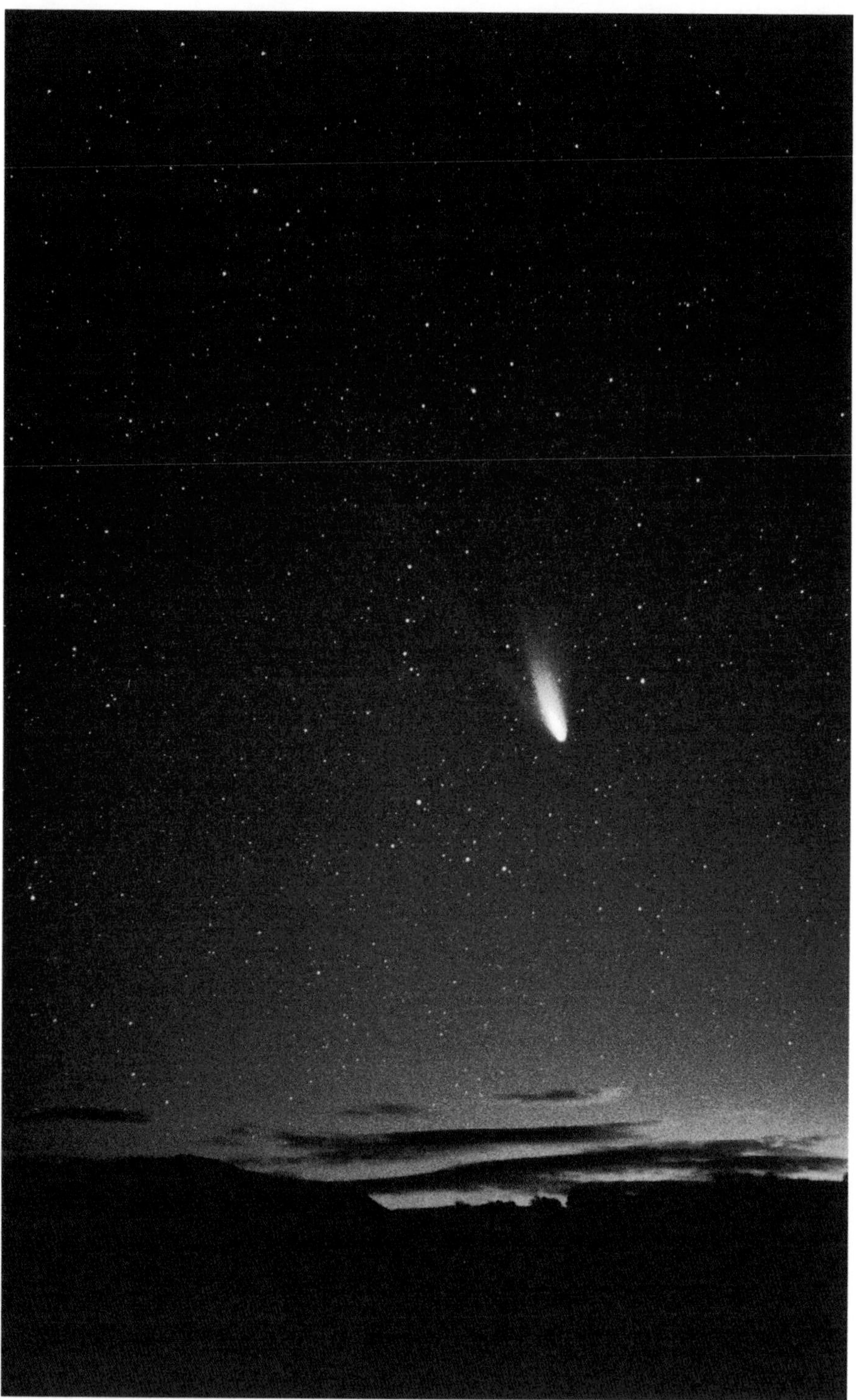

The Hale Bopp comet over central Arizona

Photo by Julias Whittington, flikr cc

Out There

Perhaps human beings have always gazed up at the night sky and have imagined the heavens above as dwelling place of the gods or spirits of the sky, or wondered about the life forms that exist out there on other planets. The following chapter explores how over identification with our own longings and conflicts projected onto the world above, can lead to imbalances and encourage what author John Welwood has called "spiritual bypassing" and "premature transcendence" (the desire to by-pass our wounded humanity). This kind of ego inflation can result in a person being flooded by archetypal contents with catastrophic and tragic results. It may be that the extreme example cited reflects a wider cultural tendency to seek to fly away from our mortality, the tensions involved in being human and the issues confronting planet Earth.

Supposed UFO sighting in Shreveport, Louisiana, 2010.

Photo by Dragon Rai, flikr cc

The Heaven's Gate suicides, which took place in March 1997, are understandable from a perspective as yet unrepresented in commentaries. The term "identification with an archetype" was originally used by C.G. Jung when he wrote about the dangers of encountering the world of images and symbols, what he called the Collective Unconscious, what some call the Imaginal World (Henry Corbin 1972). While it may be true that the seekers of Heaven's Gate were exposed to forms of mind control often found in such cults, I believe there is something else that accounts for, in addition to this, the intensity of attachment to their leader, and the apparent disregard and joy with which they "shed their containers."

The "Heaven's Gate" suicides

Marshall Applewhite, leader of the Heavens Gate cult, often broadcast his message on TV.

1. *Editors' Note:* During this event, which took place in Rancho Sante Fe, a suburb north of San Diego, thirty-nine members of a spiritual group called Heavens' Gate were found dead in the rented mansion that had been their home. They had committed suicide by swallowing apple sauce or pudding laced with phenobarbital and chased down with vodka, followed by suffocation with plastic bags. Their leader, Marshall Herff Applewhite, had taught his followers (who all had short hair and wore baggy clothes so as not to show their sexuality and to avoid lust and other earthly appetites) to prepare for a "Higher Kingdom." The group was founded in 1975, and members had lived cheaply in the house which was furnished with items from discount stores. Newspaper reports said members had supported themselves by designing websites for the Internet and were known for their efficiency and ability. The group suicide was planned to coincide with the comet Hale-Bopp's passing by close to Earth. Applewhite preached his doctrine, a strange combination of beliefs, on an Internet website in an attempt to recruit more followers. He claimed that an UFO coming from the "Next Level Above Human" was following in the slipstream of the comet and had come to take him and his followers home. This was the appointed time to shed their "containers," the word the group used for their bodies. Almost all of them were found wearing new, black Nike running sneakers and diamond shaped purple shrouds over their faces and upper bodies. Each one of the dead had packed a suitcase with clothes, notebooks, and lip-balm, with a five-dollar bill and a stash of quarters in their pockets. Evidently, Applewhite and some of the other men had been castrated years before this collective suicide.

The Hale Bopp comet passed over our heads.

Hale-bopp 3. Photo by John Tewell, flikr cc

If we are dealing with a flight from earth, a fleeing from physical, embodied experience in favor of the journey to Heaven, what is it that is going on?

Skrilex Mother Ship. Photo by Nicki Spunar, flikr cc. Modifed by enlarging elements

The archetypal context of these suicides is discernible in various cultural trends of the last few years, namely the increase in stories of abductions by aliens and the widespread belief regularly visited by alien spacecraft and that the government is covering this up. Part of this archetypal context is the scenario presented in the film, *Close Encounters of the Third Kind*, where Richard Dreyfuss' character becomes one of the first humans to leave earth in a craft belonging to a civilization more technologically and, it appears, spiritually sophisticated than our own. We might also think of the film *E.T*, where the stranded alien, strangely reptilian and possessed of wide-eyed innocence, longs to rejoin the ship that will take him to his planet of origin.

The dark side of this archetypal context is expressed in films such as *Independence Day*, where the aliens visiting earth are hostile and have as their goal the destruction of humanity and the exploitation of the planet. Even the reported abduction experiences are divided between those who describe cold, ruthless, and clinical beings who perform Nazi-style experiments on human subjects and those who talk of benign encounters with spiritual beings here to teach us about the oneness of everything and the power of love. While watching Independence Day, it seems apparent that the aliens represent a projection of our darker relationship to planet earth: we are the creatures who threaten to dominate, exploit, and create a Hell here. We are confronting the Darth Vaders of our imaginings and are trying to

We are caught between the archetypal poles of heaven and earth, spirit and matter, up and down. We are trying to work out a way to resolve the tensions which exist between these different parts of our being.

Ufo in Hawaii by Keoni Canri, flikr cc

resolve the issue of the wise use of power-or "The Force" as it is called in the *Star Wars Trilogy* (recently resurrected for a new generation).

This is linked to the Heaven's Gate cult and the desire to transcend the experience of embodied sensual life which was reflected in their lives and actions. What they outwardly displayed could be a yearning in the rest of us. Most of us, to one degree or another, are caught between the archetypal poles of heaven and earth, spirit and matter, up and down. We are trying to work out a way to resolve the tensions which exist between these different parts of our being and the splits which are present there by virtue of the fact that they are opposites-or at least apparently so. There is a tendency for us to deny the spiritual dimension and focus entirely on the material or to devalue the physical realm and elevate the spiritual. Either way, there is a degrading of what it means to be human, and a loss of soul occurs.

If we are dealing with a flight from earth, a fleeing from physical, embodied experience in favor of a journey to Heaven, what is it that is going on? What we run away from we feel a strong pull towards, or we would not need to fly away. If we try to deny its hold on us, we secretly end up serving it, albeit in a distorted way. We can end up be-

A silver plate showing Cybele and her consort Attis riding in a chariot drawn by four lions, surrounded by dancing *Korybantes*.

Cybele and her consort. Silver plate ca 362 AD, Archaeological Museum of Milan

ing possessed by an archetype or, to put it another way, what we repress ends up consuming us.

Consider the voluntary castration of several of the male cultists. While horrifying to our sensibilities, there are precedents for this in history. The priests of Cybele, following the example of the god Attis, castrated themselves in a religious frenzy in order to become servants of the Goddess and serve in her temple alongside her priestesses. Cybele, a Near-Eastern goddess whose worship spread to Greece and Rome from Asia Minor, is a Great Mother goddess with chthonic characteris-

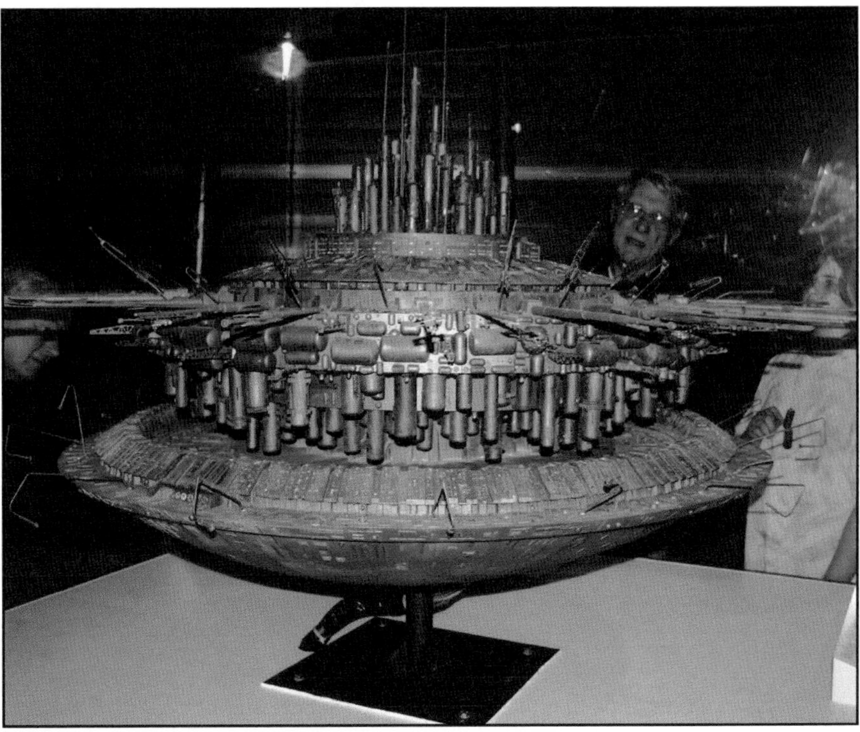

This silver model was the Mother Ship used to film "Close Encounters of the Third Kind".

National Air and Space Museum, Dulles, VA. Photo by Ryan Soma, flikr cc

tics that include her archetypal associations with birth, sex, and death. Her name has been etymologically linked to words for crypt and cave, and she has been associated with the ancient figure of the Black Goddess, whose later forms include the Black Madonnas connected with shrines in Europe (including the most famous in Einsedeln, Switzerland). When she appeared in Rome in 204 BCE, one of her images was a black meteorite—the womb (space) from which matter comes. She appears to be a kind of fertility goddess.

It seems possible that the Heaven's Gate cultists, while consciously repudiating the physical realm and sexuality, were unconsciously worshipers of a Great Mother in her dark aspect and were caught up in an archetypal drama that was catalyzed by their leaders. While this may seem surprising, other details pointing to this can be found in the patchwork cosmology that their leader, Applewhite, created.

The Myth of Cybele and Attis

The daemon *Agdistis* was both male and female. But the Olympian gods, fearing Agdistis, cut off the male organ and cast it away. By a sequence of changes that discard was reborn as Attis who was of such godlike beauty that Agdistis, in the form of Cybele, fell in love with him. However Attis was promised to wed the king's daughter, so Agdistis as Cybele, burst in on the wedding in such transcendent power that Attis in ecstacy cut off his testicles, and the king followed suit, devoting themselves to worship her. Then Agdistis repented and saw to it that the body of Attis should neither rot at all nor decay. ~ Wikipedia

Castration clamp decorated at the top with busts of Cybele and her lover Attis.

Castration clamp, bronze, ca 100-300 AD, found in River Thames, London. The busts down the handles are the Roman deities associated with the days of the week

Roman statue of Attis after his emasculation; his head glowing with starry rays.

Apse of the Shrine of Attis, Rome, photo wikimedia c

According to Applewhite the Mother Ship and its fleet, which he and his followers were to rendezvous with in the wake of the comet, had come from the core of the planet Pluto (named after the god of the Underworld). This gives the "Next Level" fleet decidedly chthonic associations. After "shedding their containers," the Heaven's Gaters were to enter the Mother Ship--which could be read as the body of the Great Mother--and return to their home in the core of Pluto. Applewhite—identified as he was with the dying/resurrecting Jesus, and thereby linking himself to a whole train of such sacrificial gods, including the self-castrator Attis whose ancient rites were celebrated between March 23 and 25 each year—

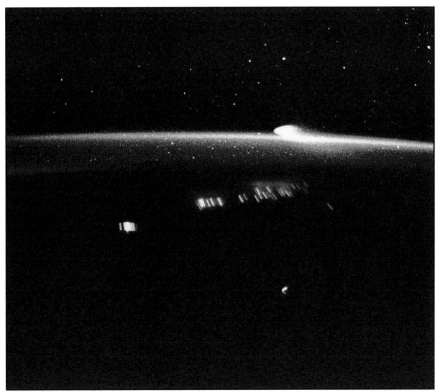

Photo of the Hale Bopp comet with airglow and city lights below.

Photo courtesy of NASA

Attis rose above the earth.

Attis; terracotta from Myrina, 1st century BCE. Pergamon Museum. Photo by Wolfgang Sauber, wikimedia c

chose this time frame to play out the archetypal drama. In the Cybele/Attis rituals, March 24 was known as the Day of Blood, since it was the day the self-mutilation occurred. Therefore, it is archetypally appropriate that it was during these few days that the Heaven's Gaters chose to move to their"Next Level", acting out the initiatory descent into the Underworld that they were trying to fly away from.

The similarities continue. The worshippers of Cybele/Attis mutilated themselves at the foot of a sacred pine tree which had been decorated with wreaths of violets two days before. The Heaven's Gaters were found dead with purple drapes over their faces. Perhaps an uncanny echo of the ancient rites, the color was later associated with the death and resurrection of Jesus at Easter. In their state of archetypal identification, did they literalize the archetype of death and rebirth, activated as it is each year by the advent of spring (when,

"The alchemical furnace of the Great Mother" displays her omnipotence, her strength and her multi-breasted nourishment. Her body shows the animal, vegetable and mineral realms that she rules as *Anima Mundi* (World Soul). Stoking her furnace is Eros, stepping into the place of his unnamed dead father whose crown and gear lie at his feet.

Actorun Chymicorum Holmiensum by Urbani Hierne, Stockholm 1712

Traditionally, one enters the Underworld by descending into the body of the Earth through openings in the ground into caverns or crypts, both literally or imaginally as in shamanic journeys.

Natural Bridge Caverns, VA. By Patrick Rohe, flikr cc

incidentally, the suicide rate tends to increase each year)?

What can be understood by these examples is that Heaven and Earth are a *syzygy* "yoked together". They are a pair of opposites which dance together and are woven into each other. Persons and groups who deny one side of the pair are in danger of being flooded with archetypal contents which they then act out. Part of the archetypal dimension of the Earth Pole of Being[1] is the tradition of the Underworld (which Christianity de-

---

1 There are two cosmic principles in Chinese philosophy: *Yin* and *Yang*. They are conceived of as two sides of a circle divided into light and dark, known as the *t'ai chi t'u* = the supreme ultimate. The Earth pole of the polarity is the dark or *Yin* segment of the circle. For a discussion of this concept, see Chapter 10 of Edward Whitmont's Return of the Goddess. See also the *I Ching* (London: Routledge, 1950), where there is a commentary by the Confucian School which refers to the archetypal principles of Heaven and Earth. "There are no greater Primal images than heaven and earth." (319)

The shaman's universe consists of three levels. Human beings live on the Earth in a middle world, between an upper world and a lower world. The three zones are linked by a central vertical axis.

The world tree Yggdrasil and some of its inhabitants by Friedrich Wilhelm Heine, 1886. wikimedia c

monized long ago and renamed Hell), thus making people in our culture vulnerable to a kind of archetypal splitting. Traditionally, one enters the Underworld by descending into the body of the Earth—both literally (as in caves or crypts)—or imaginally (through openings in the ground or descending into caverns) as in shamanic journeys. The suppression of the Earth pole of Being[2], which includes our connection to the Underworld, risks the danger that this beautiful planet

2 See Mircea Eliade, Shamanism: Archaic Techniques of Ecstasy (Princeton: Princeton UP, 1972). In this book Eliade describes the shaman's universe as consisting of three levels. Human beings live on the Earth in a middle world, between an upper world and a lower world (the latter two are often associated with the sky and the underworld). The three zones are usually linked by a central vertical axis, which is sometimes referred to as the *Axis Mundi* or Axis of the World.

The embrace of the Earth Pole of Being involves a descent into the Underworld and is an acknowledgment of the unity that exists between humans and the soul of the world.

Ta Prohm Angkor temple, Cambodia phot by Shankar S., flikr cc

we steward will become a literal Hell due to its devaluation and degradation.

Far from indulging in a kind of manic flight from our corporeal existence and then from the Earth-which is our home just as much as our home is at the level of the stars—it seems that what is required is exactly the opposite. We need to embrace our descent, and inhabit our physical presence in our world (which includes desires and attachments), and do all this with as much awareness as we can. This is the alchemical process of transforming lead into gold or dying before you die, as the Sufis image it. We are cooked in the cauldron of matter. This embrace of the Earth pole of Being[3] also involves a descent into the Underworld and is an acknowledgment of the unity that exists between humans and the soul of the world. For as R. J. Stewart points out in

3 See James Hillman on the levels of "earth" in the section "Underground and Underworld," The Dream and the Underworld. See also Hillman on "Nature Alive" in his essay "Pan," quoted in A Blue Fire (Harper Perennial, 1989).

This descent also involves embracing our mortality, as painful as this can be.

Opening of roadside tomb, Galilee, by James Emery, flikr cc

his book, *The Underworld Initiation*, there is an ancient tradition which states that, if we go deep enough into the Underworld, we emerge among the stars. Or, following the Gnostics, we do the soul work of releasing the sparks of spirit in matter. This is to accept our role as stewards of the planet.

This descent also involves embracing our mortality, as painful as this can be. The Underworld journey is a process of shedding and stripping away as much as it is also a cauldron of renewal. It is perhaps significant that a large number of Heaven's Gaters were aged forty to fifty and older. The events which led to their deaths could be viewed as a mid-life passage. It seems they chose to literalize the death/rebirth archetype that is an integral part of the midlife initiation, opting for a kind of premature transcendence[4] or pseudo-resurrection rather than suffering through the confrontation with personal death that is a painful yet essential part of human experience.

4 See John Welwood, *Towards a Psychology of Awakening* (Shambala 2002 reprint).

The Underworld journey is a process of shedding and stripping away.

Fall of the Titans by Cornelis Corneliszoon van Haarlem ca 1559. Statens Museum for Kunst, Copenhagen, Denmark. wikimedia c

The myths and legends of the place below the earth are an ancient tradition that predate later distorted cultural depictions of this Underworld .... This book offers the possibility of restoring us to a sense of the sacredness of matter and our place in the wider universe of which we are a part.

Neolithic long-barrow tomb, 3590-3400 BCE. Wayland's Smithy, Ashbury, Oxfordshire, England. Photo by AndrewBowde, flikr cc

Archetypal Underworld

> "Let me take you down, 'cos I'm going..."
> John Lennon

The myths and legends of the place below the earth are an ancient tradition that predate later distorted cultural depictions of this Underworld realm as a landscape of demonic persecution, one to be avoided at all costs. The following exploration examines the archetypal territory involved in the journey of descent to this realm and the return, as revealed in the stories and tales of many cultures, the nightly process of dreaming and the losses and traumas encountered in the course of life. This imaginal perspective offers the possibility of restoring us to a sense of the sacredness of matter and our place in the wider universe of which we are a part.

"As Above, So Below"[1]

A surprisingly large number of people in the United States of America believe in the literal existence of Hell—60% according to a Gallup Poll taken in the 1990s, rising to 69% in 2007.[2]

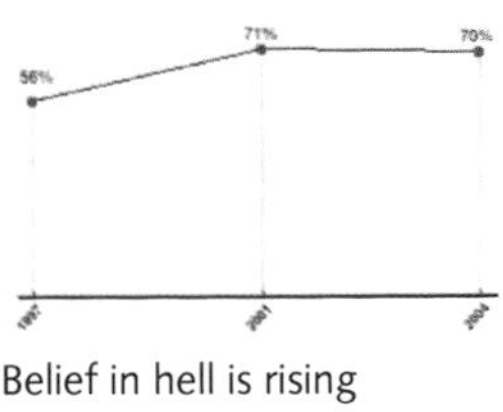

Belief in hell is rising

Gallup Poll results

Those of a scientific/materialist persuasion can put the persistence of these beliefs down to childish superstition and bewail the fact that such primitive ideas still hold sway in the 21st century. Or if we are of a spiritual bent, but drawn to less

1 From *The Emerald Tablet of Hermes Trismegistus*, an important foundation for the development of Hermetic Philosophy in the 15th and 16th centuries. According to legend, it was discovered by Apollonius of Tyana, in the 1st century AD. He entered a hidden cave and took the tablet from the hands of dead Hermes himself. See Matthews, Caitlin and Matthews, John (1986). *The Western Way: A Practical Guide to the Western Mystery* Tradition. Arkana.

2 Study quoted in Turner, Alice K. (1995). *The History of Hell.* Harvest, and in online Gallup Poll results (2004 and May 10th–13th 2007).

The religious myth of Hell as a place of punishment and demonic persecution is a recent one-sided distortion of an imagery that is fundamental to the structure of consciousness.

Detail of *The Last Judgement* by Stefan Lochner 1435, Church of St Laurence, Köln, Germany. Photo by Staedelmuseum.

fundamentalist versions of spirituality, we can comfort ourselves with the notion that we have developed a more evolved cosmology that doesn't require a concept of Hell to understand our place in the universe.[3] Either way, we can avoid looking down, wondering about the pull such beliefs exert on us, about the deep soul need people seem to have to sense themselves as existing in a mythological universe. But the findings of the Gallup Poll suggest that there is a psychomythological need for a "down there" that people want to locate themselves in relation to, even if the presence of such a location is negative.

As we shall see, this need has a long history of expression, dating back to the dawn of humankind: the traditional Christian myth of Hell as a place of punishment and demonic persecution being a much later and one-sided development of an imagery that may be fundamental to the structure of consciousness.

The etymological roots of the English word Hell—which help convey its present meaning—

3 See Hillman, James (1975). *Re-Visioning Psychology.* Harper Perennial, p. 154, *Psyche and Myths* on the inevitability of "mythologizing".

The root of the word *Hell* can be found in hill, hole, whole, heal, hall, hollow, hull of a nut, heel of the foot, and hold of a ship. They are all rooted in the Anglo-Saxon *helan* meaning to cover or hide.

Neolithic grave in Knowth, Ireland. Photo by shes_so_high, flikr cc

can be found in heel (as in that part of the foot hidden from above),[4] hill, hole, whole, heal, hall, hull (as of a nut), hollow, holt (as in a low hill covered by trees), and hold (as in a ship). They are all rooted in the Anglo-Saxon *helan*: to cover or hide.[5]

In *The Dream and the Underworld*,[6] James Hillman points out that the Latin *cella* (subterranean storeroom) is etymologically related to the old Irish *cuile* (cellar) and *cel* (death), which in turn relate to our word Hell. The *cel* is also present in the words celestial and ceiling, adding an intriguing heavenly dimension to a mythological

4 The Semang people believe that at death the soul leaves the body through the heel. The Greek hero Achilles was only vulnerable to death through his heel. See Chevalier, Jean & Gheerbrant, Alain (1994). *The Penguin Dictionary of Symbols.* Penguin.

5 Quoted in J. W. Hanson (1888). *The Bible Hel.* Universalist Publishing House.

6 Hillman, James (1979). *The Dream and The Underworld.* Perennial.

Hel is the name of the Norse goddess of the Underworld.

Hel. illustration by Johannes Gehrts 1889, published in *Walhall Germanische Gotter und Heldensagen* 1903

territory otherwise associated with a downward direction.

Hidden within this verbal landscape we have here a whole imaginary world: that of a hidden place beneath the earth, connected with death which is a storehouse as well as a realm of wholeness and healing. But it is also related to the heavenly sphere. A holy hole! It is a realm resonant with "imprisonment" (as in our word "cell') as well as with "secrets" (as in our word "occult'").

It is worth noting that Hel or Hela, daughter of the Trickster Loki—a god whose eventual fate was imprisonment—was the Norse goddess of the Underworld, the equivalent of the Greek Persephone, the Sumerian Ereshkigal and the Black Madonna of the Christian tradition.[7] Words become keys that can unlock mysteries and point to forgotten realms of correspondence.

7 For further reading see Begg, Ean (1985). *The Cult of the Black Virgin.* Arkana; Bleakley, Alan (1989). *Earth's Embrace, Archetypal Psychology's Challenge to the Growth Movement.* Gateway; Woodman, Marion & Dickson, Elinor (1996). *Dancing in the Flames, The Dark Goddess and the Transformation of Consciousness.* Shambhala; Whitmont, Edward C. (1984). *Return of the Goddess.* Crossroad. Bennett, James (1999). "Beings From Outer Space'. *Spring: A Journal of Archetype and Culture,* No. 65, Lost Souls, Spring and Summer 1999.

Isis, bronze relief ca 99—199 AD, found in Syria. Louvre Museum, Paris. Photo © Marie-Lan Nguyen, Creative Commons

Isis

The black madonnas and virgins of medieval Europe, still found in Christian churches to this day, are associated with crypts and often considered to represent a connection to a much older figure, both the great goddess Cybele, whose name is etymologically linked to the words for crypt and cave and was originally worshipped in the form of a black stone, and Isis, the Egyptian goddess, who is portrayed with dark skin and is associated with a ship festival held every year in the spring. The black virgin can be viewed as the Underworld aspect of the Great Goddess in her many forms (including the Virgin Mary in her Queen of Heaven aspect). Cybele is akin to Kali (Hindu), Hecate (Greek) and Cerridwen (Celtic) among others. According to Alan Bleakley the Black Goddess governs our night-time, our dreamworld, and our undiscovered potentials.

Were prehistoric painted caves the first temples? Places where initiates could experience visions in trance and undergo initiatory death and rebirth within the sacred body of the earth goddess?

Stone-age Cave paintings at Lascaux II, France. Photo 2008 by Jack Versloot, flikr cc

In traditions that predate the arrival of Christianity, this forgotten and devalued realm was known as the Underworld, abode of the ancestors and the spirits of the dead, and its mythological roots appear to travel back deeply into the mists of time. In a remarkable book, *The Strong Eye of Shamanism,*[8] Robert Ryan convincingly argues for the existence of initiatory rituals of descent involving early peoples' caves such as those in Lascaux, Les Trois Freres and Pech-Merle in France and the startlingly beautiful paintings that still survive there. Ryan suggests that the caves were in essence the first temples,[9] which were simultaneously incubation chambers, places where initiates could experience visions in trance and undergo initiatory death and rebirth in the sacred body of the earth goddess.

---

8 Ryan, Robert (1999). *The Strong Eye of Shamanism.* Inner Traditions.

9 Compare Willetts: "The Cretan archaeological record confirms the Greek tradition that caves were ... the earliest shrines .... " Willetts, R. F. (1962). Cretan Cults and Festivals. New York. An examination of Mithraism, "a religion of the crypt', is fascinating in terms of the notion of caves as places of worship. See Turcan, Robert (1996). *The Cults of the Roman Empire.* Blackwell.

The archetypal journey of descent in myth and fairy tales is a theme common in dreams and fantasies of modern people.

Old Stairs. Photo by Austin White, flikr cc.

Alain Danielou, in a comment that links the imagery of descent into Hell with what we are referring to here, writes: "The myth of the descent into Hell also evokes a return to the womb of Mother Earth".[10] Here womb and tomb are conceived of as being the same place. Sometimes the artist/shamans would literally have to put life and limb on the line, as there are paintings that could only have been completed at great personal risk. At the very least, the journey into the heart of the cave was arduous, involving squeezing through a narrow passage or opening. The caves are places that evoke altered states of consciousness in those who entered (an experience of what we would call ego death in psychological language) and thus moved the initiates closer to the sacred. We can imagine that they would have emerged cleansed, rejuvenated and reborn.

---

10 Danielou, Alain (1984). *Gods of Love and Ecstasy - The Traditions of Shiva and Dionysus.* Inner Traditions.

The archetypal journey of descent can appear in images of passing beneath the sea, lakes, wells or ponds.

Jonah and the Whale, from *Jami al-Tavarikh Compendium of Chronicles.* ca 1400. wikimedia c.

That this universal and archetypal journey of descent is largely hidden, due to ignorance as well as its own essential nature, does not mean it will disappear altogether. A theme common in literature and Jungian psychology[11] alike, many references are made to it in myth and in fairy tale or in dreams and fantasies of modern people. Among some of the heroes and heroines, goddesses and gods most notably connected with the journey to the Underworld are Aeneas; Dionysus; Gilgamesh; Hercules; Hermes; Inanna; Jesus; Odysseus; Orpheus and Persephone.

In people's dreams, as in fairy stories, the archetype shows up in images of passing beneath the earth, sea, lakes, wells or ponds. Sometimes

In dreams of descent cellars, basements, caves and crypts, and dark alleys feature prominently.

Untergrundbewegung in Greece.

11 In literature, among other references, we think of Dante's *Inferno*, Caroll's *Alice in Wonderland* and her trip down the Rabbit Hole, Jules Verne's *20,000 Leagues Under the Sea*, Conrad's *Heart of Darkness*, and Doris Lessing's *Briefing for a Descent into Hell.* We may also think of the Bible tale of Jonah's sojourn in the belly of the whale. Jung's autobiographical account in *Memories, Dreams and Reflections* (Vintage, 1989), p. 158, of his "big" dream of descent, on which he founded his theory of the Collective Unconscious is relevant. Among many fairy tales that deal with the theme are Sinbad the Sailor, Aladdin and the Wonderful Lamp, King Kojata, The Nixie and the Pond and Mother Holle.

In people's dreams, as in fairy stories, the archetype shows up in images of being swallowed by monsters, dragons or fierce beasts.

Detail of *An archangel locks the Hellmouth* ca 1129–1161, from *the Winchester Psalter.* British Library, London

there is fire down there, sometimes ice,[12] sometimes mists and shadows or sometimes even another world that seems to mirror this one. Cellars, basements, caves and crypts, or images of being swallowed by monsters, dragons or fierce beasts feature prominently, as do earthquakes or the collapse of buildings, images of dismemberment and death or dark alleys where unsavory characters lurk. Sometimes beings or people who live beneath the earth are encountered, like the fairy folk of old, who were linked with the mounds and barrows (chambered tombs) of ancient Europe.[13]

---

12 *In The Dream and the Underworld,* Hillman argues that the Night Sea-Journey and the Underworld Journey are essentially different in kind (see p. 168 on Ice and p.110, Hercules in the House of Hades), but I think that the journey brings an altered perspective, not neccesarily a strengthening of the heroic ego, see appendix 1.

13 See Chapter VI, Devereux, Paul (1992). *Symbolic Landscapes - The Dreamtime Earth and Avebury's Open Secrets.* Gothic Image. See also Miller, Hamish & Broadhurst, Paul (1989). *The Sun and the Serpent.* Pendragon Press, which is an exploration of "the Serpent Power" associated with sites like barrows and stone circles.

Our culture is obsessed with stories about angels and space aliens, with a fixation on spiritual practices which help us rise above our earthly limitations and purify our base concerns.

Focus on the light, we are encouraged, and reject the dark, the depths.

lower left: sculpture: *Angels*, 1841, Martyrs' Square, Brussels. Photo by Dr Leslie Sachs, flikr cc

top right: stained glass window at St Pieterskerk, Turhout, Belgium. Photo by Eddy Van 3000. flikr cc

As we shall see, it can be argued that the nightly process of dreaming is a trip we all take to the "land below"", willingly or not. From this perspective, psyche is Underworld.[14]

Despite the persistence of this imagery and theme, modern Western culture doesn't hold with the notion of an Underworld anymore—at least not consciously. The tradition persists largely in the Christian imagination of Hell, and has also found a revival in followers of neo-pagan spirituality, though this can hardly be claimed to be a mainstream cultural phenomenon. When the sacred is acknowledged in the West, it is more often associated with a movement upwards into the airy, heavenly realms "above". Our culture is obsessed with stories about angels and space aliens, with a fixation on spiritual practices which help us rise above our earthly limitations and purify our base concerns. Focus on the light, we are encouraged, and reject the dark, the depths.[15] Indeed, it

14 This is a central theme of Hillman's ground-breaking book *The Dream and the Underworld* (Perennial, 1979).

15 "As our ideals fly higher into the sky, our reality is faced with a deeper abyss in the earth". Woodman, Marion & Dickson, Elinor (1996). *Dancing in the Flames.* Shambhala, p. 60.

We are primarily an "ascensionist" culture in our driven approach to life, in our restless search for novel highs or medications to fix our boredom and emotional lows, or in our hunt for the latest self-help facelift.

Audience shaking. Photo by Martin Fish, flikr cc.

can be argued that in our driven approach to life, in our restless search for novel highs or medications to fix our boredom and emotional lows, or in our hunt for the latest self-help face-lift, we are primarily an "ascensionist" culture.

Perhaps, paradoxically, this is precisely why the stubborn belief in a "down there" persists, since heaven and hell are inextricably linked archetypally and are indissoluble mirror images of each other, the Upperworld and Underworld of ancient shamanic tradition.[16] Or is it, to quote Hillman, that "The upward-downward polarity as conceptualized in the matter-spirit opposition seems to be an archetypal schema basic to the psyche"? In our time, earth is no longer approached as a

16 See Eliade, Mircea (1972). *Shamanism: Archaic Techniques of Ecstasy.* Princeton. The world-view generally described in shamanism consists of three levels. Human beings live on the earth in a middle world, between an upperworld and lowerworld (associated with the sky and the Underworld respectively). These are linked by a vertical axis, sometimes referred to as the Axis Mundi (World Axis).

This rejection of the hidden, invisible realm beneath our feet can, among other ways, be traced back to a split that occurred many years ago between the gods and goddesses of the sky and earth.

Tor's Fight with the Giants by Mårten Eskil Winge, 1872. Nationalmuseum, Stockholm, Sweden.

sacred being and her psychic depths, her dark underbelly,[17] have long since been demonized and have come to represent all that is despised and rejected.

This rejection of the hidden, invisible realm beneath our feet can, among other ways, be traced back to a split that occurred many years ago between the gods and goddesses of the sky and earth. We can see this in the Greek myth of the battle between the Titans led by Cronus (Saturn) and the Olympians led by his son Zeus (Jupiter), after which the former were banished and imprisoned in the realm of Tartaros (the lower depths)—that part of the Greek Underworld (Hades) that was reserved for punishment. After this, Zeus reigned supreme and is depicted mainly as a god of the

17 In using the word "her" I am not excluding the possibility that earth can be imagined as having masculine being in addition. For example see Geb and Nut in the Egyptian pantheon, an Earth god and Sky goddess respectively.

Hades was sometimes referred to as "Zeus Cthonios" (Zeus of the depths).

Although Hades was later called the brother of the sky god Zeus, originally they were two aspects of one god.

Hades with his three-headed dog Cerberus. Heraklion museum of Archaelogy, Crete. Photo by Aviad Bublil, flikr cc. and wikimedia c.

sky (although his sexual exploits with humans, often disguising himself in animal forms in order to achieve them, keep him in touch with the earthly dimension).[18]

The myth of the Olympians has sometimes been interpreted, from a historical perspective, as the story of the struggle between the religion of the earth goddess and the followers of Indo-European sky-god cults. In the Norse pantheon, the same battle is depicted in the story of the struggle between the Aesir and the Vanir.[19] From an entirely different perspective, we could imagine it describing the conflict between the ancient structures of the brain and the more recently developed cerebral ones.

Fascinatingly, when you begin to look at all of this a little closer and delve beneath the surface of the Greek stories, you discover that the figure of Zeus and the figure of Hades, his brother and the Greek god of the Underworld (to confuse us god and place carry the same name meaning "unseen" or "invisible'), were originally one person, or two aspects of one god. Hades is sometimes referred to as "Zeus Chthonios" (Zeus of the depths), just as Zeus has an aspect known as "Zeus Sabazius'. Sabazius is a barley god who appears to be an early version of the Greek god Dionysus and the Roman god Bacchus, and is described by Clement of Alexandria as being an orgiastic Zeus in the form of a serpent. Dionysus is openly acknowledged as being the same figure as Hades, in a more youthful aspect, both of whom were central players in the Mysteries celebrated at Eleusis in Greece for over two thousand years.[20]

---

18 See Graves, Robert (1992). *The Greek Myths.* Penguin.

19 See Metzner, Ralph (1999). *Green Psychology.* Park Street Press. Especially Chapter VIII, "Sky Gods and Earth Deities'.

20 See Kerenyi, Karl (1976). Dionysus - Archetypal Image of Indestructible Life. Princeton/Bollingen. See also Chapter VII of Turcan, Robert (1996). Cults of the Roman Empire and Graves, Robert (1966). The White Goddess. Noonday, p. 335. On the Eleusinian Mysteries see Kerenyi, Karl (1967). *Eleusis: Archetypal Image of Mother and Daughter.* Princeton/Bollingen.

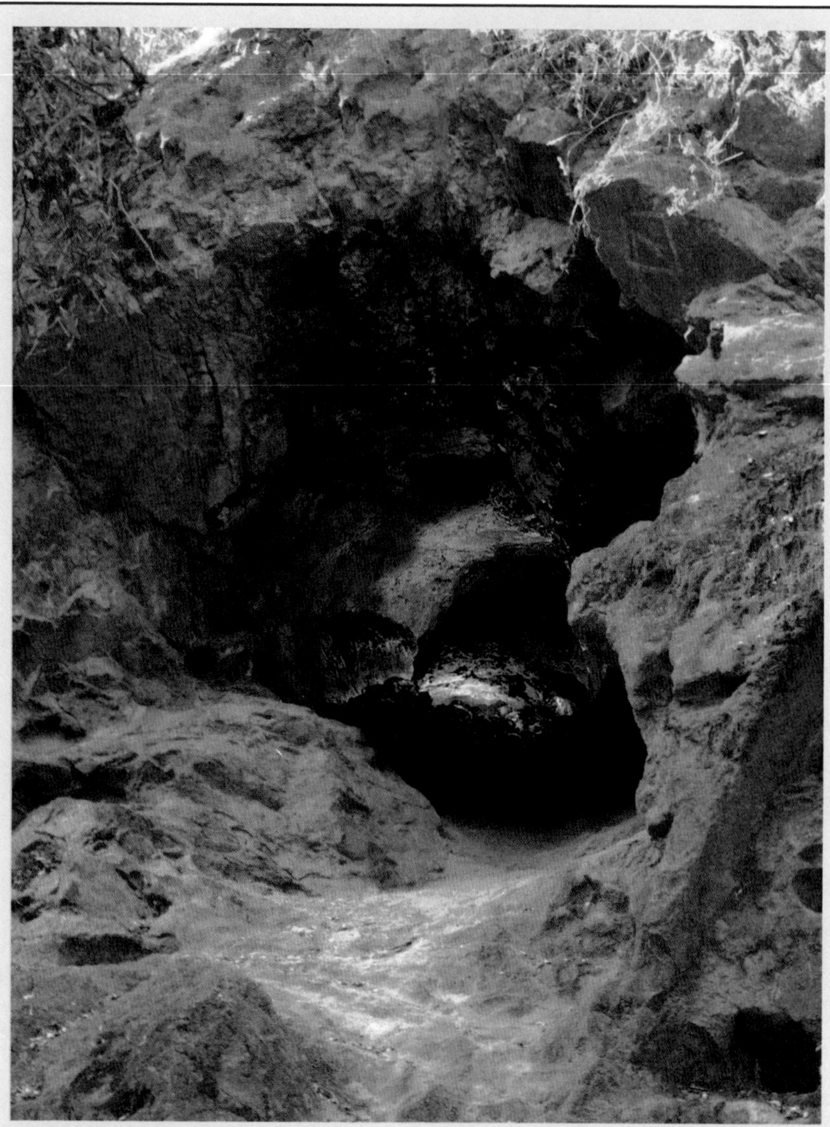

In many traditions the light that springs from darkness is imaged as a Divine Boy Child:

At Eleusis the son of Persephone and Hades was named Brimus or Iacchus or Ploutos.

In Greece the divine child born in a cave was Dionysus.

In Shivaism, Shiva has a son Skanda: god of Beauty.

In Hinduism, he is called Kumara (The Boy).

In the Celtic tradition he is known as Mabon, son of Modron or Maponus.

The Christ Child, born in a stable, sometimes called a cave, is in the same body of imagery.

Photo: composite of two: (i) The Middle Cave, Ozol, Martinez, CA 2009 by Ted, flikr cc. and (ii) Cueva de Laos Verdes, Lanzarote, Las Palmas, Spain by Macnolete, flikr cc

The dark lady of the Underworld's connection with Zeus is confirmed in an early Orphic version of the myth, in which Persephone is seduced by her father Zeus, in his subterranean aspect in the form of a snake. The later myth depicts Hades as the abductor and rapist.

Abduction of Persephone. Sarcophagus 190-200 AD: On the left, Demeter, searches desperately for her daughter. On the right, three alarmed goddesses react as Hades flees with the girl thrown over his left shoulder. The Art Institute of Chicago.

What little we know of the Eleusinian Mysteries appear too to have involved an initiatory immersion in the mysteries of the dark, perhaps involving a sacred, hallucinogenic potion,[21] during which the initiates confronted annihilation, in the form of Persephone,[22] the dark lady of the Underworld, and thereafter so we are told, lost their fear of death. The connection with Zeus is confirmed in an early Orphic version of the myth, in which Persephone is seduced by her father Zeus, in his subterranean aspect in the form of a snake. The later myth depicts Hades as the abductor and rapist. Early portrayals of Persephone display her as a snake goddess. More on snakes later.

One of the few things we do know about the initiatory details of these Mysteries is that at the climax of their experience, the initiates were granted a vision of the light, associated with the light of the sun.[23] I mention this because of an old

21 See Wasson, Gordon, Hofmann, Albert & Ruck, Carl (1978). The Road to Eleusis. New York: Harcourt Brace Jovanovich.

22 The name Persephone literally means "Bringer of Destruction'.

23 Karl Kerenyi comments "No distinction was made between the light of the Mysteries and the light of the Sun." (Kerenyi, Karl (1967). *Eleusis: Archetypal Image of Mother and Daughter,* p. 98).

The cave is bright because it is covered with quartz crystals, that is, it ultimately partakes of the mystical nature of the sky.

Rock with quartz crystals on it. Photo by Daniel R Blume of flikr creative commons

tradition that refers to the light born in darkness, the initiatory descent as paradoxically a source of illumination and healing. R. J. Stewart refers to this tradition and the teaching that there is light in the darkness below, that if you go far enough into the depths you emerge among the stars.[24] Or put another way, the stars are within the earth. He says that this theme can be found preserved in folktales, songs and ballads.

Robert Ryan, in referring to the cave journey, writes that "the dark cave is paradoxically a source of illumination because it opens inwardly people's innate relationship with the source of their own experience and of the cosmos." He also mentions that this is reflected in the cave's luminescence and quotes Mircea Eliade: "Its [the cave's] celestial character is clearly emphasized by the luminosity of the initiation cave ... the cave is bright because it is covered with quartz crystals, that is, it ultimately partakes of the mystical nature of the sky."[25]

In his electrifying book *In the Dark Places of Wisdom,*[26] Peter Kingsley writes of the Greek god Apollo, lord of illumination, the bright and golden god of the sun, from a different angle to the one we're accustomed to.[27] According to Kingsley, there are ancient traditions that connect Apollo with caves, dark places and initiatory incubations. He claims Apollo was always associated with darkness and night, with the Underworld and death.

This tradition, which links the light of the sun with the Underworld, springs in part from the notion that in its daily passage through the sky (from the vantage point of Earth) the sun appears to pass

---

24 See Stewart, R. J. (1985). *The Underworld Initiation.* Aquarian Press, 1985 and Stewart, R. J. (1992). *The Power Within the Land. Element*, 1992.

25 Ryan, Robert E. (1999). *The Strong Eye of Shamanism.* Inner Traditions.

26 Kingsley, Peter. *In The Dark Places of Wisdom* (Golden Sufi Center, 1999).

27 It is more usual to associate the Moon (Feminine) with the realm of darkness, dreams and death, and the Sun (Masculine) with consciousness and reason. While perfectly valid, these conventional associations tend to be one-sided and therefore lose some richness and relevance as a result.

In imagery portrayed in other mythologies, the sun is carried through the Underworld on a barge or ship, just as the soul travels in a boat to reach the Underworld.

Nun raises the sun at the beginning of time, from the *Book of the Dead of Anhai*. ca. 1050 BCE. The sun is represented by both the scarab and the sun disk. Photo by Richard H. Wilkinson 2003. wikimedia c.

beneath the earth at sunset, only to be born anew at the dawning of the day. In imagery portrayed in other mythologies, the sun is carried through the Underworld on a barge or ship, just as the soul travels in a boat to reach the Underworld. We may remember here that the word *helan* is the etymological root of the word *hold*—as of a ship. A painting on the ceiling of King Rameses VI's (circa 1130 BC) tomb shows the night voyage of the sun through the Underworld[28] as the journey of the ram-headed sun god Ra standing in a long snake boat. According to this myth, the sun god had to battle with his arch-enemy, the snake Apep, throughout the night. In the last hours he enters

28 See Willis, Roy (ed.), (1993). *World Mythology.* Henry Holt, p. 47, "The Sun God, His Night Voyage and The Stars'.

In one Egyptian myth, the sun god had to battle throughout the night with his arch-enemy the snake Apep. But in the last hours he enters into the great snake, then emerges rejuvenated and reborn as the dawn.

Set fighting Apep/Seth Fighting Apophis. Painted limestone. Egypt, New Kingdom, 19th Dynasty, ca 1340 BCE. Modified by emphasizing the relevant figures.

The alchemists *Sol Niger*, the black sun, is in the same tradition as the myths in which the sun god has to die to be reborn.

Sol Niger, the black sun of alchemy, by Mylius, 1618, from his *Opus medico-chymicum.*

the great snake—from which he emerges rejuvenated and reborn at dawn.

The same tradition can be discerned in the *sol invictus* (unconquered sun) of Mithraism, the *sol niger* (black sun) of the alchemists and the midnight sun of the Mysteries. In esoteric tantrism, a correspondence is drawn between midnight and the "condition of absolute repose in a state of beatitude". Rene Guenon comments that this is because the spiritual sun is at its zenith at midnight, while the material sun is at its nadir. Initiation into the Mysteries was linked to the midnight sun.[29]

From the perspective of this dark light or black sun, Apollo's Underworld connection can be understood as representing the spilt-off part of the archetype: the "death/rebirth" aspect of a god who has come to be identified purely with his heroic, light-bringing, rational consciousness-affirming aspect, made, we might say, in the image of ego. Or as Jung expressed it, the archetypes have a tendency to turn into their own opposites. And so, at the Anatolian town of Hieropolis we are told,

29 Quoted in entry under "midday/midnight" in Chevalier, Jean & Gheerbrant, Alain (1996). *Penguin Dictionary of Symbols.* Penguin. See also Marlan, Stanton (2005). The Black Sun: The Alchemy and Art of Darkness, Texas A & M, for a masterful exploration of the "sol niger" and many of the other themes touched on in this chapter.

Apollo's temples, like this one at Delphi, Greece, were places of divination and healing, where postulants would go for the answer to questions from the source of Wisdom herself, the depths beneath.

Apollo's Temple at Delphi. Photo by sunrisehomeland, flikr cc

Apollo's temple was right above the cave believed to lead down to the Underworld.

Apollo's temples, like the one at Delphi,[30] were places of divination and healing, where postulants would go for the answer to questions from the source of Wisdom herself, the depths beneath. The priestess with the sacred snakes known as the Pythoness, after the serpent Python, was representative of these depths where Apollo reportedly killed the snake. In trance, the Pythoness would respond to questions brought to her. Her oracle with its *omphalos* (navel stone) was considered to be the navel of the world.[31] Incubatory temples named after Apollo's son Asclepius, the god of healing, were sanctuaries where people would go for healing which in this case occurred through

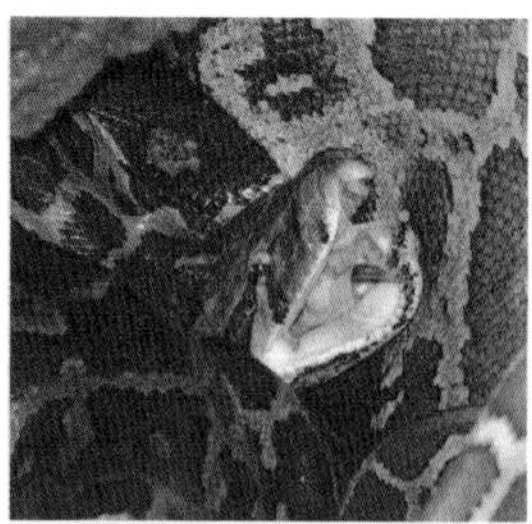

Python.

Python by Karunakar Rayker, flikr cc

30 Delphi, from the Greek *delphys* means "womb'.

31 See Willis, Roy (ed.), (1993). *World Mythology.* Henry Holt, p. 138, "Delphi - The Centre of the World'. See also Graves, Robert (1992). *The Greek Myths.* Penguin, p. 76, "Apollo's Nature and Deeds'.

At the healing Temple of Asclepius the patients were kept underground by this 80 meter walkway connecting the main building to the baths. The sacred spring of Asklepieum steams under the walkway's floor.

Temple of Asclepius, Pergamon, Turkey. Photo by Ken & Nyetta, flikr cc

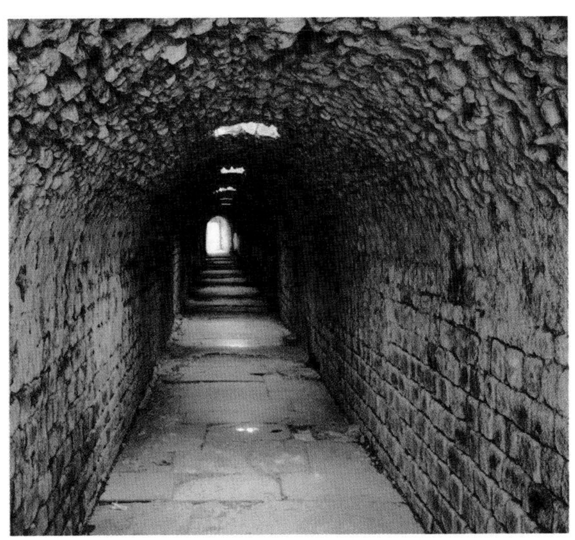

The serpent is an old god

From the Mediterranean island of Crete, ca1500 BCE, this goddess statue has a serpent knotted over her womb; its head is above her head. And the snakes around her arms become unwound in the smaller statue of her *below*. Recent archeological finds suggest that when Cretan civilization was almost destroyed by the nearby eruption the serpent goddess' religion was ceased and replaced by a male hero religion* Yet they carefully placed her two statues in a stone chamber under the new temple floor.

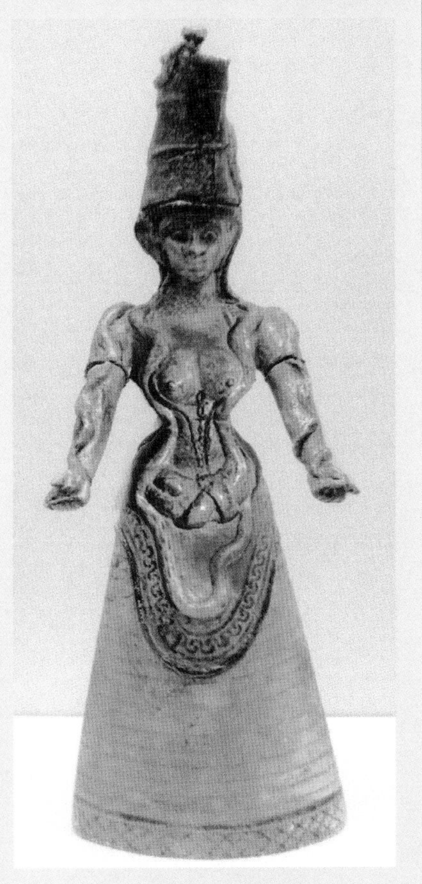

Cretan snake Goddess ca 1500 BCE. Herakleion Archaeological Museum, Crete. Composite image.

* *The Minotaur's Island*, a documentary by Bettany Hughes, Acorn Media, 2008

The serpent is one of the most important archetypes of the human soul. He is an "old god', the first god to be found at the start of all cosmogenesis, before religions of the spirit dethroned him.

Vijayanagar snakestones. Serpent deity reliefs at Hampi, Karnataka. Photo by Dineshkannambadi, wikimedia c.

the medium of sleep and dreams. Those seeking regeneration would lie in the darkness awaiting the presence of the god who would arrive in their dream taking the form of a snake[32] if healing occurred. In fact, there seems to be a universal association of the journey into the Underworld involving an encounter with snakes.[33]

Chevalier and Gheerbrant write of the serpent who "is one of the most important archetypes of the human soul",[34] that he is an "old god", "the first god to be found at the start of all cosmogenesis, before religions of the spirit dethroned him. He created life and sustained it. On a human level he is the dual symbol of soul and libido." In the Christian tradition, the angel called Lucifer, meaning "lightbearer", becomes "that old serpent" Satan, who is "cast out into the earth" by God and banished from the throne of heaven into the depths of Hell.

32 On Asclepius and Incubation see Kingsley, Peter (1999). *In The Dark Places of Wisdom.* Golden Sufi Center.

33 See entries under Snake Myths in Willis, Roy (ed.), (1993). *World Mythology.* Henry Holt.

34 See Chevalier, 1. & Gheerbrant, A. (1996). *Penguin Dictionary of Symbols.* Penguin.

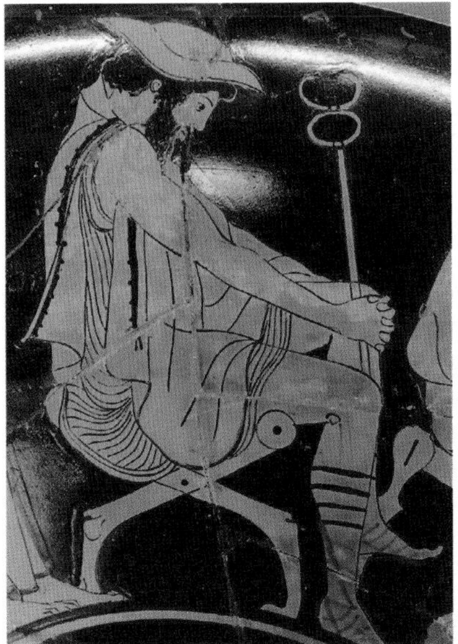

left: The wand of Hermes, the Caduceus, has two snakes intertwining atop the staff.
right The healing rod of Asclepius and his daughter Hygieia has one snake around the staff.

Two snakes around a staff topped by wings has become the emblem of the medical profession in the USA.

top left: Hermes, ceramic by Pintor de Tarquínia ca.475 BCE

top right: Asclepius and his daughter Hygieia, marble relief ca. 500 BCE

below: Hygeia. bronze by Giuseppe Morettis 1922, Pittsburgh PA.

Peter Kingsley describes how the ancient Greek accounts of incubation mention certain signs that mark the entry point into another world. One of these is a whistling, hissing sound that initiates of India associate with the awakening of kundalini energy, the serpent power, pictured lying coiled at the base of the human spine in the root chakra (muladhara, associated with the earth element). It is sometimes imaged as two snakes, one male, the other female, intertwining up the spine. This is similar to the Caduceus, the wand that belonged to Hermes and to the wand of Asclepius, an image which remains, to this day, the emblem of healing and the sign by which the medical profession is recognized. Perhaps because of the shedding of its skin and its love for dark places, the snake is an archetype of death, rebirth and healing—the bringer of Wisdom from the depths.[35] Speaking of the Hindu god Shiva, Alain Danielou writes, "it is the *Nagas* (snake gods) who preserve the

35 See Henderson, Joseph L. & Oakes, Maud (1990). *The Wisdom of the Serpent - The Myths of Death, Rebirth and Resurrection.* Princeton. See Section IV, "Personal Encounter: The Wisdom of the Serpent".

It is the *Nagas* (snake gods) who preserve the wonderful knowledge of the ancient sages and the secrets of magical power.

Nāga couple. Hoysala sculpture in Halebidu. Photo by Mohonu, wikimedia c.

wonderful knowledge of the ancient sages and the secrets of magical power".[36]

The nightly ritual of dreaming, Hillman notes, is one of the few processes left that honours this archaic wisdom, the dream being viewed from this perspective as a nightly initiation into the mysteries of the Underworld, a dissolving of our dayworld ego into the imaginal, primordial wa-

36 Danielou, Alain. *Gods of Love and Ecstasy - The Traditions of Shiva and Dionysus.* Inner Traditions.

The dream is a nightly initiation into the mysteries of the Underworld.

The Nightmare by Henry Fuseli, 1781, Detroit Institute of Arts

Inanna the sky goddess had to lose all her dignity to visit her twin the earth goddess.

Clay tablet, Iraq ca 1750 BCE. British Museum

ters of the dreamworld, a nightly dying to the image we have of ourselves, "The dream takes us downwards".[37] Sometimes we might be awash with shocking and disturbing images that shatter our composure, but these are necessary to remake us in the image of the psyche. The journey into the Underworld is not a comfortable process: during her descent through seven portals the Sumerian goddess Inanna is forced to shed an item of clothing or jewelry at each stop. Naked and furious, having been stripped of all the insignia of her status (her identity), she finally confronts her dark sister Ereshkigal, goddess of the depths, only to be hung on a stake for three days before being allowed to return to the upperworld to work something out. Canny goddess that she is, she manages to negotiate spending only half a year

37 Hillman, James (1979). *The Dream and the Underworld. Perennial.*

Mercurius rectè & chymicè præcipitatus vel sublimatus, in
sua propria Aqua resolutus & rursum coagulatus.

Ouroboros by Matthaeus Merian 1678. From Lambsprinck's *De Lapide Philosophico*

The snake is one of the central images in alchemy (the great work of turning lead into gold), usually depicted in the form of the ouroboros, or serpent biting its own tail. For the alchemists, this image expressed both the prima materia (the original matter) of the alchemical process, which the alchemists imaged as dark and chaotic, and the process itself, which Jung saw as a metaphor for the journey into wholeness (Jung called the ouroboros a basic mandala of alchemy). The salient point for our theme is that gold is to be found in the muck, in the direction of what is generally thought to be beneath us! The ouroboros was also associated with Mercurius (Mercury), the guardian of the Work, who was simultaneously substance (quicksilver), process and goal, and thus represented both the beginning and end of the journey. Bachelard wrote of the ouroboros that it is "the material dialectic of life and death, death springing from life and life from death." The ouroboros is also associated with Cronus (Saturn) in alchemy, the god who was Zeus's father, and was imprisoned in the depths along with the other Titans. Cronus is both Time and the principle of Eternal Return in this context.

For further reading on alchemy, see Jung, C. G. (1944). *Collected Works, Psychology and Alchemy*. Princeton/Bollingen. Gilchrist, Cherry (1964). *Alchemy - The Great Work*. Aquarian Press. Ponce, Charles (1983). *Alchemy - Papers Towards A Radical Metaphysics*. North Atlantic Books. Roob, Alexander (1997). Alchemy and Mysticism. Taschen.

For us moderns the decision to face the "Great Below" is seldom one we entertain voluntarily.

Returning to the womb by Stela Maris, flikr cc

down there, sending her lover Dumuzi for the other six months.[38]

For us moderns, the decision to face the Great Below, as it's called in the Inanna story, is seldom one we entertain voluntarily (even Inanna doesn't realize what the cost is going to be). We ignore our dreams. More often, like Persephone in her Kore (maiden) aspect, we are grabbed by the hand of the underworld from below when we least expect it, through the traumas, depressions and addictions life throws in our path. There are no longer initiatory structures to mediate the journey, like the Mysteries at Eleusius which honoured the dark. When archetypes are repressed, negative manifestations are more likely, both personally and socioculturally.

The journey to the Underworld, often encountered at midlife, is a confrontation with our impermanence, our mortality, a "facing of loss".[39] It is often a meeting with the Jungian Shadow archeype where resources often of great personal and cultural value have been relegated.[40] The Ro-

38 See Brinton Perera, Sylvia (1981). *Descent to the Goddess - A Way of Initiation for Women.* Inner City Books.

39 See Stein, Murray (1983). *In Mid-life.* Spring.

40 Johson (1993)

The Daimon

Each person had their own genius or guardian angel, who acted as a secret advisor, through giving the person intuitions and inspiration.

The genius giving intuitions and inspiration, artist unkown, Public Domaiin

"Ex praeterito praesens prudenter agit ne futura action deturpet ~ From the experience of the past, the present acts prudently, lest it spoil future actions."

Allegory of Prudence by Titian ca 1568. National Gallery, London

Our word demon comes from the Greek *daimon** They were considered to be divine or godlike figures with their own special powers and were seen as intermediaries between the world of the gods and humankind. A person's daimon was also identified with Divine will, and therefore with the fate of that person. Later the word was used for minor gods, and finally with the spread of Christianity, became synonymous with evil spirits. They have also been viewed as the souls of the dead. Each person had their own genius or guardian angel, who acted as a secret advisor, through giving the person intuitions and inspiration.

*Hillman, James (1996). The Soul's Code. Random House, pp. 8-11. In some ways the whole book is a meditation on the image of daimons.

We appear to be at war with our own reptilian roots, our instinctual heritage. We have become so alienated from the primordial mind that we can only view the snake divinity as our chief enemy and tormentor, rather than as a source of wisdom and healing.

Getting Knotty, Indian Pythons (Python molurus). Photo by Karunakar Rayker, flikr cc.

man name for the god of the Underworld, Hades, is Pluto—from the Greek *Plouton* (the Rich One) and aptly, the Christian mystic St. Bernard of Clairvaux writes, "The Holy Spirit draws the soul into the cellar to take stock of its riches".[41] It often takes hindsight to realize this!

So what of the magical snake energy, whether masculine or feminine, imprisoned in the cellar, in the caves and crypts of our imagination?[42] We seem to have become so alienated from the depths of the primordial mind, that we can only view it as a landscape of terror with its ancient divinity as our chief enemy and tormentor, rather than as a source of wisdom and healing. We appear to be at war with our own reptilian roots, our instinctual heritage, and are so identified with masculine, heroic sun-first consciousness as a culture, that we fight and fear anything that would loosen its hold on us, and lead us through a dying to ourselves to riches within. Perhaps it is a necessary alienation from the ground of being built into the structure of consciousness itself, part of the legacy of having developed a cortex, of being "smart apes".

41 Quoted in entry under "cellar" in Chevalier, 1. & Gheerbrant, A. (1996). *Penguin Dictionary of Symbols*. Penguin.

Images of devils and demons maybe the equivalent of "wrathful deities", the guardians of the threshold, whose job it is to prevent us from entering the realm of wholeness before we are ready. It could be they are really healers, there to purge us of guilt and shame by facing us with what we fear in ourselves.

above: A Guardian of Shrine. Lion Dog, Takemizuwake Shrine, Chikuma, Nagano, Japan. Photo by Yuya Sekiguchi, flikr cc.

below: Guardian Giant at Thai Temple, Los Angeles. Photo by by Sompop S, flikr cc.

The images of devils and demons[43] may be the equivalent of what in the Tibetan tradition are called wrathful deities, the guardians of the threshold of the Western Mystery tradition, whose job it is to prevent us from entering the realm of wholeness before we are ready. It could be they are really healers, there to purge us of guilt and shame by facing us with what we fear in ourselves. In our private *nekyias* (descents) I wonder if we are being broken by the imaginal world, dismembered psychically, so that what Buddhist scholar Tulstrim Allione calls "gaps in the fantasies of dualistic fiction"[44] are created in us to help us see through our literal mindedness and systems of identification.

We human beings are so terrified of our archetypal dimensions, of our emptiness and the death of who we think we are and what we think a confrontation with our cosmic roots entails, that we demonize the very thing that is a manifestation of our primordial belonging—our embeddedness in matter—and the coiled energy that lies at its

43 Our word "demon" comes from the Greek "daimon", see page 45.

44 Allione, Tsultrim (1984). *Women of Wisdom.* Routledge and Kegan Paul, quoted in Marion Woodman, Marion & Dickson, Elinor (1996). Dancing in the Flames. Shambhala.

We dwell in the Underworld all the time. The outer person represents the surface of existence, the inner represents the depths which incorporate us, whether we know it or not. There is only an apparent descent that needs to take place, a reflection of our identification with the surface of things.

Retrato en baño (Diana) by Antonio MaloMalverde on flikr cc.

heart: the immanent divine.[45] We remain in deep conflict about our material substance, our essential psychological androgyny, and the impermanence of our current identity that this reflects.

Nevertheless it can be argued that we dwell in the Underworld all the time. If the outer person represents the surface of existence, the inner you and me represents the depths which incorporate us, whether we know it or not. From this perspective, there is only an apparent descent that needs to take place, a reflection of our identification with the surface of things. We are only apparently

45 See Woodman, M. & Dickson, E. (1996). *Dancing in the Flames.*

We are so terrified of our archetypal dimensions that we demonise the very thing that is a manifestation of our primordial belonging—our embeddedness in matter.

Burning of the witch Prigotovleniya in Russia, 1544. wikimedia c

separate from the place of our radical wholeness.[46] Although we take our egos as real, it is paradoxically in non-existence that we are most real, with the Underworld journey as a descent through the levels of being into a reality Jung called the objective psyche, a journey into the interiority of things.[47]

By looking and venturing down, I suggest, by following the pathways of our dreams and the

---

46 By using the term radical wholeness here I am, following Hillman, attempting to reimagine wholeness as a quality that remains open to the notion of our ultimate emptiness, of each of us being made up of and dwelled in, by many different persons, which, paradoxically is what gives us our individuality. By moving to accept the multiplicity of our selves, we are taking a journey towards psyche (the images in the dreamworld), and therefore towards the Underworld, an emptying of our self-identification. In his book *Imaginal Body* (University Press of America, 1962), Roberts Avens writes of death as being "precisely that which constitutes the background and reality of our experience." Death and life cannot be separated without diminishing each and it is death that gives life its fullness. Hillman in *Suicide and the Soul* (Spring 1965), writes "Health, like wholeness, is completion in individuality and to this belongs the dark side of life as well: symptoms, suffering, tragedy and death. Wholeness and health therefore, do not exclude these negative phenomena; they are requisite for health."

47 Quote from Bleakley, Alan (1989). *Earth's Embrace.* Gateway Books.

By looking and venturing down, following the pathways of our dreams and the labyrinths of our imaginings, by opening ourselves we will recover the sacredness of matter and the healing that comes from below, recovering that loss of soul.

The forest path, Rykkinn, Akershus Fylke, Norway. Photo by Randi Hausken, flikr cc.

labyrinths of our imaginings, by opening ourselves to the creative uncertainty that's involved in stepping into the unknown, we will recover the sacredness of matter and the healing that comes from below. We will be initiated into the unseen, realm of the Black Goddess.[48] We will restore to the world and to the arena of soul, that sense of presence and of our place in the scheme of things which is so often sadly lacking in this earth exploited, manic Information Age, recovering that "loss of soul" Jung has addressed in his own initiatory descent.[49]

48 See Woodman, Marion & Dickson, Elinor (1996). *Dancing in the Flames*, Chapter 1, "The Fierce and Loving Goddess".

49 Jung, C.G. (1933). *Modern Man in Search of a Soul.* Harcourt Brace. Murray Stein, in Jung's Map of the Soul (Open Court, 1998), refers loss of soul to the modern belief in ego-consciousness as the only reality – an inflation of self. There is an enormous hunger for soul in the world now, due to the loss of meaning and aridity that ensue from this attitude.

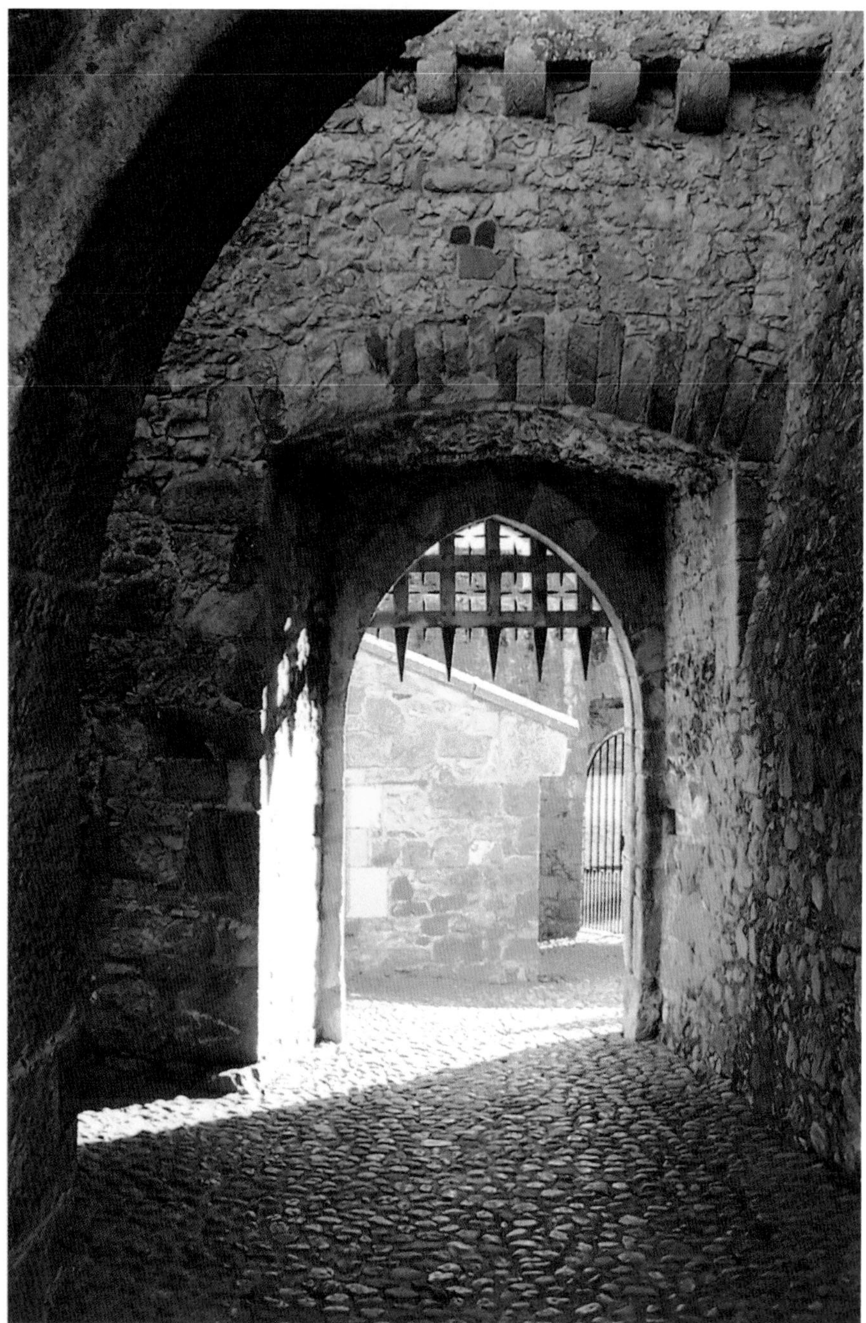

The metaphors: "Doors opening and closing", "a rite of passage", "the threshold of a new outlook", "an entrance into a new phase" reflect how deeply embedded are the archetypal images of thresholds and doorways in our psyches.

Cahir Castle portcullis, Ireland. Photo by Kevin Lawver, flikr cc.

The Space Between

In common everyday language, we talk about doors opening and closing for us, an experience being a rite of passage, that someone is on the threshold of a new outlook on life, or that a particular event is an entrance into a new phase of life. All of these metaphors reflect how deeply embedded are the archetypal images of thresholds and doorways in our individual and cultural psyches. We are beings in transition. In the pages that follow, the significance and origins of this set of images are described and expanded upon.

We all experience transitions in the course of our lives. We come into the world, we pass from childhood to adolescence, navigate the waters of becoming an adult, move into elderhood and eventually exit this world. There are also accompanying changes in role and status as we make the journey. We lose or change jobs, get married and divorced, perhaps have children, move to another country, experience loss and bereavement,

We all experience transitions in the course of our lives. We come into the world, we pass from childhood to adolescence, navigate the waters of becoming an adult, move into elderhood and eventually exit this world.

Four Seasons copyright © Mary McMurray

During liminal times, it is often as if we are in a passageway, neither here nor there. We feel disoriented, ungrounded, with an altered sense of time and identity, alone and disconnected, looking for certainties where there are none. It often feels we will be stuck in this state forever, no way out or through.

In the Emigration Passport Office, by Felix Schlesinger ca 1900. Photo by Hampel Auctions, released as Creative commons

retire or take up a new profession or identity. All these transitions, whether developmental or status based, involve the leaving of one system of identification and the adoption and integration of another, a sometimes challenging process taking time as well as inner and outer reorientation. It also may confront us with what we are holding onto, or what may be obstructing us, as well as revealing new possibilities to embrace.

The liminal (from the Latin *limen* meaning threshold, from which come the words limit, limitless and preliminary) refers to those periods of time and psychological space that lie between the ending of one stage of life, process or experience, and the beginning of another. During such between times, it is often as if we are in a passageway, neither here nor there, varying in intensity depending on person, experience and context. We feel disoriented, ungrounded, with an altered sense of time and identity, alone and disconnected, looking for certainties where there are none. It often feels we will be stuck in this state forever, no way out or through.

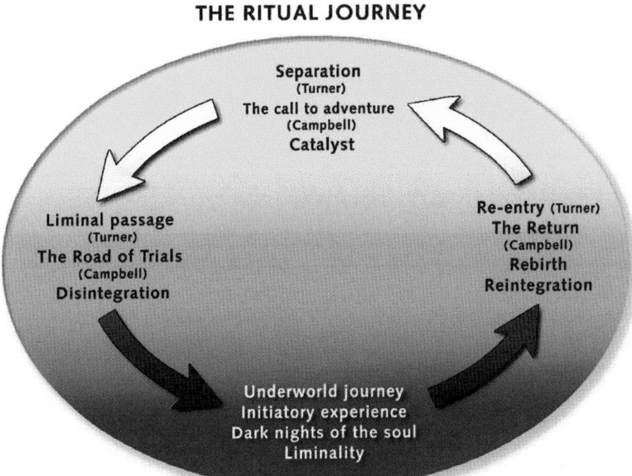

The hero's journey is envisaged as divided into phases or stages. Although the underworld is the focus of our exploration we cannot separate any part of the process without sacrificing understanding of the whole sequence.

The hero's journey, copyright ©David Kidd of Goldenaer

The concept of liminality was introduced into thought and discourse by the French folklorist Arnold Van Gennep in his 1909 book The Ritual Process and later taken up by Scottish born anthropologist Victor Turner in the 1970s and 1980s. This perspective envisions ritual as divided into three phases or stages: a preliminary one (separation from the status quo), a middle liminal one (deconstruction and searching), and finally a post-liminal stage (re-entry). Mythologist Joseph Campbell, in Hero with a Thousand Faces, reformulated this model as the Hero's Journey or Monomyth, describing the three phases as A Call To Adventure, The Road Of Trials and finally The Return.

Although the middle stage is the focus of our exploration we cannot separate any part of the tripartite process without sacrificing understanding of the whole sequence. Perhaps we can only experience and look at the liminal through its relationship to the other stages. I say look at, yet this in itself is an absurdity, perhaps only possible with hindsight. Its very all absorbing and encompassing nature is indeterminacy. We are in flux, unable to find our feet or words to name what is happening to us. Cast out from social consensus reality we find ourselves in a kind of no man's land where boundaries are dissolved, ambiguity

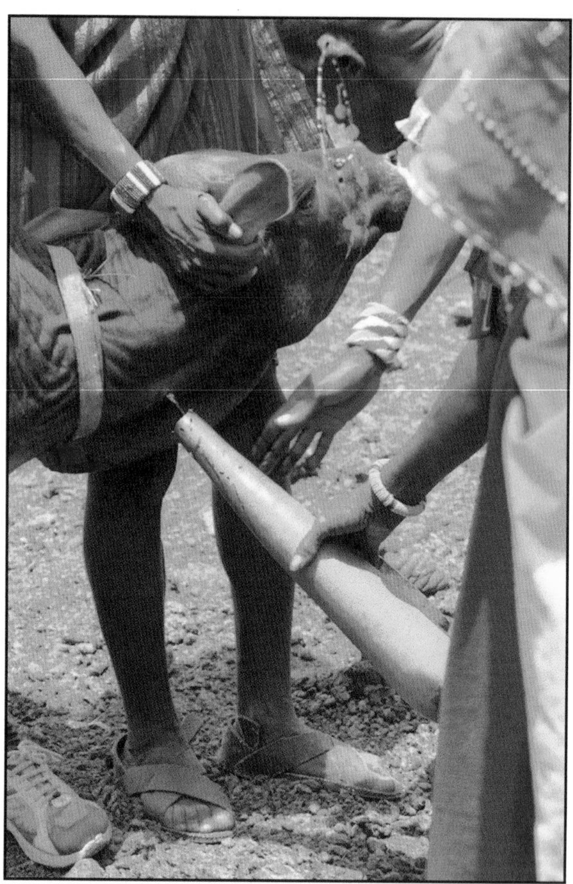

The blood often shed in birth and death is represented in Masai puberty initiation rites by fresh ox blood, here being collected into a gourd.

Collecting blood for Masai initiation rite ceremony. Photo by Frédéric Salein, Wikimedia c

and confusion reign and we feel marginalized, out on a limb.

A dramatic example of this archetypal pattern is revealed in the male and female puberty initiation rites of traditional societies. At an appointed time candidates are abruptly separated from the life they have known as children and placed into seclusion or silence, during which the tribe's adults act out the ritual death and rebirth of the young person. These mark the ending of the child stage of life, engender an encounter with the deep structures underlying surface existence and finally welcome the reborn person back into the community with new adult status and identity.

According to Turner, during the liminal period the candidates are described in terms that represent them as invisible (in terms of being and sta-

In puberty initiation rites of traditional societies children are abruptly placed into seclusion or silence, whilst adults act out their death and rebirth, engendering an encounter with the deep structures underlying surface existence.

Malawi initiation rite by Steve Evans, Wikimedia c

tus, not physically). Symbols that represent them are drawn from imagery of death and decay and as such they are viewed either as dangerous and taboo, or as carrying great blessings, or both. As transition beings they hold a liminal persona and are subjected to varying forms of ritual scarring and ceremony which must induce altered states of consciousness in them. Turner comments that seemingly antithetical processes of death and growth can be represented by the same symbolism and imagery: huts and tunnels are simultaneously tombs and wombs; the moon waxes and wanes, the snake looks as if it is dying, yet is only discarding its skin and growing a new one, the bear appears to die when it hibernates, but is reborn in the spring, nakedness can be both of a corpse ready for burial or a newborn infant. The ritual passage may be symbolized in spatial terms by exits and entrances, crossings and journeys, and in the general significance attached to crossroads, boundaries and thresholds. The candidates are also taught the sacred history of the tribe in order to grow into fully responsible members of the group, sexually and spiritually.

While many of these practices appear alien and even cruel to our modern sensibilities, and while I am certainly not advocating a return to the form of traditional puberty rites, it does seem clear that our Western culture suffers a dearth of cultural vehicles that can tap into the primal depths and effectively mark and mediate life's transitions. Without such vehicles to redress the

Western culture suffers a dearth of cultural vehicles that can mark and mediate life's transitions. Without them the danger is that some will become lost in an endless liminal passage to destruction.

Sensation White 2007, Arena Riga. Photo by Mark Vegas, flikr cc

archetypal vacuum that breeds profound need young people, often unconsciously, resort to such attempts at self-initiation as gang violence, drug and alcohol excesses, suicide and cutting. Without a culturally mediated reintegration marking the boundary that must be passed through from one state or stage to another, the danger is – and this theme of danger in threshold experience appears in the myths and customs of many cultures—that some will become lost in an endless liminal passage and literally die or self destruct (see Meade 2008).

Homes also have thresholds, and many traditions refer to a sprite or spirits, perhaps of the dead, that residing here require propitiation, confrontation or avoidance. The job of the threshold figure, known as the Guardian, is to bar those students not yet ready for the next stage of inner development or to initiate and allow passage to those who are. As the boundary between the worlds is seen to be at its thinnest at the threshold place old traditions have developed such as the one where the groom lifts the bride over the threshold the first time they enter their new house.

In ancient Rome the god of thresholds and doorways was called Janus, most often represented as a two headed figure, simultaneously fac-

The job of the Guardian is to bar those not yet ready for the next stage, or to allow passage to those who are. The boundary between the worlds is at its thinnest at the threshold place.

Border control 2005. Photo by James R. Tourtellotte, wikimedia c

ing the past and future. Depicted with emblems of key and staff he was gatekeeper, protector of doors, gate and roadways, his spirit presiding over all exits and entrances as well as the beginnings of new enterprises or stages of life. Symbolizing change and transition he watched over the passage of one condition to another and was invoked at the beginning of ritual moments such as planting time, marriages and deaths. It is from him that we derive the name January, our first month. Alexander Bell, the inventor of the telephone, stated that when one door closes, another opens.

In ancient Rome the god of thresholds and doorways was called Janus a two faced figure simultaneously facing the past and future. His spirit presided over all exits and entrances as well as the beginnings of new enterprises or stages of life. It is from him that we derive the name January, our first month.

Janus sculpture, 1st century BCE. Musée des beaux-arts de Montréal. Photo by Quinn Dombrowski, flikr cc.

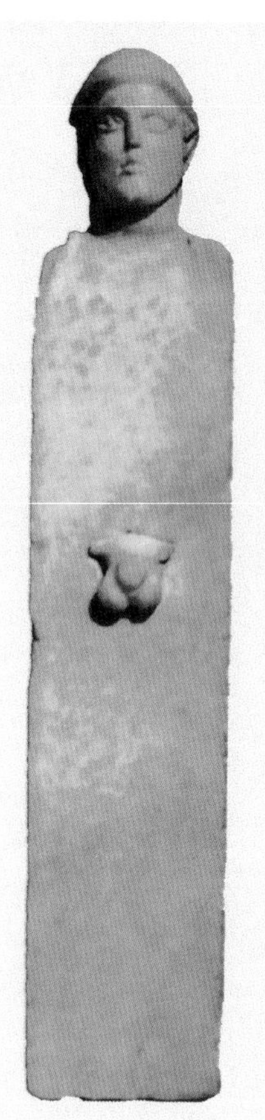

Hermes, the tutelary divinity of travellers and wayfarers, is also a guardian of boundaries whose boundary stones or *herms* were used to demarcate land in ancient Greece erected at the side of roads and crossroads.

Herm, 500-450 BCE. Archaeological Museum of Amphipolis, Macedonia, Greece

Every choice and stage of life involves both loss and gain.

Some commentators believe Janus may have connections to the Greek god Hermes (the Roman Mercury) who like Janus, the tutelary divinity of travellers and wayfarers, is often depicted with a stick or staff and like Janus has a special connection with young people. He is also a guardian of boundaries whose boundary stones or *herms* were used to demarcate land in ancient Greece erected at the side of roads and crossroads. Later Hermes became honoured as the guide of souls into the underworld and with his cap of invisibility and magic wand, mediated the boundary between waking and dreaming, day and night. As messenger also of the gods Hermes journeyed across the boundary between Zeus and mortals. Liminality and marginality, says textual scholar Richard Palmer, were his very essence.

Hermes became the guide of souls in the underworld and with his cap of invisibility and magic wand, mediated the boundary between waking and dreaming, day and night.
The Return of Persephone by Frederic Leighton 1891, Leeds Art Gallery, England,

Saturnalia, with its suspension of normal rules: role reversal; lifting of gender identification; encouragement of sexual expression; this cultural event allowed for much that was liminal.

Detail of Saturnalia by Antoine-François Callet, 1783, wikimedia c.

Another god who features in our exploration of the archetypal dimension of transition, is Saturn, god of agriculture and harvest in Roman myth. After warring with his son Jupiter Saturn fled to Rome and welcomed by Janus established a Golden Age of peace and harmony celebrated every year[1] at the feast of Saturnalia. With its suspension of normal rules—the role reversal of servants becoming masters and masters servants, the lifting of gender identification with men dressing as women, and the permission and encouragement of sexual expression in dances around a large phallus—this cultural event allowed for much that was liminal. The relaxing and loosening of boundaries in honour of archetypal realities was

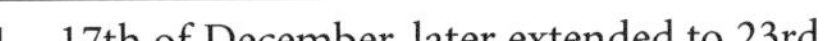

1 17th of December, later extended to 23rd.

Perhaps the archetype we know as Saturn expresses himself In Japan in the Shinto Festival *Kanamara Matsura*.

Kanayama Festival in Kawasaki, Japan. Photo by Stealth3327, wikimedia c.

Presiding over the Saturnalia was Bacchus, god of wine (the Greek Dionysus sometimes called the Loosener or He Who Unties).

Leader perhaps of the late medieval Feast of Fools which, until it was banned during the reign of Queen Elizabeth 1st of England, featured many elements of the Saturnalia.

Bacchus by Caravaggio, ca 1596. Uffizi Gallery, Italy, wikimedia c.

perhaps an unconscious acknowledgement that the deconstruction of fixed statuses and role identifications has a healing and restorative function for individuals and societies alike. Saturn, called *Cronus* or *Kronos* by the Greeks, was the Roman god of time as well as an agricultural deity, often pictured carrying a scythe, an image later incorporated into the medieval figure of Death, the great Reaper.

Presiding over the Saturnalia was Bacchus, god of wine (the Greek Dionysus sometimes called the Loosener or He Who Unties), leader perhaps of the late medieval Feast of Fools which, until it was banned during the reign of Queen Elizabeth the First of England, featured many elements of the Saturnalia. It doesn't take much stretch of the imagination to view the Bacchus/Dionysus figure as the god Hermes in a different guise. Hermes is the Trickster, among other attributes, like the archetypal figure in the person of the Fool or Jester often attached to mediaeval royalty, who acting as a licensed truth teller and levelling transgressor of royal authority and boundary, expressed the notion that there are limits even to the wisdom and absolute power of monarchs. The Fool card in the Tarot pack (the Joker in the modern one) is the first card, delineating beginnings, portrayed as a golden youth stepping out into the unknown, liminal world with abandon. Hermes also fathered sons who became messengers to Dionysus and was Dionysus' midwife and protector saving him from his jealous stepmother Hera. Hermes' child, the goat-footed god Pan (goats were sacred to Dionysus) was a member of Dionysus' retinue.

All these gods of the threshold point to a time when there was for ancient people a much closer connection to the rhythms and cycles of nature and the seasons. For agrarian farming communities the cycles of sowing and harvest, growing and dying away, were key to survival, literally a life or death issue for families and communities.

The Fool is the first card in the Tarot pack, delineating beginnings, portrayed as a golden youth stepping out into the unknown, liminal world with abandon.

The Fool tarot card by Bonifacio Bembo ca 1460. Yale University library, wikimedia c.

Pan, the goat-footed child of Hermes, was a member of Dionysus' retinue

Arte romana, mosaico con Pan. Mosaic, early Roman empire. Izmir Archaeology Museum. Photo by I. Saiko, wikimedia c.

All these gods of the threshold point to a time when people had much closer connection to the rhythms and cycles of nature. For agrarian farming communities the cycles of sowing and harvest, growing and dying away, were key to survival, literally a life or death issue.

Labors of the months from *Tres Riches Heures du Duc de Berry,* ca 1440. Assembled by Przykuta, wikimedia c.

In truth they are for us too, though in our modern world a trip to the supermarket far removed from the harvesting and eating of foods planted by us, insulates us from this awareness. For the ancients there were a number of liminal passages in the year that required special attention and the invoking and honouring of the appropriate gods or goddesses for the harvest of grain and the husbandry of cattle and sheep to be successful. At the passage time of year when the gulf between the divine and human realms were seen to be less

On Beltane May 1st, and also on November 1st, the Celts lit two bonfires and led their cattle between them, presumably a purification: a cleansing and blessing.

Two photos combined (i) *Hot feet. The 2007 Wicker Man is alight* (ii) *Fiery leg the 2009 Wicker Man burns.* Both taken at Butser Ancient Farm, Chalton, UK, by Jim Champion, flikr cc. Modified by superimposition

pronounced, great blessings or great misfortunes were most likely.

In Roman times the start of summer celebrated from April 27th to May 3rd was called *Floralia*, after Flora, goddess of flowers and vegetation, a time when the renewal of the cycle of life was marked with dancing, drinking and flowers, prostitutes were honoured, flowers adorned the temples and colorful clothes were worn. In the Celtic world the May 1st festival, *Beltain*, marked the first great door of the year and beginning of summer. Bonfires were lit, yellow flowers gathered from fields and hedgerows and placed on the doorsteps of houses and cow barns. People cleansed themselves and their flocks by walking between two bonfires. On May eve, boughs of may bush (the white hawthorn) or rowan (mountain ash) were placed near the door of the home to keep out bad luck.

Another important passage for ancient peoples was of course the transition from autumn to winter that recognized the end of summer and the approaching spectre of winter, celebrated in various cultures as harvest festivals. In ancient Rome, festivals were held to honour Mania, the goddess of death, on August 24th, October 5th and November 8th in order to appease the manes, the spirits of the dead. Echoing our own Halloween traditions it was believed that on these days the passageway into the Underworld lay open and the spirits of the dead were free to roam the earth. Families would hang wooden dolls represent-

Fontinalia honours Fons, god of springs and wells, during which people tossed garlands into springs, the archetypal ever-renewing sources of life and soul.

Initiation well from below. The Initiation Well at Quinta da Regaleira, Sintra, Portugal. Photo by Thomas Claveirole, flikr cc.

ing current family members to the doors of their homes in the hope that the manes would carry these off instead of the occupants of the house.

In October there were also a number of festivals honouring Bacchus, god of wine and on October 13th a festival called *Fontinalia* to honour Fons, god of springs and wells, during which people tossed garlands into springs, the archetypal ever-renewing sources of life and soul. In the Celtic world, the autumn festival was called *Samhain,* the Celtic New Year and the other major door of the year. It was celebrated on October 31st to November 1st, was a harvest festival and denoted the end of the lighter half of the year. Bonfires were lit and again people and cattle walked between two fires, presumably a form of purification and blessing, and slaughtered livestock bones were consumed in the fires.

In addition to certain seasonal liminal thresholds to be navigated and celebrated in time, there are also places where liminal space, culturally and mythologically, is more likely to be encountered and experienced, as in the example of springs and wells above. Traditionally these threshold places are the meeting ground or boundary between two elemental realms. So for example springs encompass water and earth, mountain tops air and earth, shorelines water and earth and volcanoes fire and earth. In such places where again the boundary between outer and inner worlds are thought to be thinner, supernatural or transpersonal experiences were considered more likely, particularly at

Supernatural or transpersonal experiences were considered more likely, particularly at dawn or dusk, at a meeting ground between two elemental realms:

- springs encompass water and earth
- mountain tops air and earth
- shorelines water and earth
- volcanoes fire and earth

A meeting grounds between two elemental realms. Photo copyright © James Bennett

dawn or dusk, the daily liminal change points. In folk songs based on ancient ballads and seen in myths and stories the world over, these are places of both wonder and terror, where encounters with dark strangers, fairy-folk, or magical beings may occur.

In modern life there are situations and contexts both positive and negative that reveal liminality to us. Anthropologist Victor Turner made a distinction between what he called true liminality, existing as a phenomena only in highly structured traditional cultures denoting transformation, and liminoid, exemplified in modernity, for instance, by the rock concert which is liminal-like without leading to profound changes in identity and status.

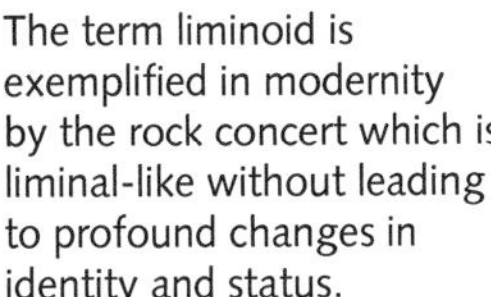

The term liminoid is exemplified in modernity by the rock concert which is liminal-like without leading to profound changes in identity and status.

Planet Webs, The Underground, Oklahoma City, 2012. Photo by Justin Waits, flikr cc. 2.0.

Since archetypes do not die but keep finding different forms and places in which to express themselves we may look to airports, railway or bus stations as liminal places, as are national borders, ports and harbours.

The Internet is a liminal zone par excellence.

Airport Lounge. Gate 5, IAD, Pleasant Valley, VA, USA. Photo 2013 by Robert S Donovan, flikr cc

However since the purpose of this exploration is to attempt an outline of the archetypal background of liminality, and since archetypes do not die but keep finding different forms and places in which to express themselves, whether the individual is transformed or not, we may look to airports, railway or bus stations as liminal places, as are national borders, ports and harbours. Theaters, cinemas, concert halls and even sports are-

Unwelcome life experiences and events are a liminal experience.

Exiles, oil on canvas 1908 by Karel Myslbek (1874–1915) National Gallery in Prague, Czech Republic.

Liminality may also be experienced in mystical and trance states and sexual intercourse.

Bliss. Photo by Alex Barth, flikr cc.

nas too are liminal cultural spaces. The Internet a liminal zone par excellence. Spies and undercover officers live in liminal space, as do hostages and soldiers in combat. Unwelcome life experiences and events such as illness, trauma, addiction and bereavement may lead through liminal experience to profound transformation and healing, initiations of a different sort. Liminality may also be experienced in mystical and trance states, sexual intercourse and states of wonder and reverie that interact with the natural world around us.

Liminality may also be experienced in states of wonder and reverie that interact with the natural world around us.

Cedar Swamp Forest. Wisconsin. Photo by Joshua Mayer, flikr cc.

The perception that life is but a dream is a common theme in theology, myth, literature and the arts.

Vishnu's Dream. Gupta style sculpture ca 500 AD. Uttar Pradesh, India. Photo 2007 by Bob Kingi, flikr cc.

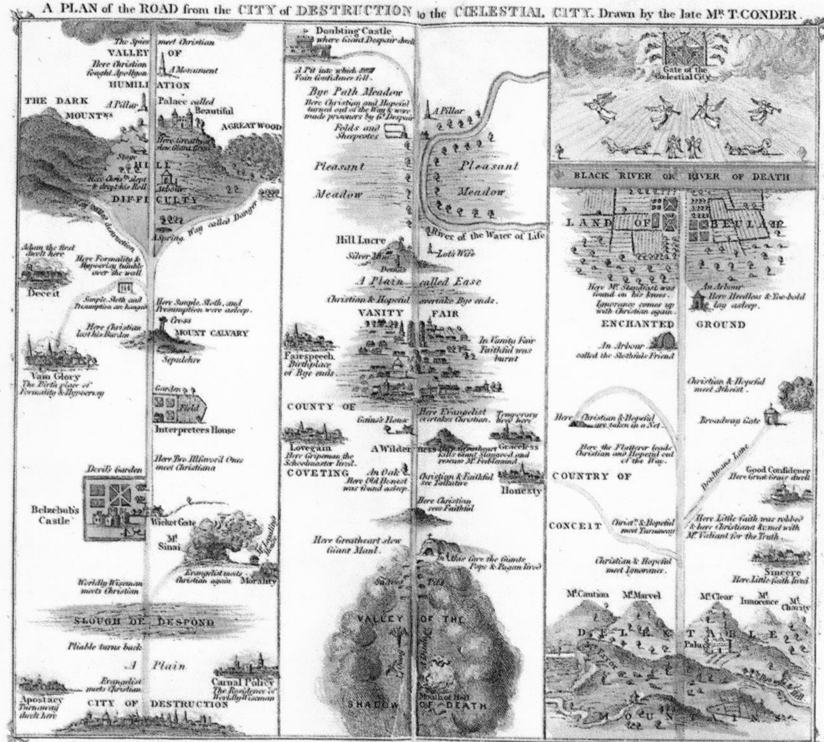

Some Christian perspectives have viewed life as a Valley of Tears to be endured and tolerated, while hoping for a reward in the afterlife.

Map of the Pilgrim's Progress by Thomas Conder 1778, Colorized for an 1844 reprint. Photo by Jo Guldi, flikr cc.

The poet John Keats reframes this earthly life and world as the Vale of Soul-making. We are here to discover and express who we are in our essential nature.

Sunrise by Marilyn Peddle. Okeford, Dorset, England, flikr cc. Modified: retouched tree

Ultimately we are all passing through this world. We are beings in transition whether we are consciously aware of it or not. Loss and change, which Buddhists refer to as impermanence, is a fact of life, and the perception that life is but a dream is a common theme in theology, myth, literature and the arts. The Taoist sage Chuang-Tzu tells how he dreamed he was a butterfly and when he awoke he no longer knew if he was a man dreaming he was a butterfly, or a butterfly dreaming he was a man. Some Christian perspectives have viewed life as a Valley of Tears to be endured and tolerated, while looking to the real reward that will come in the afterlife. In contrast, the poet John Keats in a letter to his brother and sister-in-law[2] reframes this earthly life and world as the Vale of Soul-making. We are here to discover and express who we are in our essential nature The possibility of liminality is that it opens us to soul, and in the process we are dissolved and then remade.

2 Apppenix 2

A procession of young men who have just been initiated in Rumsu, Kapsiki, Camaroon, W Africa.

Kapsiki initiation, Camaroon, W Africa. Photo by Zeratime, wikimedia c.

Appendices

APPENDIX 1

Page 23 The journey back with an altered perspective has nothing to do with strengthening the heroic ego

In *The Dream and the Underworld*, Hillman argues that the Night Sea-Journey and the Underworld Journey are essentially different in kind.

While agreeing with Hillman that the importance of the distinction he makes between a downward journey made to initiate the traveller into the mysteries of death, in order to learn from the Underworld, and a journey made in order to bolster up the ego for more effective functioning in the dayworld, (which Hillman refers to Hercules and to what he calls the heroic ego), it seems that his distinction rests almost entirely on the example of Hercules and his dishonorable actions in the realm of Hades (which Hillman uses to illustrate the cultural and psychological denial of psychic depth). As Hillman himself acknowledges, he was the only one of the Greek heroes to behave so badly there, and certainly from a cross-cultural perspective, most participants, unlike Hercules, are transformed through their contact with the realm below. Whatever the entry point through which the traveller embarks on the journey down, and it seems there are different entrances and a variety of different regions once you arrive there, and therefore different initiations (perhaps one for each of the four elements), the hallmark of the journey is a radical transformation of the person involved, an emptying of the self (a death), and a "return" as a changed being. Hillman argues that with the true Underworld journey there is no return, that the *nekyia* (descent) takes the soul down for its own sake. This is consistent with the intent of his book which is I think, to perform an alchemical dissolution on dayworld consciousness. In my reimagining of the Underworld, the journey is about going there and coming back (sometimes), albeit with an altered perspective that contextualizes our egos.

With regard to Hillman's assertion that the Night Sea Journey connects only to a building of interior heat as opposed to a journey down into the icy zones beneath, (the building of internal fire as a defence against the icy depths), there are differing perspectives through the ages as to which of the four elements is fundamental to the realm of Hades[1]. It seems to me that the outcome of a fire initiation depends on the awareness of the person undergoing the process. The Night Sea Journey doesn't have to be about strengthening the heroic ego. Perhaps it is significant that Hercules' final fate was to be consumed by fire and in many traditions fire has been conceived as an agent of purification and transformation (hellfire and the fires of Divine Love are sometimes seen as the same experience from a different point of view!). In the Hindu tradition, the fire element is associated with the 3rd *chakra* (*manipura* at the solar plexus), which has to do with dominance/submission and the use and abuse of power (the burning heat of the battle frenzy?). A transformation of our relationship to the warrior archetype whether in the form of the Herculean ego, or that of the military/industrial complex, is a major issue for our time.[2]

---

1 Kingsley, Peter (1996). *Ancient Philosophy, Mystery and Magic.* Oxford University Press

2 Von Franz, Marie-Louise (1986). *The Transformed Beserk,* her essay in Human Survival and Consciousness Evolution. SUNY.

APPENDIX 2

Page 67. **Life is not a Valley of Tears but a Vale of Soul-making**

In contrast to the view that life is a Valley of Tears to be endured and tolerated the poet John Keats re-frames this earthly life and world as the Vale of Soul-making.

Sunday Morn Feby 14th 1819

My Dear Brother & Sister -

The most interesting question that can come before us is, How far by the persevering endeavours of a seldom appearing Socrates Mankind may be made happy—I can imagine such happiness carried to an extreme—but what must it end in?—Death—and who could in such a case bear with death—the whole troubles of life which are now frittered away in a series of years, would the[n] be accumulated for the last days of a being who instead of hailing its approach, would leave this world as Eve left Paradise—But in truth I do not at all believe in this sort of perfectibility—the nature of the world will not admit of it—the inhabitants of the world will correspond to itself. Let the fish Philosophise the ice away from the Rivers in winter time and they shall be at continual play in the tepid de light of Summer. Look at the Poles and at the Sands of Africa, Whirlpools and volcanoes—Let men exterminate them and I will say that they may arrive at earthly Happiness—The point at which Man may arrive is as far as the parallel state in inanimate nature and no further—For instance suppose a rose to have sensation, it blooms on a beautiful morning it enjoys itself—but there comes a cold wind, a hot sun—it cannot escape it, it cannot destroy its annoyances—they are as native to the world as itself: no more can man be happy in spite, the worldly elements will prey upon his nature—The common cognomen of this world among the misguided and superstitious is "a vale of tears" from which we are to be redeemed by a certain arbitrary interposition of God and taken to Heaven—What a little circumscribed straightened notion! call the world if you Please "The vale of Soul—making" Then you will find out the use of the world (I am speaking now in the highest terms for human nature admitting it to be immortal which I will here take for granted for the purpose of showing a thought which has struck me concerning it) I say "Soul making" Soul as distinguished from an Intelligence—There may be intelligences or sparks of the divinity in millions—but they are not Souls till they acquire identities, till each one is personally itself. Intelligences are atoms of perception—they know and they see and they are pure, in short they are God—how then are Souls to be made? How then are these sparks which are God to have identity given them—so as ever to possess a bliss peculiar to each ones individual existence? How, but by the medium of a world like this? This point I sincerely wish to consider because I think it a grander system of salvation than the chrystain religion—or rather it is a system of Spirit—creation—This is effected by three grand materials acting the one upon the other for a series of years—These Materials are the Intelligence—the human heart (as distinguished from intelligence or Mind) and the World or Elemental space suited for the proper action of Mind and Heart on each other for the purpose of forming the Soul or Intelligence destined to possess the sense of Identity. I can scarcely express what I but dimly perceive—and yet I think I perceive it—that you may judge the more clearly I will put it in the most homely form possible—I will call the world a School instituted for the purpose of teaching little children to read—I will call the Child able to read, the Soul made from that school and its hornbook. Do you not see how necessary a World of Pains and troubles is to school an Intelligence and make it a soul? A Place where the heart must feel and suffer in a thousand diverse ways! Not merely is the Heart a Hornbook, it is the Minds Bible, it is the Minds experience, it is the teat from which the Mind or intelligence sucks its identity—As various as the Lives of Men are—so various become their Souls, and thus does God make individual beings, Souls, Identical Souls of the sparks of his own essence—

John Keats, April 21, 1810

Bibliography

- Allione, Tsultrim (1984) Women of Wisdom. Routledge and Kegan Paul
- Avens, Roberts (1962) Imaginal Body. University Press of America
- Begg, Ean (1985) The Cult of the Black Virgin. Arkana
- Bennett, James (1999) Beings From Outer Space. Spring: A Journal of Archetype and Culture
- Bleakley, Alan (1989) Earth's Embrace. Gateway Books.
- Brinton Perera, Sylvia (1981) Descent to the Goddess - A Way of Initiation for Women. Inner City Books.
- Campbell, Joseph (1973) The Hero with a Thousand Faces. Bollingen.
- Carroll, Lewis [Charles Lutwidge Dodgson](1865) Alice in Wonderland. Macmillan
- Chevalier, Jean & Gheerbrant, Alain (1994). The Penguin Dictionary of Symbols. Penguin.
- Conrad, Joseph (1899) Heart of Darkness,
- Corbin, Henry (1972) Mundus Imaginalis or the Imaginary and the Imaginal. Spring
- Danielou, Alain (1984) Gods of Love and Ecstasy - The Traditions of Shiva and Dionysus. Inner Traditions.
- Dante [Durante degli Alighieri] (1308 – 1321) Divine Comedy: Inferno, Purgatorio, Paradiso
- Davidson, Hilda Ellis (ed 1993) Boundaries and Threshold, Papers. The Thimble Press

- Devereux, Paul (1992) Symbolic Landcapes - The Dreamtime Earth and Avebury's Open Secrets. Gothic Image
- Eliade, Mircea (1972) Shamanism: Archaic Techniques of Ecstasy. Princeton
- Gilchrist, Cherry (1964) Alchemy - The Great Work. Aquarian Press
- Graves, Robert (1960) The Greek Myths. Penguin
- Graves, Robert (1966) The White Goddess. Noonday
- Henderson, Joseph L. & Oakes, Maud (1990) The Wisdom of the Serpent - The Myths of Death, Rebirth and Resurrection. Princeton
- Hillman, James (1965) Suicide and the Soul
- Hillman, James (1979) The Dream and the Underworld, Perennail
- Hillman, James (1975) Re-Visioning Psychology. Harper Perennial (1977) William Morrow Paperbacks
- Hillman, James (1979) The Dream and The Underworld. Perennial
- Hillman, James (1996) The Soul's Code. Random House
- Johnson, Robert A (1933) Owning Your Own Shadow: Understanding the Darker Side of Psyche. Harper
- Jung, C.G. (1944) Collected Works, Psychology and Alchemy. Princeton/Bollingen.
- Jung, C.G. (1933) Modern Man in Search of a Soul. Harcourt Brace
- Jung, C.G. (1989) Memories, Dreams and Reflections, Vintage
- Keats, John (ed Gittings, Robert 2002) Selected Letters. Oxford World Classics
- Kerenyi, Karl (1967) Eleusis: Archetypal Image of Mother and Daughter. Princeton/Bollingen
- Kerenyi, Karl (1976) Dionysus, Archetypal Image of Indestructible Life. Princeton/Bollingen

- Kerenyi, Karl (1996) Hermes, Guide of Souls. Spring Publications
- Kingsley, Peter (1996) Ancient Philosophy - Mystery and Magic. Oxford University Press
- Kingsley, Peter (1999) In The Dark Places of Wisdom. Golden Sufi Center
- Lessing, Doris May (1971) Briefing for a Descent into Hell. Jonathan Cape Ltd.
- Mahdi, Louise Carus; Foster, Steven; Little, Meredith (eds 1987) Betwixt and Between: Patterns of Masculine and Feminine Initiation. Open Court
- Marlan, Stanton (2005) The Black Sun: The Alchemy and Art of Darkness. Texas A&M
- Matthews, Caitlin (1989) The Celtic Tradition. Element Books
- Matthews, Caitlin and Matthews, John (1986). The Western Way: A Practical Guide to the Western Mystery Tradition. Arkana.
- Meade, Michael (2006) The Water of Life: Initiation and Tempering of the Soul. Greenfire
- Metzner, Ralph (1999) Green Psychology. Park Street Press
- Miller, Hamish and Paul Broadhurst (1989) The Sun and the Serpent. Pendragon Press
- Onians, R.B. (1994) The Origins of European Thought: About the Body, the Mind, the Soul, the World, Time and Fate. Cambridge University Press
- Otto, Walter F. (1995) Dionysus: Myth and Cult. Indiana University Press
- Palmer, Richard E. (1980) The Liminality of Hermes and the Meaning of Hermaneutics. Western Michigan University
- Ponce, Charles (1983) Alchemy - Papers Towards a Radical Metaphysics. North Atlantic Books
- Roob, Alexander (1997) Alchemy and Mysticism. Taschen
- Ryan, Robert E. (1999) The Strong Eye of Shamanism. Inner Traditions

- Stein, Jan O. and Stein, Murray (1987) Psychotherapy, Initiation and the Midlife Transition (in Betwixt and Between). Open Court
- Stein, Murray (1998) Jung's Map of the Soul. Open Court
- Stewart, R. J. (1985) The Underworld Initiation. Aquarian Press,
- Stewart, R. J. (1992) The Power Within the Land. Element
- Turcan, Robert (1996). The Cults of the Roman Empire. Blackwell.
- Turner, Alice K. (1995) The History of Hell. Harvest,
- Turner, Victor W. (1967) Betwixt and Between: The Liminal Period in Rites of Passage. Cornell
- Turner, Victor W. (1969) The Ritual Process: Structure and Anti-Structure. Aldine De Gruyter
- Van Gennep, Arnold (1909) The Rites Of Passage. Reprint 1960 Routledge & Kegan Paul
- Verne, Jules Verne (1870) 20,000 Leagues Under the Sea, *Vingt mille lieues sous les mers: Tour du monde sous-marin*. Pierre-Jules Hetzel
- Von Franz, Marie-Louise (1986) The Transformed Beserk, in Human Survival and Consciousness Evolution. SUNY
- Wasson, Gordon, Hofmann, Albert & Ruck, Carl (1978) The Road to Eleusis. Harcourt Brace Jovanovich
- Welwood, John (2002) Towards a Psychology of Awakening. Shambala
- Whitmont, Edward C. (1984) Return of the Goddess. Crossroad
- Willetts, R. F. (1962) Cretan Cults and Festivals. Barnes & Noble
- Willis, Roy (ed.) (1993) World Mythology.
- Woodman, Marion and Elinor Dickson (1996) Dancing in the Flames, The Dark Goddess and the Transformation of Consciousness. Shambhala

Sources of Images

Front Cover

The Return of Persephone by Frederic Leighton 1891 Leeds Art Gallery, England, wikimedia. Modified by highlighting the caduceus.

Introduction

o. *Lycurgus Consulting the Pythia,* oil on canva 1835/1845, by Eugène Delacroix. University of Michigan Museum of Art, wikimedia c.

Unless marked *copyright* © all images in this book are either public domain[1] or from flikr.com licensed by the creators of their work as creative commons sharing permitted for commercial use.[2]

1 PUBLIC DOMAIN
All paintings and sculptures shown in this book, because their copyright has expired, are in the public domain in the USA, Australia, the European Union, and non-EU countries with a copyright term of life of the author plus 70 years or less.

2 CREATIVE COMMONS
All photographs in this book are by photographers who have permitted the sharing of their work under the Creative Commons (CC) licence.

Creative Commons license, summary

You are free to: Share—copy and redistribute the material in any medium or format

You are free to: Adapt—remix, transform, and build upon the material for any purpose, even commercially.

The licensor cannot revoke these freedoms as long as you follow the license terms. Under the following terms:

Attribution — You must give appropriate credit, provide a link to the license, and indicate if changes were made. You may do so in any reasonable manner, but not in any way that suggests the licensor endorses you or your use.

ShareAlike — If you remix, transform, or build upon the material, you must distribute your contributions under the same license as the original. No additional restrictions — You may not apply legal terms or technological measures that legally restrict others from doing anything the license permits.

ii. *Attis*. Terracotta statue from Myrina, 1st century BCE. Collection of Classical Antiquities. Pergamon Museum, Berlin, Germany. Photo by Wolfgang Sauber, wikimedia c.

iii. *Nãga couple.* Hoysala sculpture in Halebidu. Nãga is a deity or class of being taking the form of a huge king cobra. Photo by Mohonu, wikimedia c.

iii. *Cybele, Ceres and Flora on a chariot surrounded by many forms of natural abundance, corybantes and cherubs, symbolising the element earth.* Engraving by A. Tempesta after himself, 1592. Wellcome Library, London, Creative Commons licence cc 4.0

Out There

iv. *The Hale Bopp comet over central Arizona.* Photo by Julias Whittington, flikr cc.

1. *UFO sighting in Shreveport, Bossier Port, Louisiana, USA on Oct 23, 2010.* Photo by Dragon Rai, flikr cc.

2. *Marshall Applewhite leader of the Heavens Gate cult, often broadcast his message on TV.* Photo copyright © David Kidd

3. *Hale-bopp 3.* Photo by John Tewell, flikr cc. Modified by saturation.

4. Skrilex Mother Ship. Photo by Nicki Spunar, flikr cc. Modifed by enlarging some elements.

5. *Ufo in Hawaii* by Keoni Canri, flikr cc.

6. *Cybele and her consort Attis ride in a chariot drawn by four lions, surrounded by dancing Korybantes.* Silver plate ca 362 AD, Archaeological Museum of Milan, wikimedia c.

7. *The Mother Ship model used to film "Close Encounters of the Third Kind".* At the National Air and Space Museum, Dulles, VA. Photo by Ryan Soma, flikr cc.

8. *Roman statue of Attis reclining after his emasculation.* Apse of the Shrine of Attis, Rome. wikimedia c.

8. *Castration clamp,* bronze, ca 100-300 AD, is decorated with busts of Cybele and her lover Attis while busts of other Roman deities represent the days of the week. Found in the river Thames, London Bridge, England. Photo from *British Art and the Mediterranean* By Fritz Saxl and Rudolf Wittkower, 1948, Oxford University Press.

9. *The Hale Bopp comet with airglow and city lights below.* Photo courtesy of NASA.

9. *Attis; terracotta from Myrina, 1st century BCE.* Pergamon Museum Collection of Classical Antiquities. Photo by Wolfgang Sauber, wikimedia c.

10. *The alchemical furnace of the Great Mother.* Illustration from *Actorun Chymicorum Holmiensum* by Urbani Hierne, Stockholm 1712.

11. *Natural Bridge Caverns, VA.* Photo by Patrick Rohe, flikr cc.

12. *The world tree Yggdrasil and some of its inhabitants* by Friedrich Wilhelm Heine, 1886. wikimedia c.

13. *Ta Prohm Angkor temple, Cambodia* Photo by Shankar S., flikr cc.

14. *Opening of roadside tomb, Galilee.* photo by James Emery, flikr cc.

15. *Fall of the Titans* by Cornelis Corneliszoon van Haarlem, ca 1559. Statens Museum for Kunst, Copenhagen, Denmark. wikimedia c.

Underworld

16. *The entrance to Wayland's Smithy,* Neolithic tomb, long-barrow, 3590-3400 BCE. Ashbury, Oxfordshire, England. It was named after Wolund the smith-god by the Saxons some four thousand years later. Photo by AndrewBowde, flikr cc.

17. *Gallup Poll results 2007.* The Gallup Poll asked people in the USA whether Hell is something they believe in, something they're not sure about or something they don't believe in. In the 1990's they found that 60% believed, rising to 69% in 2007.

18. *The Last Judgement* by Stefan Lochner 1435, Church of St Laurence, Köln, Germany. Released by the Staedelmuseum on flikr cc.

19. *Neolithic hill grave in Knowth, Ireland.* Photo by shes-so-high, flikr cc.

20. *Hel.* Book illustration by Johannes Gehrts 1889. Published in 1903 in *Walhall Germanische Gotter und Heldensagen* by Felix Therese Dahn.

21. *Isis, bronze relief ca 99—199 AD, found in Syria.* Louvre Museum, Paris. Photo © Marie-Lan Nguyen, licensed under the cc attribution 2.5 generic license.

22. *Stone-age Cave paintings at Lascaux II, France.* Photo 2008 by Jack Versloot, flikr cc.

23. *Old Stairs.* Photo by Austin White, flikr cc.

24. *Jonah and the Whale,* from *Jami al-Tavarikh Compendium of Chronicles.* ca 1400. wikimedia c.

24. *Untergrundbewegung in Greece.* Photo by Thomas Quine, flikr cc.

25. Detail of *An archangel locks the Hellmouth* ca 1129–1161. Miniature ca 30 x 20cm, from *the Winchester Psalter.* British Library, London

26. *Beautiful sculptures of angels,* artist unknown ca 1840. Details added in 1841 to the monument in Martyrs' Square, Brussels. Photo by Dr Leslie Sachs, flikr cc.

26. *Angel blessing,* stained glass window in St Pieterskerk, Turhout, Belgium. Photo by Eddy Van 3000, flikr cc. Modified by flopping.

27. *Audience shaking.* Photo by Martin Fish, flikr cc.

28. *Tor's Fight with the Giants* by Mårten Eskil Winge, 1872. Nationalmuseum, Stockholm, Sweden.

29. *Hades with his three-headed dog Cerberus.* Heraklion museum of Archaelogy, Crete. Photo by Aviad Bublil, flikr cc. and wikimedia c.

30. Composite made by Goldenaer of two images (i) *The Middle Cave, Ozol, Martinez, CA 2009*, photo by Ted, flikr cc. and (ii) *Cueva de Laos Verdes, Lanzarote, Las Palmas, Spain,* photo by Macnolete, flikr cc.

31. *Abduction of Persephone.* Sarcophagus 190-200 AD: On the left, Demeter, goddess of the harvest, searches for her daughter. On the right, three alarmed goddesses react as Hades flees with the girl thrown over his left shoulder. The Art Institute of Chicago.

32. R*ock with quartz crystals on it.* Photo by Daniel R Blume of flikr creative commons

33. *Nun raises the sun at the beginning of time,* from the *Book of the Dead of Anhai.* ca. 1050 BCE. The sun is represented by both the scarab and the sun disk. Photo by Richard H. Wilkinson 2003. wikimedia c.

34. Set fighting Apep/Seth Fighting Apophis. Painted limestone. Egypt, 19th Dynasty (ca 1340 BCE). Modified by emphasizing relevant figures.

35. *Sol Niger, the black sun of alchemy, by Mylius,* 1618, from his *Opus medico-chymicum.* Public domain.

36. *Apollo's Temple at Delphi,* Photo by sunrisehomeland, flikr cc.

36. *Python.* Photo by Karunakar Rayker, flikr cc.

37. *Temple of Asclepius, Pergamon,* Turkey. Photo by Ken & Nyetta, flikr cc.

37. Cretan snake Goddess ca 1500 BCE. Herakleion Archaeological Museum, Crete. A composite image of many photos.

38. *Vijayanagar snakestones.* Serpent deity reliefs at Hampi, Karnataka. Photo by Dineshkannambadi, wikimedia c.

39. *Hermes and his caduceus* by Pintor de Tarquínia, Çeramic ca 480-470 BCE. Louvre Museum. wikimedia c.

39. *Asclepius and his daughter Hygieia.* Marble relief rom Therme, Greece, end of the 5th century BCE. Istanbul Archaeological Museums Photo by Prioryman, wikimedia c. Modified by graduated contrast and brightness.

39. *Hygeia* detail of *Memorial to World War Medical Personnel,* bronze by Giuseppe Morettis 1922. Pittsburgh PA. Photo by Takomabibelot, wikimedia c.

40. *Nãga couple. Hoysala sculpture in Halebidu.* Nãga is a deity or class of being taking the form of a huge king cobra. Photo by Mohonu, wikimedia c.

41. *The Nightmare.* oil painting by Henry Fuseli 1781. Detroit Institute of Arts, wikimedia c.

41. *Inanna* [Sumerian] or *Ištar* [Akkadian] Old Babylonian, 1800-1750 BCE. Southern Iraq. Large plaque of baked straw-tempered clay. She was originally painted red and the background in black. British Museum: Photo by Helen Simonsson, flikr cc.

42. *Ouroboros,* by Matthaeus Merian 1678. From Lambsprinck's *De Lapide Philosophico*, published in the *Musaeum hermeticum, reformatum et amplificatum. Francofurti: Apud Hermannum à Sande.*

43. *Returning to the womb* by Stela Maris, flikr cc.

44. *The genius giving intuitions and inspiration.* Artist unkown, Public Domain. Printed in Fortean Times, July 2006

44. *Allegory of Prudence* by Titian ca 1568. In the backround is lettering: "*Ex praeterito praesens prudenter agit ne futura action deturpet* ~ From the experience of the past, the present acts prudently, lest it spoil future actions." National Gallery, London

45. *Getting Knotty, Indian Pythons (Python molurus).* Photo by Karunakar Rayker, flikr cc.

46. *A Guardian of Shrine. Lion Dog,* a decorative sculpture above the door of one of the shrine pavilions in Takemizuwake Shrine, Chikuma, Nagano, Japan. Photo by Yuya Sekiguchi, flikr cc.

46. *Guardian Giant at Thai Temple,* Los Angeles. Photo by by Sompop S, flikr cc.

47. *Retrato en baño (Diana)* by Antonio MaloMalverde on flikr cc.

48. *Burning of the Witch Prigotovleniya*, 1544, Russia. wikimedia c.

49. *The forest path,* Rykkinn, Akershus Fylke, Norway. Photo by Randi Hausken, flikr cc.

Liminality

50. *Cahir Castle portcullis,* Ireland. Photo by Kevin Lawver on flikr cc.

51. *Four Seasons*, oil on masonite 1997. Copyright ©Mary McMurray. Four panels, each 6 ft x 2 ft.

52. *In the Emigration Police Passport Office.* Oil on canvas ca 1900 by Felix Schlesinger (1833–1910). Photo by Hampel Auctions, released as Creative commons

53. *The hero's journey,* digital 2015 by David Kidd. Copyright ©David Kidd of Goldenaer Publishing.

54. *Collecting blood for Masai initiation rite ceremony.* "The cow's head is pulled up to open the crack previously made in the jugular vein. After collected the crack is closed and the

animal is unharmed" Photo by Frédéric Salein, wikimedia c.

55. *Malawi initiation rite*, Republic of Malawi, southeast Africa, formerly known as Nyasaland. Photo by by Steve Evans from Citizen of the World. wikimedia c.

56. *Sensation White 2007,* Arena Riga. Photo by Mark Vegas, flikr cc.

57. *Border control 2005*. U.S. Customs and Border Protection, United States Department of Homeland Security. Photo by James R. Tourtellotte, wikimedia c.

57. *Janus sculpture,* 1st century BCE. Musée des beaux-arts de Montréal. Photo by Quinn Dombrowski, flikr cc.

58. *Herm,* 500-450 BCE. The Archaeological Museum of Amphipolis, Amphipolis, Central Macedonia, Greece.

58. *The Return of Persephone* by Frederic Leighton 1891 oil on canvas. Leeds Art Gallery, England. Public Domain. Photo by cgfa.sunsite.dk.

59. Detail of *Saturnalia* by Antoine-François Callet, 1783, wikimedia c.

59. *Kanayama Festival* in Kawasaki, Japan. A Shinto Festival held first Sunday in April. Photo 2013 by Stealth3327, wikimedia c.

60. *Bacchus* by Caravaggio ca1596. Uffizi Gallery, Italy, wikimedia c.

61. *The Fool tarot card* by Bonifacio Bembo ca 1447–1477. From the Visconti-Sforza tarot decks, whose symbolism is Neoplatonic. Yale University library, wikimedia c.

61. *Arte romana, mosaico con Pan.* Mosaic early Roman empire. Izmir Archaeology Museum. Photo by I. Saiko, wikimedia c.

62. *Labors of the months* from *Tres Riches Heures du Duc de Berry,* ca 1440. Assembled by Przykuta, wikimedia c.

63. Combination of two photos taken at Butser Ancient Farm, Chalton, UK.: (i) *Hot feet. The 2007 Wicker Man is alight, the beardy man in the gown is keeping his distance.* (ii) *Firey leg. The 2009 Wicker Man burns.* Both photos by Jim Champion, flikr cc.

64. *Initiation well from below*. The Initiation Well at Quinta da Regaleira, Sintra, Portugal. Photo by Thomas Claveirole, flikr cc.

65 *A meeting grounds between two elemental realms.* Photo copyright © James Bennett

65. *Planet Webs, The Underground, Oklahoma City, 2012*. Photo by Justin Waits, flikr cc. 2.0.

66. *Aiport Lounge. Gate 5, IAD, Pleasant Valley, VA, USA.* Photo 2013 by Robert S Donovan, flikr cc

67. *Exiles,* oil on canvas 1908 by Karel Myslbek (1874–1915) National Gallery in Prague, Czech Republic.

67. *Bliss*. Photo by Alex Barth, flikr cc.

67. *Cedar Swamp Forest.* Norway Point Bottomlands, Wisconsin State Natural Area #151, Burnett County. Photo by Joshua Mayer, flikr cc.

68. *Vishnu's Dream.* Gupta style sculpture ca 500 AD. Temple Complex Panchayatan, Deogarh, Uttar Pradesh, India. Photo 2007 by Bob Kingi, flikr cc.

68. *Map of the Pilgrim's Progress.* Engraving 1778 by Thomas Conder, for *The Pilgrim's Progress* by John Bunyan. Colorized for the 1844 printing. Photo by Jo Guldi, flikr cc.

69. *Sunrise* at Okeford, Dorset, England. Photo by Marilyn Peddle, flikr cc. Modified: retouched tree.

70. *Kapsiki initiation,* Camaroon, W Africa. Photo by Zeratime, wikimedia c.

85. *Departures*. Tel Aviv Ben Gurion airport, Israel 2012. Photo by Joshua Piano, flikr cc.

Index

86. Detail of: *A Mythological Subject* by Piero di Cosimo, ca 1495. National Gallery, London, England. It is untitled and its subject is disputed. wikimedia c.

Back Cover

James Bennett, the author. Photo copyright © Rachel Bennett

Liminality expresses itself in airports, railway and bus stations, national borders, ports and harbours.

Tel Aviv Ben Gurion airport, Israel 2012. Photo by Joshua Piano, flikr cc.

The dream is our nightly initiation into the mysteries of the Underworld, a dissolving of our dayworld ego into the imaginal, primordial waters. The archetypal territory is a nightly dying to the image we have of ourselves. The sometimes disturbing images are necessary to remake us in the image of our psyche. This altered state of consciousness, what we call ego death in psychology, moves us closer to the sacred. We emerge cleansed, rejuvenated and reborn with a sense of the sacredness of matter and our place in the universe.

Detail of: *A Mythological Subject* by Piero di Cosimo, ca 1495, National Gallery, London, England

Index

Made in the USA
Lexington, KY
24 March 2015

#3

ALSO BY M. K. GRAFF:

The Blue Virgin
The Green Remains
Writing in a Changing World (co-author)

The Scarlet Wench

M. K. Graff

Bridle Path Press, LLC
8419 Stevenson Road
Baltimore, MD 21208

www.bridlepathpress.com

Direct orders to the above address.

Printed in the United States of America.
First edition.
ISBN 978-0-9852331-7-4

Library of Congress Control Number: 2014933753

Illustrations and design by Giordana Segneri.

FOR KATHLEEN M. L. TRAVIA

You may have tangible wealth untold;
Caskets of jewels and coffers of gold.
Richer than I you can never be—
I had a Mother who read to me.

Strickland Gillilan, *The Reading Mother*

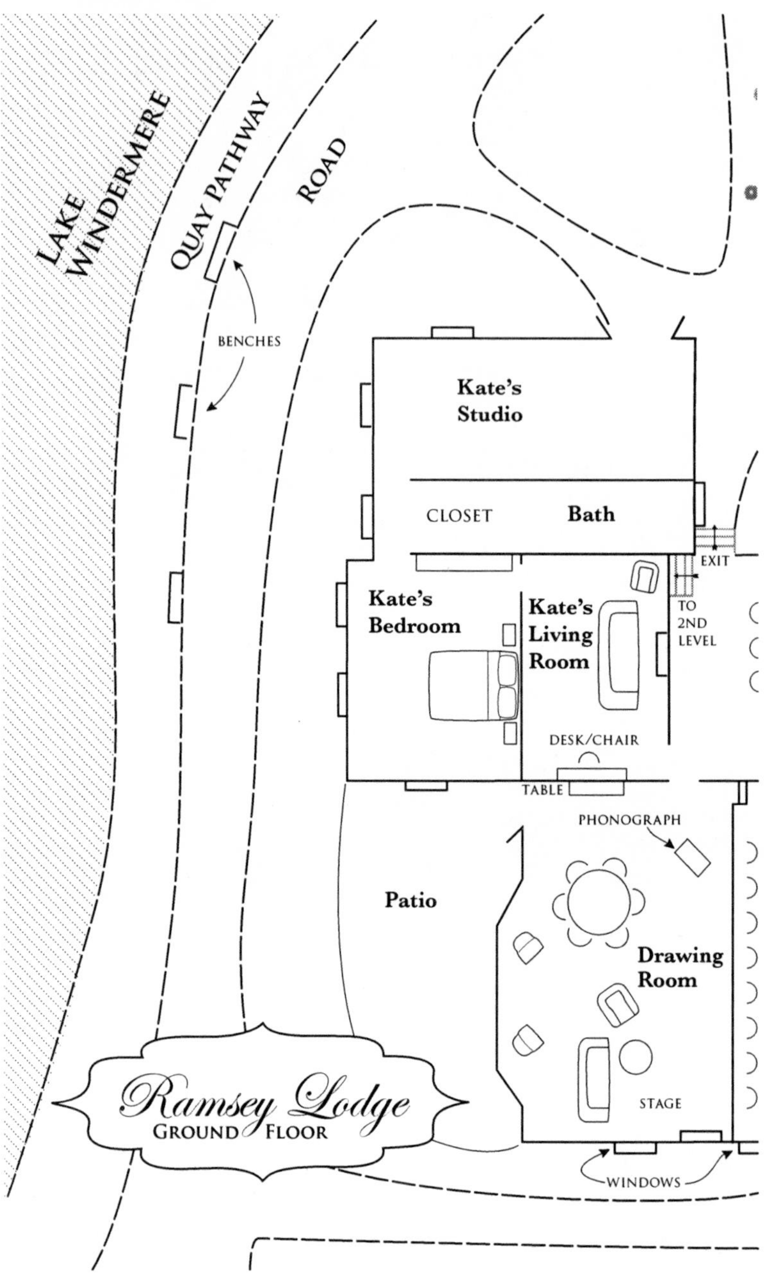

LAKE WINDERMERE
QUAY PATHWAY
ROAD
BENCHES
Kate's Studio
CLOSET
Bath
EXIT
TO 2ND LEVEL
Kate's Bedroom
Kate's Living Room
DESK/CHAIR
TABLE
PHONOGRAPH
Patio
Drawing Room
STAGE
WINDOWS
Ramsey Lodge
GROUND FLOOR

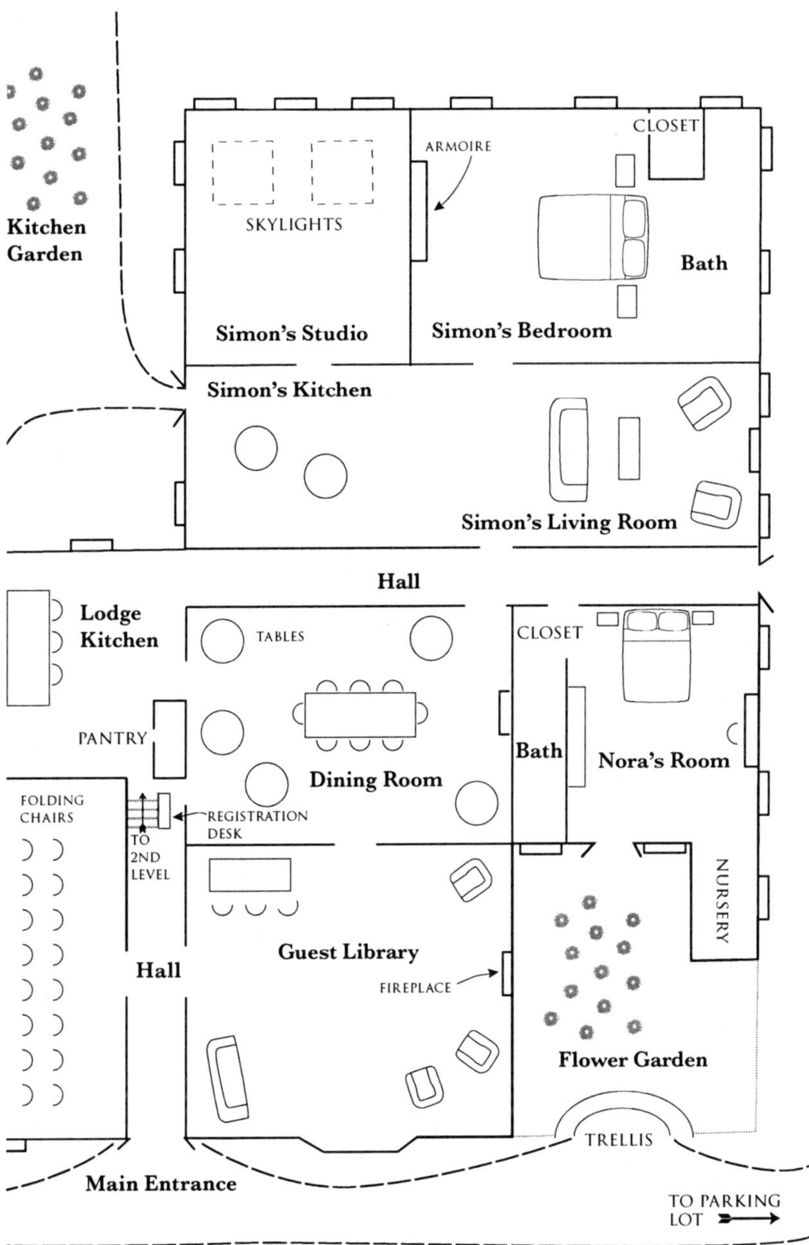
Kitchen Garden
SKYLIGHTS
Simon's Studio
ARMOIRE
CLOSET
Bath
Simon's Bedroom
Simon's Kitchen
Simon's Living Room
Hall
Lodge Kitchen
TABLES
CLOSET
PANTRY
Bath
Nora's Room
Dining Room
FOLDING CHAIRS
REGISTRATION DESK
TO 2ND LEVEL
NURSERY
Guest Library
Hall
FIREPLACE
Flower Garden
TRELLIS
Main Entrance
TO PARKING LOT

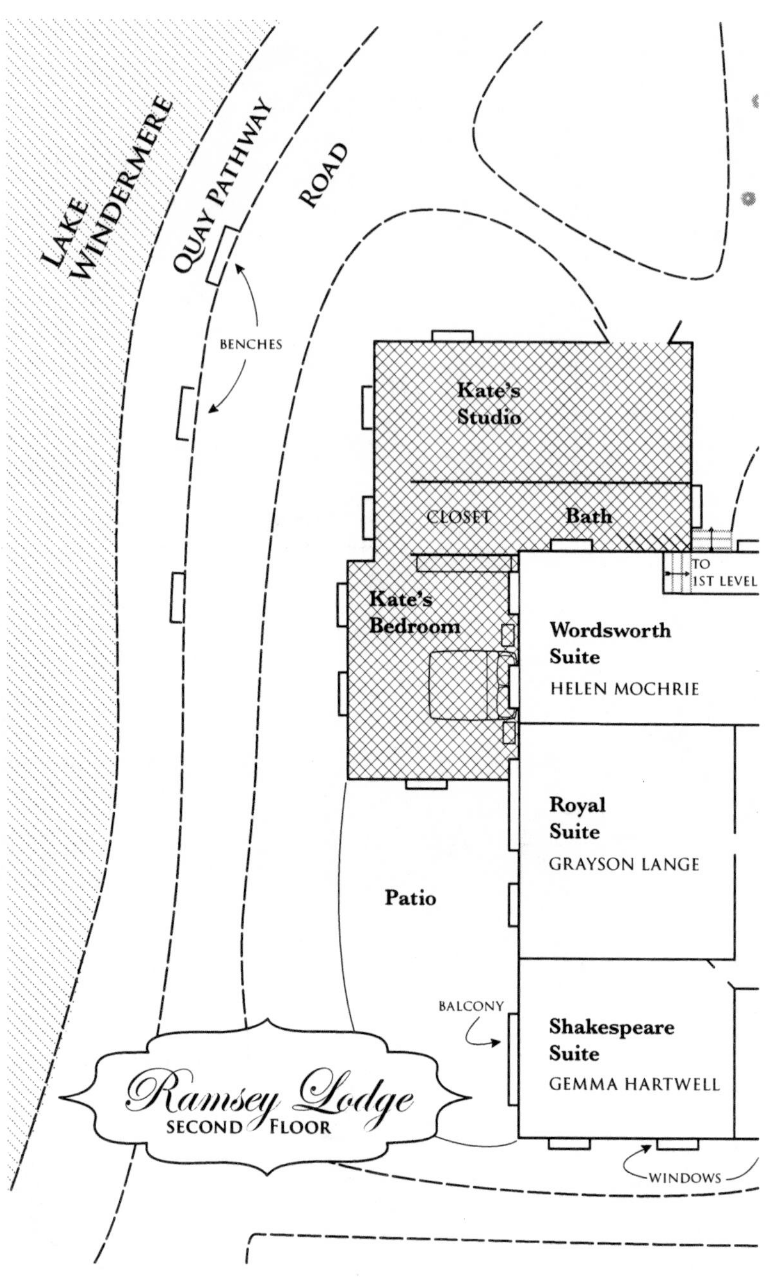

LAKE
WINDERMERE
QUAY PATHWAY
ROAD
BENCHES
Kate's
Studio
CLOSET
Bath
TO
1ST LEVEL
Kate's
Bedroom
Wordsworth
Suite
HELEN MOCHRIE
Royal
Suite
GRAYSON LANGE
Patio
BALCONY
Shakespeare
Suite
GEMMA HARTWELL
Ramsey Lodge
SECOND FLOOR
WINDOWS

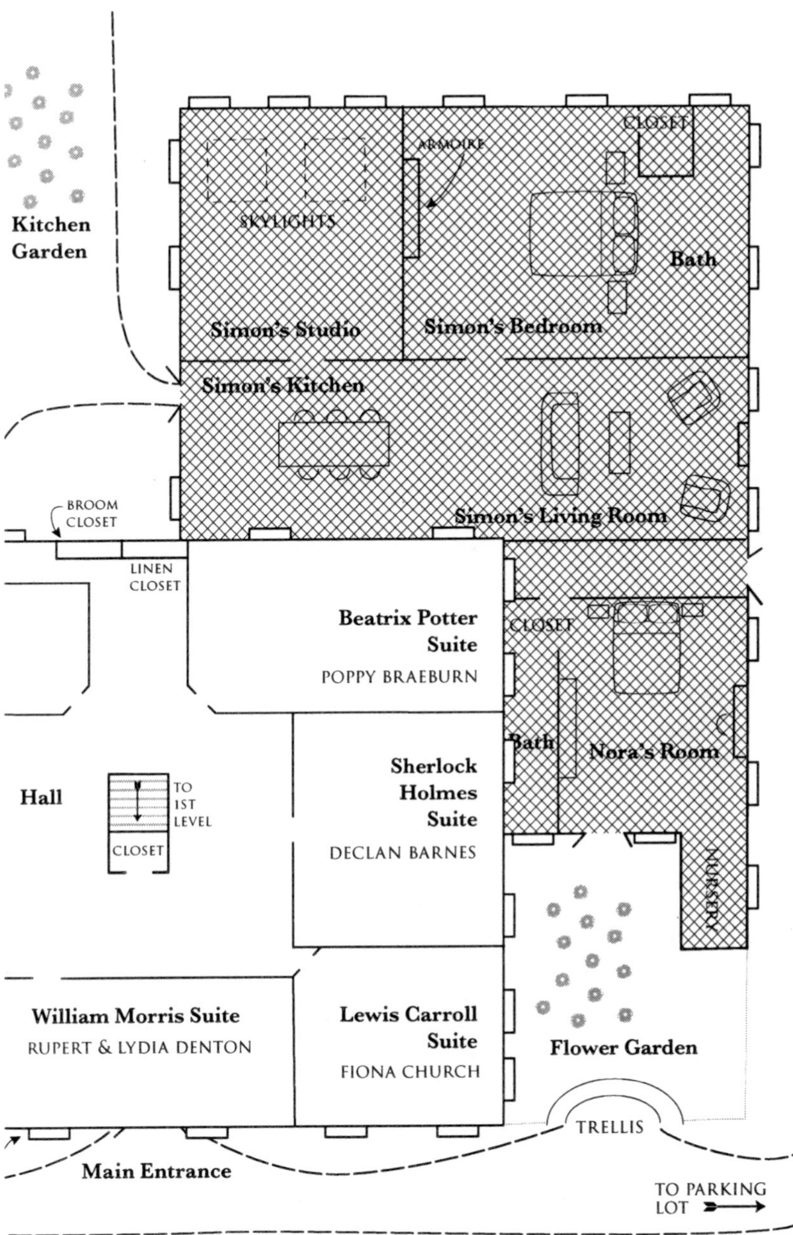
Kitchen Garden
SKYLIGHTS
ARMOIRE
CLOSET
Bath
Simon's Studio
Simon's Bedroom
Simon's Kitchen
Simon's Living Room
BROOM CLOSET
LINEN CLOSET
Beatrix Potter Suite
POPPY BRAEBURN
CLOSET
Bath
Nora's Room
Hall
TO 1ST LEVEL
CLOSET
Sherlock Holmes Suite
DECLAN BARNES
NURSERY
William Morris Suite
RUPERT & LYDIA DENTON
Lewis Carroll Suite
FIONA CHURCH
Flower Garden
TRELLIS
Main Entrance
TO PARKING LOT

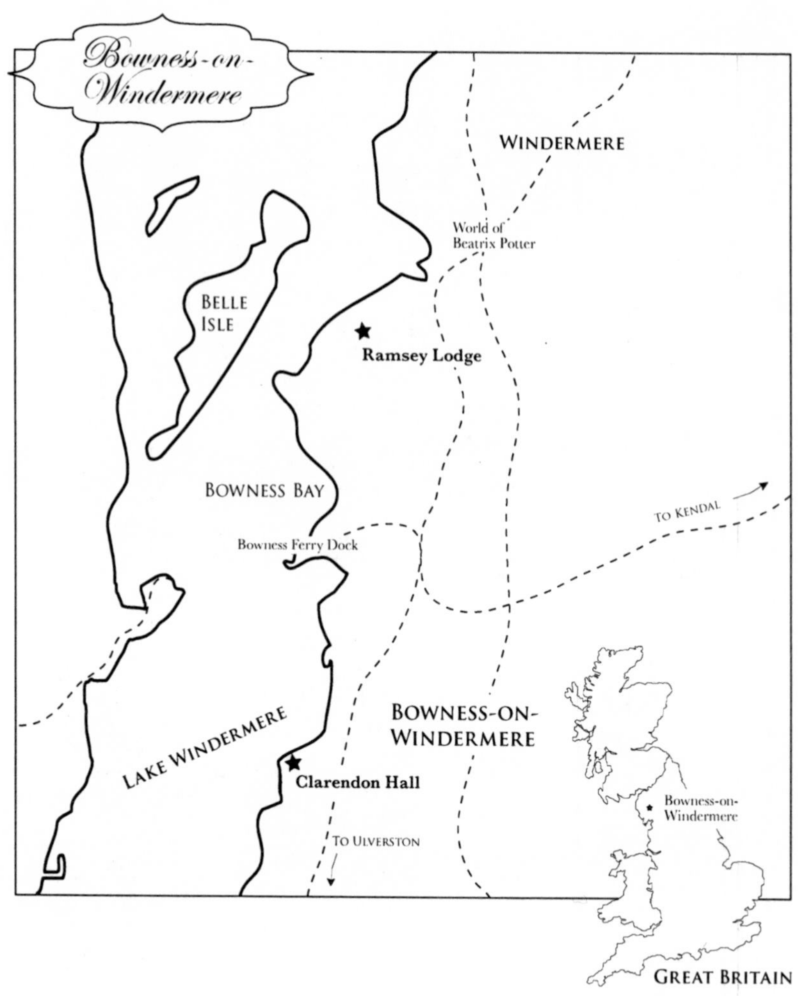
Bowness-on-
Windermere
WINDERMERE
World of
Beatrix Potter
BELLE
ISLE
Ramsey Lodge
BOWNESS BAY
Bowness Ferry Dock
TO KENDAL
BOWNESS-ON-
WINDERMERE
LAKE WINDERMERE
Clarendon Hall
TO ULVERSTON
Bowness-on-
Windermere
GREAT BRITAIN

Cast of Characters

in order of appearance

NORA TIERNEY — American writer

SEAN — her son

VAL ROGAN — textile artist; Nora's best friend in Oxford

DETECTIVE INSPECTOR DECLAN BARNES — detective inspector in Oxford, Thames Valley Police Criminal Investigation Department

AGNES — cook at Ramsey Lodge

POPPY BRAEBURN — actress playing Edith and theatre troupe's costumer

SIMON RAMSEY — co-owner of Ramsey Lodge; artist and illustrator of Nora's children's books

RUPERT DENTON — actor playing Dr. Bradman

LYDIA BROWN — his wife; actress playing Mrs. Bradman

CALLIE BARNUM — Ramsey Lodge part-time staff; Nora's mum's help

GRAYSON LANGE — director and actor playing Charles Condomine; head of Lange's Traveling Theatre Troupe

GEMMA HARTWELL — actress playing Elvira Condomine

FIONA CHURCH — actress playing Ruth Condomine

HELEN MOCHRIE — actress playing Madame Arcati

BURT MARSH — Bowness resident hired to stage manage

MAEVE ADDAMS — manager of Ramsey Lodge and Simon's girlfriend

DR. MILO FOREMAN — Home Office pathologist

DAISY — owner of The Scarlet Wench Pub

DETECTIVE SERGEANT STEPHEN HIGGINS — Cumbria Constabulary Criminal Investigation Department, Kendal

DANIEL KEMP — solicitor representing Muriel and Harvey Pembroke, parents of Nora's deceased fiancé, Paul

All chapter epigrams are lines from
Blithe Spirit: An Improbable Farce in Three Acts
by Noel Coward

The Scarlet Wench

Here is a woman who's lost her head
She's quiet now because she's dead

— plaque in the hall of The Scarlet Wench Pub, also reproduced on their matchbooks

"You can have scenes with English people but they are nice, quiet scenes. Under all that surface calm they are simply seething with feeling and emotion and warmths and it pops out all the time."

— Avis Devoto, in a letter to Julia Child, 1953

Chapter One

"I shall never be able to relax again, as long as I live."
Charles: Act 1, Scene 2

Bowness-on-Windermere, Cumbria

Monday, 9th April

8:59 AM

She was the worst mother in the whole world.

"My whole life is changing, and how did this child get cereal in his ear?" Nora Tierney cradled her mobile phone against her ear as she spoke to her Oxford friend, Val Rogan. She held her infant son close to her chest to soothe his grizzling while she smoothed Sean's shiny-penny hair, lighter than her own. Nora frowned at the bit of dried cereal mashed into his ear and the spit-up on the front of his sleeper. His nursery in an alcove off her room in Ramsey Lodge seemed to have shrunk in on both of them today.

"I gather that's your usual disjointed rhetorical question," Val said, "but you said you skipped his bath last night. Easily explained: baby rice from mouth to hand to ear. And I know you haven't had sex in a while, but why is seeing the delicious Declan going to change your life?"

"You know I don't take these … interludes lightly. It's important. And don't call Declan that or it'll become a nickname and stick."

Nora stole a glance at the Peter Rabbit clock over Sean's changing table. "It's not just Declan, it's the theatre troupe, too."

"I think their play has already been cast, Nora."

"I heard that stifled laugh. You never know what can happen. I *did* play Elvira in college."

"Did you know whining brings out your American accent? Why is my godson so fractious?"

"He's been fine on formula for two weeks, but last night he wouldn't settle and he woke very early. I thought he'd take an early nap—I should be helping in the lodge." The rice cereal won out. Nora put the phone on speaker, undressed the baby and walked with the phone into the bathroom, reveling in the feel of Sean's soft, downy skin against her own as he grabbed a hunk of her hair. Such unconditional love for this small, squirming child who could frustrate her one minute, then reduce her to jelly with his joyful smile the next.

"Maybe you need to change his formula?" Val's voice echoed from the mobile.

"I'll call the health visitor if it keeps up. There's no change in his bowel—"

"Stop right there. I've no need to hear about his dirty nappies or their contents."

Nora laughed. "Some godmother. Wait till your world is filled with nappies and feeding schedules." Nora ran warm water in the sink, wet a washcloth and sat Sean in the sink for an abbreviated bath. She cleaned off the cereal as she talked and the baby wiggled. She washed his hands and nappy area for good measure. "If I didn't have my writing and this play to look forward to, I'd go barmy. The parenting websites say he should be past the colic stage by now." She wrapped Sean in a towel and walked back to his changing table.

"You can't believe everything you read on the Internet. He's not quite six months old, Nora. Give the little bugger a break. New book done?"

"Thankfully. Simon's working on the illustrations. I get a break from writing, although I'm waiting to hear about a freelance assignment the end of next week." Nora dried Sean off and dressed him, pausing to kiss his rounded belly. The baby giggled his pleasure. "I'm excited for this theatre troupe to arrive. I read the woman playing Madame Arcati is a real character, and *Blithe Spirit* is my favorite Noel Coward play." She paused, lost in memory.

"Your acting past explains why you're such an accomplished liar."

"Unfair." But perhaps true. "I haven't seen the director, Grayson Lange, since I interviewed him for *People and Places*."

"I'm sure you can give him pointers." Val yawned. "This place is boring me today. Remind me why I wanted to start an artists' cooperative?"

"Because you're a talented textile artist and like to keep busy."

"All true. Noel Coward? Is that the one with the exes honeymooning in the same place?"

"No, that's *Private Lives*. In this one, writer Charles Condomine has a medium—that's the Madame Arcati role—perform a séance as research for his new novel. She unwittingly calls up the ghost of his first wife—that's the Elvira part—to the chagrin of his new wife, Ruth," Nora explained. "Never seen the movie with Rex Harrison?"

"No. You played a ghost? What fun. I'd pay to see that."

"It's all done with one set, perfect to perform in a small space like Ramsey Lodge. Great marketing for Simon, too. He's keen on the whole project."

"But that's not the entire reason you've got your knickers in a twist. When's Declan due to appear?"

"Not till tomorrow. I can't wait for that, either," Nora admitted. "Although it's not all about the sex."

"Yankee, it's always about sex," Val proclaimed. "I'll want all the gory details. Customer here, we'll talk again." She hung up.

Nora dressed Sean after kissing him again. His responding

giggle reassured her. There was so much to this parenting thing. Websites and books left her feeling incompetent at times, accomplished at others. Sean often didn't fit what Mumsnet.com described, but he seemed to be thriving and had a toothless grin for everyone he met. The moments when he wouldn't settle seemed to happen when she needed him to do so most, and Nora wondered if he picked up on her higher stress level—like today's.

Her anticipation of the troupe's arrival had increased in addition to the whirl of activity these last weeks, culminating with Saturday's wedding at the lodge. Simon's sister, Kate, had married her detective boyfriend, Ian Travers. The siblings owned and ran the lodge together. They'd been so good to her that Nora was happy to help out while Kate was on her honeymoon. Assisting where she could with anything related to the play was a role she'd assigned herself. She'd re-read the play and the lines were instantly familiar, taking her back to a time when acting had shaken her out of her grief after her father's death. She tried to reconcile her memory of the eager and naïve college student she'd been then with the person she was now: a writer with a decent editorial and writing resume behind her, author of a children's book series, single parent to Sean. A very modern woman, indeed.

She looked around the nursery, a nook off her bedroom that the friends with whom she lived had helped her decorate. Simon's artistic nature had led to the fluffy clouds on the pale-blue ceiling; Kate had refinished the vintage dresser that held Sean's clothes and doubled as a changing table. That was Kate *Travers* now, Nora reminded herself.

But the guest she anticipated most arrived tomorrow. Detective Inspector Declan Barnes would be in Cumbria for a walking holiday booked during his visit the past November. His was the only room not occupied by a member of Grayson Lange's cast. A rush of anticipation ran through her.

Time changed everything, Nora's father used to tell her, and she had to admit that always proved true. She juggled caring for Sean with writing book manuscripts and taking on freelance assignments from the magazine for which she used to work, providing her a modest income. Royalties from the first children's book had been small but consistent. She hoped the series would take off with Book Two.

Nora sat in her comfortable wing-backed chair and settled Sean in the crook of her arm. She shouldn't worry so much. Her adopted family at Ramsey Lodge had provided serious help after his birth. Even the visit from her mother and stepfather, who had come from Connecticut at Christmas for the baby's christening, had gone well. She had expected her mother to be critical of her parenting. Instead, Amelia Tierney Scott had been supportive, proud of Nora and delighted with her first grandchild. Nora felt a giant hurdle had been crossed.

The biggest changes were in her body and in the men in her life. She had a waist again and could see her feet but struggled with a few lingering pregnancy pounds. Simon had finally accepted that while she truly cared for him, she didn't love him romantically. He was her confidante, protector and good friend but would never be her lover.

Into that void had stepped Oxford Detective Declan Barnes. He had showed up at Ramsey Lodge soon after Sean's birth, ostensibly to flush out details of an embezzling investigation reaching from Oxford into Cumbria. Nora, however, sensed his visit had been to check on her after the dramatic events leading up to Sean's quick delivery: almost drowning at the hands of a murderer.

She inhaled Sean's sweet baby scent as she conjured up an image of the detective. In her mind, Declan wore a frown, and she knew that was because she often frustrated him. After he had returned to Oxford, they had begun an email correspondence that had become more personal as the months passed. After Sean fell asleep each night, Nora looked forward to writing to the detective with the square jaw and grey eyes. When she felt she must be the only person awake during Sean's middle-of-the-night feeds, there was often a late-night reply from Declan after hectic work hours on a case.

She smiled at the memory of how she had irritated him when they had first met in Oxford and she had pushed her way into his investigation of the death of Val's partner. Nora decided her loyalty to Val, and ultimately proving her innocence, had changed Declan's mind from annoyance to respect. At least, she hoped that was true.

She enjoyed their verbal bantering. Their emails had evolved from laid-back notes about the details of their day to longer missives in which they revealed likes and dislikes that went beyond a mutual appreciation for Adele's music or a fondness for Indian food. She had confided the memory of her mother's miscarriages while trying to give her a sibling and how that had been a factor in Nora's decision to have Sean, despite having to raise him alone. He understood how her father's death left her guilt ridden for years after she had turned down his invitation to go sailing and he'd drowned that very night. It was the one area where she failed at compartmentalizing things that bothered her.

Declan was the reason she worked so hard to lose those last pounds clinging to her slight frame. Although their emails had taken on a more personal tone, she hadn't seen him since November. It was easy to flirt online. The thought of seeing him tomorrow thrilled and scared her with its possibilities. Would he be everything she had built up in her imagination? What would happen if they became intimate, and more to the point, how could they accomplish that with her infant sleeping a few feet away? She blushed at her wild fantasies.

Nora realized Sean had stopped fussing. He gazed solemnly at her as she scrutinized his face: those eyebrows that were the exact shape of Paul's, the dimples when he smiled that reminded her of her fiancé, who had died fourteen months earlier in a plane crash. Sean had her coloring, and the shape of his lips belonged firmly to the Tierney side, but there could be no mistaking this was Paul Pembroke's son. The thorny issue of letting Paul's parents know they had a grandchild was an area she'd managed to wall off while she decided how to deal with it. Not expecting financial help from them had allowed her to assuage her moral duty to let Paul's parents know that though their son was dead, he'd left a child behind. The longer she avoided it, the worse she felt and the more she ran away from dealing with it.

But this week she had to figure out how to be a good mom while being a help to Simon and also find time alone with Declan to explore their relationship. Biting her lip, she reached for the baby sling and eased Sean into it. He was old enough to face the outside world, and the baby chortled and reached out his hands as she adjusted the straps and left the sanctity of her room.

9 AM

Declan Barnes resisted the impulse to check in with the station. Today you are not a detective inspector, he reminded himself. You are a guy taking a much-deserved hiking holiday in the Lake District. His team was in the capable hands of his detective sergeant, and all had been quiet when he spoke to Watkins last night.

"Get an early start, guv. No need to come in today. All's quiet and covered."

Bless Watkins. He looked at his open suitcase and bulging rucksack. Hiking required one kind of clothing and boots, but what of smarter clothes? He knew Nora had a mother's help who babysat on occasion and often watched Sean when Nora was writing. Perhaps he should throw in a jacket in case he could convince her to leave Sean for a romantic dinner, provided he could peel her away from this theatre troupe she was barmy about. Didn't babies mostly sleep in the evening, anyway?

Declan rifled through his cupboard. He didn't object to children as a rule, although he and his wife had divorced before having any. There had been women since then but none he felt compelled to see more than a few times, contrary to station gossip over his supposed stable of women. As if. Over time, he had understood that any woman he would have a long-term relationship with would have to accept the demands of The Job, as his colleagues referred to policing, and the uncertain hours that came with it. Until recently, he had seen himself staying single.

Then he met Nora Tierney, the journalist with the stubborn temperament, who had a desire to delve into everything and the audacity to butt in everywhere. He grew frustrated with her ability to lie at the drop of a hat, a talent Nora merely scoffed at. She called it "improvising to fit a situation" when she interfered in his investigation. Despite her tendency to be such an actress at times, he grudgingly came to respect her tenacity as well her fidelity to those she loved. She reminded him at times of a puppy who wouldn't let go of its toy, but his thoughts had become decidedly more carnal in nature as they had flirted online.

After seeing her in November, he wanted to know what made her tick. He was surprised at how much he had revealed to her during their running correspondence. He felt comfortable with Nora, but that had all been on screen until now. The chemistry he felt in her presence glowed through her words, but she was an accomplished writer. What would reality bring once they were in each other's presence for more than an hour at a time?

Declan hummed as he chose his best jacket. He felt energized, ready for a new adventure. Maybe he'd catch a dose of Nora's enthusiasm and even enjoy this bloody play. Nora had recently gone back to using contact lenses when the baby started grabbing her glasses, and he looked forward to seeing her green eyes, one of the first things he'd noticed when they had met in Oxford.

Folding the jacket, Declan saw his reflection in the mirror and tried to judge what Nora would see. His thick brown hair, with a few greys over the ears, had been freshly cut over the weekend. Upping the length of his morning run had allowed him to drop half a stone, despite his awful eating habits, which revolved around too many take-aways or not eating at all. All right, he had a tendency to frown, but surely, given he was nearing forty, he was entitled to some life experience showing. His grey eyes were clear, and from the front, the slight bump on his nose from his rugby days was hardly noticeable.

He stood up and mentally surveyed what he'd packed, then opened his night table drawer and optimistically threw in a box of condoms.

9:45 AM

Darby, Simon's Lakeland terrier, pranced around Nora and Sean as she headed to the lodge kitchen to see Agnes. Approaching the main hall, she heard the noise of the vacuum running upstairs. Hoovering, the Brits called it. Despite her years in England, her American roots were firm. Although she had appropriated many British phrases into her vocabulary when she spoke, she remained pure Connecticut in her thoughts.

Agnes would feed the theatre troupe, but the lodge would suspend its usual evening dinners to the public for ten days. Nora found the lodge's cook at her worktop, flipping pages in a well-thumbed cookbook. The woman perked up at the sight of them. She opened the back door to let the dog into the garden.

"There's the little laddie. How's he doing today?"

"Won't nap and fusses on and off."

"Such a sweet bairn. Maybe his tummy's off? My gran used to heat a bit of olive oil when one of us had a tummy ache." Agnes tickled the baby under his chin. "We'll all have a tummy ache when that group of barking actors arrives."

Nora wondered what the health visitor would think of the home remedy. "Don't get your knickers in a twist, as Val says. I'm looking forward to the actors being here."

"They say trouble follows that Grayson Lange," Agnes insisted. "I read that magazine you used to work for, and he's trouble."

"When I interviewed him, he was fine." Just a terrible flirt, she recalled. Time to change the subject. "When does Darby go to the Barnums?" Callie Barnum was Nora's mum's helper who also worked for the lodge when her nursery school certification classes allowed it. This week, she was on spring break.

"Callie's brother's coming for him. Just because one of these posh actresses is allergic to dogs, our Darby has to leave."

The desk bell clanged, saving Nora from a reply. Fiona Church's allergy had been a sticking point until Simon agreed to farm the terrier out for her tenure at the lodge.

"I'll get it." Nora made a hasty retreat.

A young woman who reminded Nora of Audrey Hepburn stood by the desk, all slender arms and legs, her short, dark hair grazing her long neck. Her camel skirt sported sewn-on bows of different materials in a riot of color and patterns. Cream patterned tights ended in lime-green ankle boots. A woven oatmeal sweater had a high neck and concealed any curves she might have.

"Can I help you?" Nora cupped Sean's toes through the material of his stretchy onesie. She admired the woman's bright and original outfit. It made her feel dowdy in her old jeans and shirt. "I'm Nora Tierney, helping the owners this week." That felt bright and professional, despite the infant strapped to her chest.

"I'm Poppy Braeburn," the woman answered. "Sorry to be early, but there you go. Sweet baby."

"Thanks." Nora didn't think she looked sorry at all, but it didn't matter because she knew Poppy's room was ready. She was the first of the actors to arrive, and Nora wanted to make a good impression. "You're in the Beatrix Potter Suite. I'll have Simon bring your bags up. Follow me." She led Poppy up the stairs to the northeast corner room, holding onto the railing with her precious cargo leading the way. Voices from the front of the lodge told her Simon and Callie were finishing the last room.

Poppy carried her backpack and a portable sewing machine. Nora had poured over the cast list and knew Poppy would play the maid, Edith, and also doubled as the troupe's costumer on the road.

Poppy seemed pleased to have her own bathroom and didn't comment on her room's location at the back of the lodge. "Great room," she told Nora, taking in the white iron bed and green-and-white striped wallpaper. A frieze of characters from the Potter books ran along the chair rail. There was a trundle bed under the queen bed that made the room ideal for parents traveling with children.

Nora lifted the bed skirt and pointed it out. "I can have that removed if you'd rather."

"No, leave it."

Nora nodded. "Can I get you anything?"

Poppy plopped her sewing machine onto the wide windowsill and yawned. "Think I'll take a nap until the others get here."

"I'll leave you to it, then." Nora approached the woman to hand her the room key. That was when Sean, with an extravagant belch, threw up on Poppy Braeburn's sweater.

Chapter Two

"… something very peculiar happened to me."
Charles: Act II, Scene I

10:20 AM

All things considered, Poppy Braeburn reacted with grace. Nora decided Sean's wide smile after he cleared his bubble had been a factor. She helped Poppy gingerly remove the wet sweater.

"I'm so sorry. I'll wash this right now." Nora checked the inside seam for care details while Sean gurgled happily.

Poppy washed her hands and brought a wet cloth for the baby's face, gently wiping his chin. "No worries. Goes in the washer and dryer in a snap, one reason I wear it often." Stripped to her camisole, Poppy smiled at the baby. "What's his name?"

"Sean, and you're very kind. Not our best foot forward, I'm afraid. Certain I can't get you anything?" she insisted. "A sandwich or some grapes? A new sweater?"

Poppy laughed and pulled an apple from her backpack. "I have all I need, and I'll probably crash out for a while."

Nora closed the door behind her and met Simon at the head of the stairs.

"Someone here already?" He pushed his sandy hair off his forehead in a familiar gesture and reached out to tickle Sean's foot. "Hello, Munchkin, thought you'd be asleep by now."

"Don't ask." They started down the stairs together, Simon a lanky head taller than Nora. "Poppy Braeburn checked in early, and Sean welcomed her by spitting up on this." She held up the damp sweater.

"A personal welcome to Ramsey Lodge. Well done, Sean!"

Simon's reward for his light tone was a huge grin from the baby as they reached the hall.

"I'll just chuck this in the washer," Nora said. Simon's good mood was infectious.

He stopped her. "Since he's awake and the next crew isn't due for hours, do you want a lift to St Martin's to get Kate's things? I need to pick up the Dentons from the station, and you can walk back with Sean and post the text to the publisher on the way."

Nora had promised to retrieve the Ramsey heirloom Kate had used on the altar, a lace runner that was her way to represent her parents at the ceremony. Work on Book Two of Nora's *Fairies of Belle Isle* series was done, and she needed to get the text to her editor while Simon finished the illustrations. "I'll get his buggy and meet you at the car in ten minutes," Nora said. "Maybe he'll fall asleep on the walk home."

"I'll take these bags up." Simon took Poppy's suitcase and a thick garment bag labeled "Costumes."

The kitchen stood empty; through the window, Nora saw Callie Barnum listening respectfully as Agnes gave a discourse by the herb garden. Darby had been whisked away; Callie's brother must have arrived while Nora was upstairs.

Nora started the sweater washing on a small load in the household machine. She went back to her room and took Sean out of the sling, changed his nappy and added a sweater and hat to his outfit. She opted to throw on her old zip-front Exeter sweatshirt, softened and faded through many washes. After checking the nappy bag, she added a bottle of water from her dorm fridge and her manuscript envelope, then stowed them in the back of the buggy, remembering how Simon had teased her for calling it a stroller. She was becoming more and more British every day. Diapers and cribs and strollers had been replaced by nappies and cots and buggies.

Nora gave the baby one more kiss and strapped him into the seat of the buggy. Sean had learned this was the sign of an outing and kicked his legs in anticipation.

She tried to keep the clutter of having an infant confined to her suite. It was enough that Kate and Simon had urged her to spend this past year with them. While she paid toward groceries and utilities from her small income and savings, they refused to accept formal rent, insisting they had no immediate use for the suite she occupied, the rooms of a former live-in housekeeper. By the end of the summer, she'd have to find her own lodgings, day care for Sean and a better job to earn a real income, a prospect she dreaded. How could she write her books and mother Sean if she were gone all day? She'd just have to cross that bridge when it rose before her.

Nora stopped by the door and darted into the bathroom to run a brush through her hair, then clipped it back off her face. The bags under her eyes were just one of the many "delights" motherhood had brought her. She thought of her Caesarean scar and wondered what Declan would make of it if she found herself in a position for him to notice.

Pushing the buggy through the dining room, Nora stopped in the hall near the front door to wait for Simon. The majority of the drawing room furniture had been piled into Kate's studio barn a day earlier after clearing up Saturday's reception. Folding chairs were stacked against one wall in anticipation of the audiences that would fill them for the play's weekend performances. Simon's enthusiasm had infected everyone but Agnes when he'd shown them the plan for the set, a drawing room built on a slightly raised stage in front of the large windows that looked out over England's largest lake, Windermere. Wrapped up in her wedding, Kate had readily agreed and had left the details to Simon to sort out.

"This outing's a tryout for a West End run he hopes to mount." Simon had relayed what Grayson had explained during their negotiations. "From my point of view, the play should bring in fresh faces and exposure for the lodge." Simon had confided to Nora it was the reason he'd agreed to share prop-rental costs with Grayson, a detail she knew he hadn't mentioned to Kate.

The view beyond those picture windows showcased downy white clouds reflected in the azure blue of the lake's surface. Nora watched a steamer pull away from Bowness Bay and head out on tour. She hoped she and Declan would have time to take Sean on a ride. The mild spring had brought tourists out in as much force as the yellow forsythias lining the lodge's driveway. She could still be impressed with the sheer beauty of the nature around her and often felt like a visitor on vacation.

She had put out feelers for a freelance commission for an interview with Grayson and the troupe in the hope she could parlay that into another paycheck. Nora recalled her previous meeting with the director. Grayson Lange was tall and big boned with a long, carved nose and high cheekbones. His trademark salt-and-pepper goatee was impeccably groomed.

She remembered his loud laugh and hooded brown eyes under a deep brow that gave him a bedroom look that had seduced more than one young actress. Nora hadn't fallen under his spell, but his strong personality exuded an undeniably sexy and dynamic force.

"Want me to drive?" Simon appeared next to her, pulling on a windcheater.

"Sure." It had taken Nora ages to qualify for her U.K. license after using her out-of-country license for well more than the approved year. She still smarted that she'd had to take the test twice. While she'd aced the written exam, the practical drive had been filled with laborious things she had never performed, like driving in reverse around a corner. Driving on the opposite side of the car on the opposite side of the road still didn't feel natural. She tossed Simon the keys to her used Volvo, happy to let him drive.

Nora buckled Sean into the rear seat, and Simon stowed the buggy in the cargo area. As they slid into the vehicle and he adjusted the seat for his long legs, Nora wondered how he really felt about his beloved sister's marriage. Ian Travers was a decent guy and a good detective who had acted more than fairly last autumn when Simon had fallen under suspicion of murder. Still, Nora thought the new situation would take getting used to for Simon.

"The Dentons play the neighbor couple, right?" Simon asked.

Nora pulled lip balm from her sweatshirt pocket and applied it liberally. "Rupert and Lydia; she uses her maiden name, Brown, on stage. Married for decades."

Simon grinned. "You really soak this stuff up, don't you?"

Nora shrugged. "I used to work for a magazine that coveted details of any kind of celebrity. It sticks. And I've always loved the theatre. Have you heard from Kate today?"

"She's having fun in Paris. I don't expect to hear from her again until they're in Provence next week."

They drove on the cobbled street uphill toward the church, passing The Scarlet Wench Pub. "Look at that." Simon pointed to the banner that hung over the door: Welcome Lange's Traveling Theatre Troupe.

Nora clapped her hands, making Sean squeal in response. "Daisy said she hoped you'd bring the group there. I know it's one of your favorite places, but I've never asked you how the pub got its name."

"In the 1860s when you lot were having your Civil War, the lake froze and people walked or skated across it. Some locals crossing the deep middle claimed they saw a headless woman under the ice, wearing a red dress and waving to entice them to drown with her. Daisy named the pub after the legend."

Nora gave an exaggerated shudder. "Brutal."

"Probably some idiot's scarf, lost before the water froze."

"So cynical. And all this time I had you down for a romantic."

"I've become much more practical—" He stopped to allow an elderly woman to cross the street. "—which is why this theatre troupe is such a bloody good idea."

The tenor of his voice struck Nora; she felt a glimmer of revelation. "Simon, is Ramsey Lodge in financial trouble?"

Silence as the woman reached the sidewalk. Then a casual shrug of his shoulders.

"Not deep trouble, just getting too close to our overdraft for my comfort."

Nora's stomach tightened. She'd been so wrapped up in Sean these past months. Did their presence add to the strain? She remembered pledging her silence to Simon about the fact that he was fronting half the prop rental for the play, an expense he thought justified, as the lodge would get a cut of the ticket sales. Just how badly off was the lodge? "I didn't realize, Simon. If there's anything I can do … "

They pulled up in front of the medieval church.

"There is one thing you can do, Nora."

"Name it."

"Pray this play is a rousing success and brings new life to Ramsey Lodge."

He left the car, whistling a cheery tune that didn't fool Nora for a minute. She thought back over the winter. Bookings were down, but she'd attributed that to the rhythms of the tourist season. While Simon coming under suspicion in last October's murders certainly had an effect on November bookings, she'd not spent a winter there before and so had thought the holiday season sent tourists to warmer spots. How could she not have realized her good friends were hurting? She doubted Kate was fully aware. It would be just like Simon to keep this downward trend from his sister, especially when she'd been caught up in the whirl of planning her wedding.

Simon retrieved the wheeled base of the buggy and helped Nora set the bucket seat. She thanked him for the ride, as it would have been the uphill walk; going home would be downhill, requiring a death grip on the buggy and giving her a good workout for her stomach and leg muscles. She feared she'd never get that small roll by her waistband to disappear.

Nora waved as Simon honked and drove away toward the train station in Windermere. She would keep Simon's financial worries at the back of her mind for the next week and hope ticket sales kept increasing. Handing Sean his favorite stuffed bunny, she decided to do everything in her power to make this play a success and attract new customers to Ramsey Lodge.

10:50 AM

Nora approached St Martin's, admiring the sandstone exterior and unusual lead roof while she mulled over the lodge's precarious situation. There had been a church on this site since the early 1200s; it had evolved to a mix of modern touches with a reverence for its roots. Nora had used the church for Sean's December christening, and Kate had married Ian here two days ago.

The original wooden doors sported etched-glass inner doors commemorating the new millennium, echoing the mix of old and new. Nora pushed Sean into the church's cool interior. The baby seemed awed by the dark nave, unaware he'd been the center of attention when the vicar had poured holy water over his forehead from the font that had survived a fire in 1480. All eyes had been turned toward Val and Simon, his godparents. Sean had frowned and gurgled his annoyance, then gone promptly back to sleep, setting up a ripple of laughter in the congregation. Nora carefully lifted the font's lid and, as promised by the altar guild ladies, found Kate's lace, folded in blue tissue paper inside a carrier bag.

Nora passed memorials, set into the walls, dating back to 1631 and admired the east window; its crucifixion scene in jeweled stained glass glowed in the late-morning sunlight. She'd used the church as a setting for her second book. Her cranky gnome, sightseeing off Belle Isle by sneaking from the private island onto the Sawrey ferry, falls into one of the church's organ pipes and has to be rescued by the rest of the fairies. Simon had labored over illustrations of the church's ceiling beams, stenciled in religious quotations in gold. As homage to Nora's American background, they'd decided to include the coat of arms of John Wessington, ancestor to George Washington, displayed in the interior. Nora felt pleased she'd been able to incorporate the space's strong history to young readers without hitting them over the head with it.

A sound like sobbing reached Nora from outside. She stopped in her tracks to listen but the noise ended, and she wondered if it was the spring breeze she'd heard, whistling through an ancient window. She glanced at Sean; his eyelids flickered in the dim light. She sat down in a pew next to him to allow him to fall asleep, stowing the carrier bag under the buggy. The mixed scents of burned candles, cool stone and old wood surrounded her and brought her back to Saturday's wedding.

There had been enough tartans and kilts to make her dizzy, and Simon had explained the extras that went into the outfit, like the purse called a sporran that hung in front of the kilt and the oddly named knife, a sgian dubh, that was stuck into knee socks. There had been a lot of jokes about what kilted men wore—or didn't—underneath, but she'd never received a straight answer. If Declan had been there, she might've been tempted to find out.

Kate had been lovely in her mother's dress, a simple 1970s empire gown with an embroidered overlay she'd made her own by running a length of Forbes tartan from one shoulder to under her bust. She'd pinned it in place with a fresh nosegay that matched the flower circlet that held her grandmother's veil in place. Forbes was her new mother-in-law's clan, and Kate's tribute had endeared her to Ian's family. Ian had worn a kilt in the same tartan as he'd waited at the altar. Nora's great joy for the newlyweds had felt tinged with sadness that she had skipped this traditional step on her way to motherhood.

But then marrying Paul would have been a truly bad idea, one she'd acknowledged before he'd died. His handsomeness had matched an intelligence she'd admired, but his obsessive work ethic had left her cold. She was as conscientious as the next person, but even when they'd managed time together, she'd felt his mind wandering, his intensity elsewhere. Their so-called engagement hadn't merited a ring, and he'd resisted taking her to Cornwall to meet his parents. At times she had felt there was some mystery surrounding them he hadn't shared, but Paul had said they were country folk and blamed his work commitments. He'd insisted he'd get around to introducing them at some point. She'd missed out on so much, she thought, a brief hormonal wave hitting her and making her tear up. He'd had the bad grace to go off on a business trip for the Ministry of Defense and die in a plane crash before she could formally break their engagement, she thought unreasonably, then shook herself. Paul had found a way to haunt her thoughts forever. She'd found out three weeks after his memorial service that she was pregnant.

She roused herself from her daydream and scrutinized the baby that was Paul's legacy. His small head tilted to one side, his breathing regular. She checked her watch. She'd been here longer than anticipated, dwelling in the past. Simon would be on his way to the lodge, and she needed to get Sean back for his lunch and to help with the check-ins of the new arrivals.

The steep downhill walk back would let her work up a good sweat after a stop at the post office. She left the church and paused outside on the path as she heard the crying once again. Walking nearer the graveyard, she came to an abrupt stop.

Centuries-old yew trees stood there. Underneath one, an elderly man lay stretched out across its roots on his stomach. Nora set the buggy brake and was about to run and help him when she realized the keening sounds were cries of grief. She stopped herself from flying to his side.

The man's cries echoed in the churchyard; his hands clawed into the dirt. The noise fell away to a pitiful moaning. Obviously he thought his outpouring had been conducted in private. Nora turned silently away and passed through the gate to the street before the man could see she'd been a witness to his despair.

CHAPTER THREE

"As you talk of her she sounds enchanting."
Ruth: Act I, Scene I

11:45 AM

Simon Ramsey opened the Volvo door and turned sideways in the seat to stretch his long legs outside. The train from Carlisle via Oxenholme was late; what else was new with British Rail? His mobile beeped a message, and he read that the electrician had finished the upgrades needed for the hot stage lights. With luck, this might be the first of many productions held at Ramsey Lodge.

He might as well use this brief respite to do something useful. He checked the Notes app and scrolled down the list of ideas he'd made for Nora's illustrations after reading her story text. He'd completed the cover and several other specific pages they'd agreed on featuring the church, but he still needed an image for the ferry ride from Sawrey.

His fingers itched to get back to work. The Oxford gallery that showed his landscapes had been on to him for a while about a fresh round, and he would start those after he finished Nora's book. More income for the flagging coffers, he rued.

Simon knew Nora would keep his confidence about the state of his financial affairs and he was trying hard not to dwell on it. Even though he'd agreed to share in the prop rental, the nice fee they'd receive for hosting Grayson Lange's Traveling Theatre Troupe would more than balance that out. His take of the tickets made up for closing their weekend dinner service to the public with a little left over. If sales continued to be brisk, it would all be profit for the lodge. Plus, the marketing and free publicity at someone else's expense would draw attention to them and drive in new business. With any luck, he'd have time to get back to his painting right after the troupe left. Thank goodness Nora was willing to step in for Kate and help him run things smoothly.

Nora. She'd put her life on the line, and her baby's, too, to ferret out the real murderer last year to prove his innocence. He'd seen her at her worst over the past months: crying through postpartum blues, adjusting to breast-feeding, feeling sleep deprived but thrilled with her infant son. It had forced him to see her as a real person, not as the romantic notion he'd harbored. He would always look at her differently—that one night together assured that—but his ardor had cooled as he understood his feelings weren't reciprocated. Nora loved him, but it had taken him time to realize she wasn't *in love* with him, and he knew there was a distinct difference. He'd taken a giant step back from putting any kind of pressure on her. At the same time, becoming a murder suspect had renewed his instincts for survival and made him inspect his own future. Nora would always be there for him, but she'd seemed relieved when he'd started dating his manager, Maeve Addams.

He'd dated the brunette with the shiny hair briefly in school. When Kate hired her years later to help manage the lodge, he'd protested. Now he could see what Kate had seen, that Maeve was industrious and organized. Her presence allowed both Simon and Kate time off, and for Simon, that meant valuable hours to pursue his painting.

Maeve quickly proved herself an asset to Ramsey Lodge and made no secret of her interest in Simon. He'd missed having a real relationship and envied Kate and Ian. When he'd asked her out, they'd seemed to click, and their dating hadn't impacted his working relationship with Nora. If anything, they were more at ease with each other than ever.

Having someone in his life reciprocating his desire for affection and companionship wasn't half bad. All good things on the horizon these days, and with financial relief in sight, Simon felt his spirits on the rise. Now where was that bloody train?

12:20 PM

Simon pulled up in front of Ramsey Lodge and turned to the ruddy-faced man with white hair sitting next to him.

"Here we are. Ramsey Lodge in all its glory."

"Delightful," Rupert Denton said, exiting the car and opening the rear door for his wife.

Lydia Denton gazed around her and made a beeline for the end of the drive, where she scrutinized the lake across the road. "Rupert, look!" She waved for him to join her.

Simon watched the couple talking and pointing as he retrieved their suitcases. They had shared an amiable chat on the way from the station. Lydia must be over seventy but still had a lovely English rose complexion. He'd seen the sparkle in her blue eyes in the rearview mirror when she'd talked of honeymooning in Bowness.

"We stayed at the Belsfield Hotel and walked by the lake every afternoon," she said.

"Didn't have money to travel far in those days," Rupert added. "Still, did us just fine, didn't it, Lydia?"

"Forty-three years this May," she agreed.

The lodge door opened, and glimpsing a flash of reddish hair, Simon expected to see Nora welcoming the visitors, but it was Callie Barnum who came out to help with the suitcases. Callie had been a boon to him getting the lodge ready before and after Kate's wedding.

Simon pulled up the handles on the Dentons' rolling cases as Callie reached for one. "Thanks." He threw a garment bag over his shoulder. "Nora back yet?"

"Nope." Callie bumped the suitcase up the stone steps and into the hall.

Simon stopped at the desk to check Kate's list. The Dentons entered behind him, and Simon introduced Callie. "She'll be around all week, so don't hesitate to ask her if you need anything."

"You're Dr. and Mrs. Bradman," Callie said with a light blush. "I read Nora's copy of the play."

"Easy parts for two old-timers like us. Not too many around that let us work together," Lydia said, looking around her. "Who's Nora?"

"She's the writer who lives here with her baby," Callie answered.

Simon reflected that Callie's remark neatly summed up the situation. "You're in the William Morris Suite," he announced and led the way upstairs.

Chapter Four

"It's all a question of adjusting yourself."
Elvira: Act 1, Scene 2

12:35 PM

Declan smiled at the BMW that cut him up as he approached Bowness. Let the bugger get ahead. Nothing could spoil his good mood. Traffic had been light, and he'd breezed through the drive from Oxford with only one brief pit stop, reveling in using his vintage MGB. His sergeant continuously marveled at how Declan squeezed his large frame into the small vehicle, but once settled in the leather bucket seat, Declan enjoyed driving the car he'd restored. He didn't often get the chance to take it for this kind of long run.

He'd told Nora he preferred to be introduced to the other guests without his official title. It put people off to know there was a policeman around. He didn't want to be seen as a detective inspector this week, just as a chap enjoying his holiday, much like anyone else.

Declan parked and retrieved his suitcase and rucksack, then walked past the small flower garden on the east side of the lodge. He remembered Nora's suite looked out on this space, and he glanced through the trellis, hoping she might be there with Sean. Empty, except for a few chairs and a table littered with pale pink clematis flowers coming into bloom, giving off a faint, sweet scent.

Declan continued on the curve past the library with its bay window, wondering how Nora would react when they first saw each other. What a great surprise, showing up the day before she'd expected him. He looked up, and there she was, getting ready to lift the buggy up the front steps. His heart lurched and he quickened his pace. She'd be so happy he'd arrived a day early.

He reached her side. "Let me help." The baby was fast asleep in the buggy, a thin line of drool spilling out of his mouth.

Nora wheeled around, her face flushed, glowing with vitality. She'd never looked lovelier, filled out with the curves motherhood left on her slight frame. But for a fraction of a second, Declan thought that instead of being thrilled to see him she actually looked horrified.

12:40 PM

Nora wiped the startled expression off her face, softening it to one of welcome. She became acutely aware of the damp wisps of hair that escaped her clip and curled around her sweaty face and salty lips; her Caesarean scar itched.

"Declan! I didn't expect you until tomorrow," she said aloud. She bit back saying aloud: *If I had, I'd have shaved my legs and not been a mass of perspiration when you first saw me.* She sucked in her belly and wiped her hands on her jeans. So much for the silky dress she'd bought to impress him. In contrast, Declan's chinos and shirt hardly looked wrinkled. She resisted the urge to take off her baggy sweatshirt and wipe her face with it. A smile lit his face and gave her butterflies in her stomach.

"Work was quiet, and I have so much time off owed," he explained. "Is that a problem? Kate said the room was saved for me … "

"Of course not, you just—surprised me," she said. "Pleasantly," she hastened to add. Now that she was faced with him in the flesh, she felt awkward. She reached up to kiss him briefly on the cheek in welcome, hoping he couldn't smell perspiration or Sean's dribble.

Declan crouched down to inspect the sleeping baby. "He's huge."

Nora nodded. "Wait till he wakes and you see him smile."

"Let me get this." Declan scooped the buggy up over the steps as Nora held the lodge door open.

Callie ran to greet her. "Oh, he's so cute asleep. Want me to put in him his cot, Nora?" She nodded to Declan. "Hello, Mr. Barnes."

"Declan is fine. Nice to see you again," Declan said.

Nora was pleased Callie remembered to leave out *Detective*. "Thanks, Callie." The deep purring of a throaty engine caused Nora to turn back to peer outside. "That must be Grayson with Gemma Hartwell and Fiona Church. They're riding in from London together."

Declan followed her out onto the stoop to see a silver Jaguar XKR turn into the drive at a fast clip. It shrieked to a stop in front of the lodge with a belch of petrol fumes. Declan made a face, and Nora supposed he disapproved of the way the driver abused his tires. Or was it that she'd used the director's first name? Three of the car's four doors opened, spilling out the male driver and his two female passengers. The boot swung open as the driver ran around the car and up the steps.

"As I live and breathe, it's the red-haired fox," the man pronounced.

Chapter Five

"You always behaved very badly."
Charles: Act II, Scene 2

12:45 PM

Declan gritted his teeth when Grayson Lange scooped Nora into a bear hug that swept her off her feet. He relaxed his jaw when Nora caught his eye and rolled her own. The director's long nose and angular jaw were offset by eyes that crinkled with laughter as he deposited Nora back on the ground.

"Good to see you, too." Nora smoothed her hair.

Grayson put his hands on his hips and surveyed the area. "Just as charming as I remember it from last autumn. We missed you then, Nora."

"I was busy in hospital having a baby, Grayson. Let me help you with your luggage." She pulled a small bag and a laptop case out of the boot, and the director dipped back for a large suitcase.

Declan pushed the door wide and looked around for a door-stop. Nora winked as she passed him; the director followed, rolling the large case with another bag balanced on top.

"Hello," Grayson said, looking Declan up and down. "Come along, Gemma."

Declan bit back a protest that he wasn't the bellboy. He held the door for the woman from the front seat. Her full-lipped face held light-hazel eyes; chin-length wavy blonde hair topped a voluptuous figure. Gemma Hartwell wore a fitted, navy-and-white polka-dot dress that nipped in at her waist and revealed a wealth of cleavage. In one hand, she carried a large flowered case. The other held a soft leather bag.

"Hello, sailor," she purred as she passed him.

Declan watched her saunter down the hall after Grayson, hips swinging. The woman exuded sex appeal of a rather obvious sort that left him cold. Simon came down the stairs and met them at the registration desk.

"Could I get some help here?" a woman's voice said.

Declan turned at the request of the second woman, a brunette with a thick fringe and shoulder-length hair cut bluntly straight. Fiona Church, he assumed from Nora's description of the actors. Her silky, green tunic and pants were wrinkled but clung in all the right places to her slim frame. She stood by the backseat holding a leather train case and tapped one pointed shoe on the pavement to underscore her impatience. He decided to be a gentleman.

"Actually, I'm another guest," he explained as he reached for her bags.

"Don't bother, then." She tried to hoist a huge leather sack out of the footwell of the backseat.

"My pleasure," he insisted, hauling the bag out. What did she have in here, a dead body? He admired the car's interior, soft, charcoal leather with ivory stitching. Directing must be lucrative.

She slung her purse over her shoulder and slammed the door. Declan followed her into the lodge, studying her smart look and trim figure. Too bad she came across as such a stuck-up tart.

Nora came down the stairs as they reached the desk. "You must be Fiona." She held out her hand in greeting. "I'm Nora Tierney, and I see you've met our guest, Declan Barnes."

The actress ignored Nora's outstretched hand and looked back over her shoulder at Declan. "I thought we were the only people here this week."

"You're in the Lewis Carroll Suite," Nora replied smoothly. She reached for the leather bag. "I'll take that, Declan."

"I have it," he insisted. "It's quite heavy."

Fiona glared at him. "It holds all the stage makeup," she said, ice dripping from each word. She swept past them and started up the stairs. "And I hope my room isn't filled with little creatures from *Alice in Wonderland*."

Behind her back, Nora stifled a laugh and whispered to Declan: "Oops—"

2 PM

Sean's midday bottle, greedily consumed, settled easily on his stomach. Nora showered and decided to save her new dress, opting instead for capris and an untucked lavender shirt that brought out her green eyes. She scrutinized her image in the mirrored door of the antique armoire that held her clothes. Not as full-figured as Gemma Hartwell or with as pretty a face, Nora readily acknowledged, even as she noted that Gemma seemed awfully chummy with Grayson. Nora's damp auburn hair would wave around her face as it dried, not at all sleek like Fiona's bob, and she wasn't as tall as the dark-haired beauty. Would Declan's head be turned by the comparisons? God, she hated feeling like a schoolgirl again.

When Nora reappeared in the dining room, pushing Sean in his buggy, Declan was finishing one of the sandwiches Agnes had assembled for the guests.

"Want me to take him for a walk?" he offered. "You said you're supposed to help Simon."

"That's Callie's job today. With a full belly and fresh air, he'll be satisfied."

Nora felt flattered he'd offered. After all, she was a package deal. "You can keep me company instead."

"No problem there." His smile lit his eyes, and he suddenly crouched down to tweak the baby's face. "You were right."

"About what?" she asked.

"I'm a sucker for his smile—and for his mother."

Callie appeared from the kitchen before Nora could stammer a reply. "He's all ready for you, Callie," Nora said.

"Off we go, then. Wave bye-bye to Mummy." Callie thanked Declan for holding the heavy lodge door for her as she left.

He turned back to Nora. Her heart hammered in her chest. "Let me show you where the play will be held." She held out her hand and he clasped it.

They were barely inside the drawing room doorway when he drew her to him. Nora fell into his embrace and the kiss that followed. "Nice to have you here in the flesh instead of on a computer screen," she murmured. God, that was inane, but Declan merely nuzzled her neck.

Simon passed the doorway carrying a huge earthen jug, and they broke apart. Bloody teenagers, Nora thought, but she felt herself grinning. Simon propped the door open, letting in a gentle breeze that brought with it the sweet scent of bluebells flowering under the hawthorn tree in the front yard.

"I'd better get to work," she whispered, then louder: "So the chairs go here, and risers will elevate a stage in front of the windows."

"Very nice." Declan walked with her into the hall. "Thanks for that sandwich. I'll unpack unless I can do something constructive." He raised an eyebrow, his look filled with meaning.

"See you later." She joined Simon at the desk. If he noticed her high color, Simon chose not to comment.

Nora consulted Kate's listing. "Gemma Hartwell plays Elvira, the first wife's ghost who makes life miserable for Charles Condomine. That's the part I played. She's in the Shakespeare Suite. Kate said Grayson chose the rooms, right?"

Simon nodded. "He gave himself the suite with the best water view."

"I think it's interesting he installed Gemma right next door and put Fiona in the farther corner, with the Dentons separating them."

"Don't go looking for trouble, Nora."

"I'm not." Her face was all innocence. "It's just that in the play he's still in love with his dead wife and gets exasperated with his second wife. That's who Fiona plays—"

Simon stopped her rush of words with a "time out" gesture. "It's a *play*, Nora, not reality."

A taxi honked, and they turned to watch it deposit a striking older woman with a slightly hunched posture. "That's Helen Mochrie," Nora said. "She plays—"

"Madame Arcati, the medium. Our turn to play our parts." Simon strode to the driveway.

Nora followed in his wake. With her snowy hair, the actress could be any age between sixty-five and eighty. Helen appeared already in character, sweeping ahead of them into the lodge with a swirl of printed skirt, a long, yellow scarf wrapped around her neck, her blue eyes glittering.

They took her luggage and showed her to the Wordsworth Suite. When Simon opened the door to the narrow, yellow room, Helen ran to the west window that looked out onto Windermere.

"Brilliant!" she proclaimed, turning to take in Kate's hand-painted daffodils splashed upon the walls. "Delightful!" she trilled, waving her hands to point to the lines of poetry stenciled as a border near the ceiling. Simon met Nora's eye with a barely concealed smirk; she had to look away.

"Kate Ramsey was a stage decorator before running the lodge with Simon," Nora explained. "She decorated all the suites."

Simon opened a door. "Here's your private bath—"

"Glorious!" Helen boomed, sweeping past Nora and into the bathroom. "If you don't mind, I'll just check with my control." She shut the door with a slam.

Simon gave in to his chuckle. "Her control?"

"Hush, she'll hear you." They left the room, and Nora closed the door behind her. "Her 'control' is the ghost she uses at séances to reach the spirit world."

"You're taking this much too seriously." Simon started downstairs. "But she's aptly cast. The play's not subtitled *An Improbable Farce in Three Acts* for nothing."

Nora's mouth gaped open. Long ago, Simon had told her he was a wealth of trivial information. He'd just confirmed it.

The lodge phone rang. Simon quickened his pace and answered. "Ramsey Lodge."

Nora joined him at the desk.

"I'll see if she's in. Hold, please." Simon punched a button. "For you, a solicitor named Daniel Kemp." He held the phone out to Nora.

"Who?" Why would a lawyer call her?

"He says he represents Mr. and Mrs. Harvey Pembroke."

Nora's throat constricted. Paul's parents? Why were they calling her now, and through a lawyer? She'd met them for the first and only time at Paul's memorial service, and it had not been a heartwarming experience for either side. His parents blamed Nora for keeping Paul from them. Nora hadn't had a chance to explain it was Paul who hadn't wanted to bring her to Cornwall before Muriel Pembroke had advanced on Nora, eyes blazing, and only Val plunging in to pull Nora out of the way had prevented an altercation. She hadn't known she was pregnant that day, but that meeting explained why almost six months after Sean's birth, she still dithered about telling them they had a grandson.

These thoughts flitted through Nora's mind in an instant. She gulped. "Why are they having a lawyer call me? Did they find out about Sean?" The lump that had been in her throat plummeted to her stomach; her hands were clammy as she reached for the phone.

Simon whispered, "You won't know what they know until you take the man's call."

CHAPTER SIX

"You took her by surprise."
Ruth: Act 1, Scene 1

2:55 PM

Simon left the hall to give Nora privacy with her call. She almost called him back as she clicked the button for line one, wondering how the lawyer had found out where she lived. Then she flashed on last autumn's murder and realized a simple Google search would provide headlines with the details. She drew a breath. "Nora Tierney."

"Miss Tierney, this is Daniel Kemp. I'm the solicitor representing Muriel and Harvey Pembroke in the matter of settling the estate of their son, Paul." The man's cheerful voice bore none of the gloomy tenor she expected from an estate lawyer.

Nora struggled to keep her voice calm. "I see." She really didn't but wanted to appear cooperative. "How can I help?" she asked, instead of shouting the line, "*What do you want from me*?" Her thoughts clutched on the term "estate." Could Paul's parents think she'd stolen from their son's flat? They'd never lived together; the few things of hers that had landed there she'd taken home and nothing more.

"The Pembrokes were named in Paul's will as his executors. They're anxious to settle things and sell his flat. There's a matter I've been instructed to discuss with you. I understand you were engaged to the deceased at the time of his death?"

"You could say that." Nora realized Paul must have at least told his parents of their engagement. What difference could that make now?

"I need to obtain your signature." There was the sound of fingers tapping a keyboard. "I could travel north to Cumbria next Monday if that would be convenient?"

"Next Monday? I suppose so." Nora bit her lip. "Mr. Kemp, can you tell me what this is about?"

"I prefer to discuss these matters in person, but I assure you I won't take up much of your time. Are there rooms at Ramsey Lodge to let? It's a long ride, and I owe Mrs. Kemp a break."

"I'm afraid we're fully booked for the next week, but I can give you the number of the Belsfield Hotel." Nora gave him the address of Ramsey Lodge and her mobile number while she looked through the list of the lodge's competitors.

"Thank you. I'll see you Monday after lunch. Shall we say by 2 o'clock?"

The solicitor rang off, leaving Nora looking at the phone in her hand. She slumped in the desk chair. This must be a release of sorts, to stop her from putting in any claim on Paul's estate. Yet in an age of express mail, scans and faxes, she thought signing papers could be handled without a personal visit. Perhaps Kemp's real reason for driving more than five hours was to give his wife a few days away.

But that didn't address the deeper issue. Even if the solicitor hadn't hinted at the issue of a child, Nora couldn't continue to avoid telling the Pembrokes they had a grandchild. She walked to the open door and looked across the road to her right. Handfuls of tourists walked along the quay at Bowness Bay. Bright, gauzy clouds were perfectly reflected in the deep blue of the water's surface. The setting was serene, and she loved living here, even if it was temporary. Why couldn't life be as simple as the placid lake?

Then she remembered the October morning when she'd stumbled over a corpse on her morning walk at the water's edge. Nothing was simple when you looked beneath the surface.

"There you are." Declan joined her at the door.

She turned to look at him, and he took her face in his hands and brushed her lips with his. "You look very serious."

She didn't answer and turned away as movement on the driveway took her focus. A large lorry with **FITZPATRICK'S RENTALS** painted on the side pulled up the drive. "I have to let Simon know the props are here."

4:30 PM

Nora watched Declan help Simon and another man sort the props. She leaned against the doorway, taking a brief break. After Callie returned with a drowsy Sean, Nora put him in his cot to finish his nap, then answered lodge emails and matched the stack of checks Simon gave her with their appropriate bills, ready to be mailed out. She gathered brochures on the lodge and the general area into a packet to send to a choral group from Dorset wanting to book this June. If this play came off well, Simon may have hit on a grand marketing idea, having Ramsey Lodge host different performing groups.

Nora watched the two men she cared for in different ways, a study in contrasts: Simon with his sandy hair and lanky build, Declan with his darker looks and broader frame. Then she took in the third man, who was older and reminded Nora of Mr. Rogers. Something about him looked familiar.

"Just stack those cartons in a corner, Declan," Simon instructed. "We need to leave this space clear for the risers that will form the stage." He indicated a large area that took up more than half the room, from the windows to past the fireplace.

Declan winked at Nora as he hoisted a carton marked "Linens/

Lamp." Simon and the other man carried a sofa between them to near the stacked folding chairs.

"How you managing, Burt?"

"We're fine," Burt answered.

Nora was surprised by his words; she remembered Agnes had told her that Simon had hired local Burt Marsh to be stage manager but she thought Agnes had said he was a widower.

"Burt's done stage managing, and his late wife, Estelle, enjoyed acting for the community theatre after they retired," Agnes had said. "Both teachers. Poor thing died a few months ago."

They'd been interrupted before Agnes could impart more details, but Nora decided the third man must be Burt. Declan followed Simon outside to continue emptying the truck, and Nora saw Burt attempt to measure the length of the large bow window that overlooked the patio and lake. She walked into the room and grabbed one end of the measuring tape.

"Let me hold that for you," she said. "I'm Nora, by the way."

Burt Marsh nodded. "Thanks."

Nora held the tape, and Burt walked with it to the far end, pulling it taut and noting the distance. It was only when he turned away from Nora to jot the number down on a slip of paper from his pocket that she saw the back of his head and realized why he'd looked familiar.

Burt Marsh was the man grieving in St Martin's graveyard.

CHAPTER SEVEN

"This is going to be a flop. I can tell you that here and now."
Elvira: Act III, Scene I

6:45 PM

Simon surveyed the dining room as Maeve straightened a tablecloth. The silver gleamed, and the candles would lend a lovely ambiance when lit, highlighting the clusters of daffodils and tulips Maeve had arranged on each round table.

"Certain I can't convince you to stay and eat with us?" Simon brushed his hair off his forehead. He didn't want to beg.

Maeve gave his arm a reassuring squeeze. "I can't miss my class, Si, but I promise to bring an overnight bag Wednesday, all right?"

"I didn't know learning French was so important to you."

"It's like most things; practice makes perfect." She raised an eyebrow.

Simon started to pull her into an embrace.

"This will never do at all!" Grayson Lange had crept into the room, and his booming voice startled them both.

"Whatever's wrong?" Maeve asked.

"My dear, it's these little tables." The director shook his head. "My cast and crew must be seated together at the same table to take notes and promote the family feel that is the hallmark of my troupe."

"No problem at all, Mr. Lange." Maeve fluttered her long lashes at him and drew Simon toward his rooms. "Just give us a sec."

"What are you thinking?" Simon followed her into his kitchen and watched her speedily move his fruit bowl onto the counter.

"Move those, please," Maeve said, pointing to a stack of sketches and pencils at one end of the table. "I'm thinking Grayson Lange is already a bloody pain in the arse and he hasn't been here more than a tic." She dumped an empty tea mug in the sink. "This table fit through that door?"

Simon gauged the opening of his pocket door. "With a bit of maneuvering."

"Maneuver away. We switch the long table for two of the round ones and he's satisfied."

"What do I do in the meantime for a table?"

"You put the two rounds in here, one to eat at and one to work on when you're not in your studio." She gestured to one end of the table. "Now grab hold. Ramsey Lodge aims to please."

They scrambled to bring in the long table and switched it for the two rounds, moving dishes and flowers and candles, then rolled the rounds into Simon's kitchen. Grayson lounged against the doorframe without offering help. Maeve found a pale green cloth that didn't match the others but did fit the table. She placed her vases down the center and lit the candles while Simon reset the table.

Thank goodness Maeve was on the ball. Simon thanked her as the first actors came into the room.

"I'll see you tomorrow." She slipped away.

Satisfied with the new arrangement, Grayson created his pecking order by seating Gemma and Fiona on either side of him, with Poppy and Helen next on one side and the Dentons on the other. Burt was allowed the other end. Simon knew the stage manager didn't plan to eat at the lodge every night.

Grayson kissed Nora's hand as she came into the room after putting Sean to sleep.

"So lovely to see you again, my dear," the director practically purred.

Nora blushed and pulled her hand away before sitting down at the round table where she would eat with Simon and Declan. Simon noted Declan's scowl at the director. Grayson opened his mouth to speak, only to be interrupted by Helen.

"I think we should all join hands and thank the spirits for bringing us together." Shiny discs on the turban she wore glistened in the candlelight and bobbed with her movements, throwing blue streaks into the room.

"I think you're dotty." Gemma raised her wine glass and knocked back half.

"Helen, please—" Grayson warned. He took his place at the head of the large table, leaving no doubt in anyone's mind as to who was in charge.

8:30 PM

Simon moved among the guests seated along the long table, refilling teacups and wine glasses. Fiona Church picked at her food, but Gemma Hartwell ate with gusto, and Callie took mostly empty plates back to the kitchen after the main meal. Everyone seemed to enjoy the raspberry crumble they were eating for dessert; Agnes would be chuffed.

At one of the remaining round tables in the corner, Nora and Declan lingered over the same dessert Simon had wolfed down. Simon poured tea for Poppy and listened to the conversation. Grayson Lange held court over his cast and minor crew while the Dentons made a stab at polite conversation.

"I understand you live locally, Mr. Marsh?" Lydia asked.

Burt looked up from his plate. "Burt." Then, "Windermere."

"A man of few words," Rupert chimed in. "I like that. We actors tend to be verbose, you'll find, Burt."

"Tell me about it," Poppy said, accepting more tea from Simon.

"I, for one, hardly ever talk unless I have something important to shay—say," Gemma declared, waving her wine glass.

"Spit it out, Gemma," Fiona said. "We're all panting to hear your words of wisdom."

Simon saw Nora stifle a giggle at the exchange and watched Declan reach for her hand under the table. Maeve would have enjoyed these shenanigans.

Gemma threw down her napkin. "You're just ticked off you're not Elvira!"

Fiona leered across the table at her. "For someone used to playing maids, are you really up to being the star?"

Grayson clapped his hands. "That's enough, ladies, no bickering."

Simon paused to refill the Dentons' tea.

"Wonderful meal. I'll gain a few stone if I'm not careful." Lydia's smile was infectious.

Simon returned it. "I'll pass your compliments on to our cook, Agnes."

"Mine, too," Helen chimed in across the table. "I had a premonition this would be a wonderful home for us. Your cook must be very stable emotionally."

Simon didn't feel compelled to answer, thinking of Agnes' prolific swearing in her Scottish accent when things went awry.

"I'll have a refill." Burt held out his cup.

Simon leaned over to fill it.

"Tell Agnes it was nice to have a proper dinner instead of a microwave ready-meal." He lowered his voice. "What a crew, eh?"

They looked down the table at the rest of the cast, who leaned toward their director, listening in varying degrees of rapt attention as he expounded on his start in theatre.

"Decidedly different," Simon agreed just as quietly. "But very talented, I'm sure." These were, after all, his paying guests.

CHAPTER SEVEN

8:45 PM

Burt Marsh wasn't certain these idiotic fools were so talented. If they were, they'd be acting at a real theatre in Covent Garden or Drury Lane instead of rolling around the countryside playing to small audiences in this kind of place. A string of constant holidays it looked like to him, all right for some. What a lark. Find a nice place to put on your play, then con the management into thinking they'd increase their business and spend your time lolling around. Two or three performances and you were on your way to the next stop down the road. Skiving off, every one of them on the fiddle.

His Estelle had loved the theatre, the real stuff. When they had met, he had been twenty-eight and Estelle a twenty-four-year-old English teacher who had arrived at Windermere St Anne's School with her trunk full of plays and classics for her classroom.

By the time they'd retired nine years ago, it was simply Windermere School, and they'd spent thirty-six years there, riding to school together every day, their holidays the same, their lives entwined with school activities and its calendar. Estelle had directed the school plays, too, and that was when he'd become a dab hand at lights and props. They had been quite a team.

He could still summon up his first sighting of the slim woman with long, fair hair falling into her eyes as she struggled to drag a huge trunk along the hallway. Burt had gallantly taken hold of the heavy burden and carried it into her classroom.

"My hero." Estelle had introduced herself. "Thank you for the rescue." It was a mantra she had repeated often. He'd rescued her from her loneliness, from her singleness, from being a solitary woman from Newton Abbot at a posting in a rural area she hadn't known but had grown to love.

"What's in here?" Burt had been puzzled as to why a teacher would think it necessary to carry her own tools. All he had needed for science were the textbooks and lab equipment the school had provided.

"The whole world's in here! Travel, history, culture, the ways of man." She had thrown open the lid to show him books by Dickens, Shakespeare, Tolstoy, with plays by Chekhov, Miller and Williams. There had even been three from an American named Neil Simon. "My students will have access to all of these."

He'd fallen in love with her a little bit then, but they'd dated for almost two years before marrying. By that time, he hadn't even blinked when she'd confided her idea of a perfect honeymoon: a week in London attending the theatre. Each day they'd stood in line at the box office of a different theatre, getting discounts for that night's available seats. After a day touring the Tower of London or the British Museum, they'd rushed back to their tiny rented room to wash and change for their evening out.

He could still conjure up Estelle's face the night they'd scored tickets high in the balcony to see *Funny Girl* at the Prince of Wales Theatre, its glowing corner tower making them feel cosmopolitan and worldly. When that tiny woman with the big voice had opened her mouth to sing, Estelle's eyes had opened wide.

"If I didn't love you, Burt Marsh, I could be in love with Barbra Streisand."

A loud guffaw from Grayson brought Burt back to dinner. His life was quiet now, too quiet. He wondered what his wife would have made of these whiners and pretenders. In his head, he carried on conversations with her, but he knew she was gone. A tremor ran through his body. He ached with loss for Estelle.

Chapter Eight

"I'm sure I hope you both enjoy yourselves."
Ruth: Act II, Scene 3

8:55 PM

Declan winced when Grayson Lange tapped his knife against his water glass. Voices around the table fell silent. Beside him, Nora sat up straighter.

"I think a few comments are in order before we retire. First off, thanks to Simon Ramsey for hosting us this week and to his staff for making us comfortable. I'm sure if your rooms are anywhere near as comfortable as my Royal Suite, we'll enjoy a relaxing break combined with a successful play."

Simon acknowledged the remarks with a nod of his head to a smattering of applause. Declan thought Burt Marsh actually smiled for the first time that evening. Grayson's toothy, white smile was either the result of recent bleaching or a full set of crowns.

As the director explained the daily schedule, Declan inhaled Nora's citrusy scent when she leaned in closer to him and spoke quietly.

"I saw Burt earlier today at the graveyard at St Martin's." She explained the man's piteous howls.

"Poor chap. But he seems to be engaged now."

"Grayson has that effect on everyone. He swoops you in."

"And did he swoop you in when you interviewed him?" Declan steeled himself for her answer. They were adults and both had pasts.

"No way. But I wonder who'll share the Royal Suite tonight."

Declan looked at the grouping. "You seem certain he won't be alone. Who's on your short list? Or might you change your mind and fall under his spell?"

"As if. There's only space for so much ego in one room." She pointed her chin at the table. "Besides, there are enough candidates over there."

Declan followed her gaze. "I see you need a mystery to unravel even when there isn't one. Motherhood hasn't changed you a bit. So your likely suspects are?"

"Three possibilities. Poppy Braeburn's the right age, but she's too uptight. I say it's down to either Fiona Church or Gemma Hartwell. I thought it must be Gemma because Grayson put her in the room next to him, but Simon disagrees." She sipped her tea and met his eyes over the rim of her cup.

Declan admired the mischievous glint in Nora's eyes and considered her statement. "He's in for a rough time if it's Fiona. She strikes me as beautiful but cold." Not Nora. She was anything but cold.

"Interesting. You think Gemma's more his type, too?"

They watched Gemma lean over to whisper in Grayson's ear, placing a hand on his arm in a proprietary manner. The director laughed heartily at her remark.

Declan nodded. "I think that decision's been made. I'm just not sure who made it."

10:45 PM

Declan returned his sherry glass to the tray in the library and tried to catch Nora's eye. She remained in deep conversation with Poppy about the costume Gemma would wear as Elvira.

"Empire, loose and frothy, delicate and ethereal," Poppy explained. "A very light grey, and we'll keep her makeup pale, just highlight her eyes and do bright red lips."

"Perfect." Nora sighed. "My outfit in college was run together from an old net curtain that had been used in the previous play."

"And I have no doubt it looked lovely on you," Declan interjected, finally catching Nora's attention and giving her what he hoped was a meaningful look.

"I should turn in." Nora stood. "Thanks for the update."

Lydia Denton stood also. "We've had a long day, Rupert."

Her husband rose, and the two murmured their goodnights. They left the library with Nora and Declan on their heels.

Declan walked Nora to her suite. This was a bit awkward. Could he expect to be invited into her room?

At her door, she hesitated, looking across the hall to Simon's door. He followed her glance.

"Firmly closed." He drew her into his arms for a long kiss. "I've wanted to do that all evening."

"Sorry I've been distracted." Nora returned his kiss.

Declan realized she was standing on her tiptoes to reach him. "Maybe you'd be more comfortable elsewhere?"

Nora bit her lip and opened her bedroom door. A nightlight shone in the alcove, throwing the shadow of the baby's cot onto one wall. Sean cried out, and she stiffened.

They waited in the doorway, listening to the baby shuffle around. Declan mentally crossed his fingers, hoping Sean would fall back to sleep.

The baby's movements increased and so did his cries.

Nora squeezed his hand. "I've got to go to him."

"Of course." He hoped he'd hid his disappointment. "I'll see you in the morning."

Sean howled, and Nora closed the door.

11:10 PM

Folding down the covers, Lydia Denton observed her husband puttering around their suite. It looked out over the front drive of Ramsey Lodge, and she approved of the Morris wallpaper below the chair rail that matched the blue birds and red, flowered vines on the drapes and coverlet.

"I believe that's the same Kelmscott Tree pattern Morris had in his own bedroom." She remembered their visit to Kelmscott Manor early in their marriage when she'd become an aficionado of Morris' designs.

"Very nice, dear." Rupert fussed with arranging the top surface of the tall dresser, where Lydia had stored his clothing.

She could have been talking about the weather. She watched the man she'd loved for so long move the framed photograph to different positions until he was satisfied, biting her tongue to refrain from chastising. It wasn't healthy, this obsession of his. It wasn't healthy at all.

11:59 PM

Nora looked at her sleeping son, his lips pursed as he dreamt.

He'd fallen back to sleep after only a few minutes of rocking. Missing the breast, she supposed, and he wouldn't take to using a dummy, as the Brits called a pacifier. With luck, he'd sleep until 6 AM.

That left her with a full six hours during which she could

be sleeping. She changed into her nightgown and brushed her teeth, remembering the rush of feelings that swept over her when Declan had taken her in his arms and how that warred with her reticence to welcome him into her bed with Sean sleeping just feet away.

She thought of how she'd categorized herself earlier today: writer, author and single parent. She'd left out one important aspect: woman.

Before she could change her mind, Nora turned on the baby monitor and grabbed the receiver. She threw off her old nightgown and slipped into her robe, the newest thing she had, a Christmas gift from her mother and Roger. The blue robe had *Mum* embroidered on its chest.

"Mums have sex, too," she whispered and crept out of her room past Simon's door.

The glow of a small lamp on the hall desk showed her the way. She shot up the stairs, picturing Declan in the Sherlock Holmes Suite where Kate had insisted he belonged.

She knocked softly, mirroring the hammering of her heart. Declan's surprised expression quickly changed to delight. She waved the receiver at him and watched his smile grow wider. The mahogany four-poster with its tattersall curtains centered in the room looked like a haven to Nora as she walked in and closed the door behind her.

CHAPTER NINE

"Behave perfectly ordinarily, as though nothing had happened."
Ruth: Act II, Scene 3

Tuesday, 10th April

9:20 AM

Nora looked in the bathroom mirror and smoothed on a hint of blush. Was that the face of a sated woman looking back at her? She smiled at her own reflection. Naughty could be good—very good.

Her favorite jeans fit, which brought another huge grin. Strange how a piece of clothing made a person feel confident. It was going to be a great day, despite hardly sleeping. True to form, Sean had woken at 6:15 AM just as Nora had stepped out of the shower. These morning hours when the rest of the lodge was quiet were her favorite time with her son. He had her undivided attention, and every day she could see growth and change as his personality formed.

After his morning bottle, she dressed him and sat with Sean in her wing chair and alternated taking bites of an apple with reading a book to the baby, making animal noises as she pointed to the colorful pictures. At times, Sean grunted in return. He really was the most amazing child. She felt suffused with love for the entire world. Val would say she'd put on her rose-colored glasses today. She had Declan to thank for that—Declan, who smoothed away any hint of embarrassment with laughter, who woke up bits of her she'd forgotten she owned, who made her feel that part of her that had been missing had been returned.

When Sean's eyes got heavy, Nora put him in his cot, then

turned on the musical mobile and left the room so he would learn to fall asleep by himself. Being aware of his cues would help her keep him on a schedule. She took her old friend, the monitor receiver, into the lodge.

This morning over breakfast, Declan described the hike he would take today. She knew he needed this respite from work. After the flurry of emotions of last night, she sensed that rather than trying to escape from her, he was giving her space.

Grayson had told his cast at dinner last night that his expectation was to start their first rehearsal promptly at 9:30. Right after eating, everyone had gone back to their rooms to prepare. Nora passed through the empty dining room and into the drawing room.

Burt Marsh had been in early to work; the risers were set up and locked into place. Nora had seen him getting started early this morning when she'd wandered in her robe into the kitchen to heat Sean's bottle. Now she found him pawing through one of the stacked cartons.

"Can I help, Burt?" She wondered if he knew she'd been privy to his emotional breakdown the day before. How awkward.

He looked into the depths of the carton. "You'd be a lifesaver if you could find the cloth that's supposed to go over that table." He pointed to a round table and looked at a listing on a clipboard.

His unembarrassed demeanor led Nora to decide he hadn't seen her at the church. "What color is it?"

"Not noted, damn it." He slapped the clipboard down and pulled over a second carton.

"I'll check this one." Nora opened the one Declan had moved yesterday. She found throw pillows packed around a table lamp. Wedged next to them was a slim cardboard tube with a piece of linen wrapped around it. "Could this be it?" She unrolled the cloth.

Burt hastened over. "Let's see if it fits."

Nora draped the cloth over the table. "This must be it."

"It's so wrinkled." Burt grimaced. "Estelle could press those out in a pinch."

"I'll press it." Nora whipped the cloth off the table. "Agnes has an iron in the kitchen."

"*Excuse me*—I'm supposed to handle the costumes and any material." The waspish statement came from Poppy, who stood in the doorway with her arms crossed. The Dentons hovered close behind her.

Nora stopped in her tracks by the kitchen door. So much for the woman's nice behavior yesterday when Sean had thrown up on her. Nora looked uncertainly back at Burt, who had his head down, rooting around in another carton. Then Grayson appeared with Gemma hanging off his arm.

"Now, Poppy, don't go all schoolmarmish on us. Let Nora be your handmaiden if she wants—you have plenty to do and we need to start blocking rehearsal." His voice had a remarkable effect, calming Poppy, who nodded and moved away.

Nora wished she could slam the swinging kitchen door to let Grayson know what she thought of his remark. Handmaiden, indeed. Her morning glow evaporated.

She remembered more clearly his insufferable attitude during their interview, especially his condescending demeanor toward women. Poppy's pickiness rankled, too. She could be nicer; Nora had seen that firsthand. After today, Poppy was bloody well welcome to iron everything in Ramsey Lodge.

Callie wiped the counters after breakfast cleanup. "Simon and Maeve took Agnes to the market," she said. "I made Declan sandwiches for his pack before he left. I'll start making beds up next if Sean is asleep."

"He's napping. I suspect you'll find one of those beds hasn't been slept in." Seeing Gemma and Grayson together confirmed her feelings about them. She took out the iron and board, plugged in one and folded out the other. "Need to iron this." And no need to tell Callie her own bed hadn't been slept in.

"Let me do that," Callie offered, tying her auburn hair into a ponytail.

"No, you start the beds, and I'll come up to help, but I'll tell you what you can do later." Nora licked a finger to test the heat of the iron before applying it viciously to the cloth. "When this iron cools down, please take it with the board up to the Potter Suite and leave it for Poppy's use." Nora smiled at her initiative, back in control of her emotions.

"Will do." Callie set off up the back stairs, whistling lightly.

Nora ironed the creases out of the tablecloth, then unplugged the iron and set it to cool on top of the board. She burst through the swinging door back into the drawing room in time to see Grayson stalk into the hallway and bellow up the stairs.

"Fiona! Get your lazy arse down here!" He strode back into the drawing room in a huff.

Nora helped Burt spread the cloth on the table. He smiled his thanks.

Upstairs, a door slammed, then footsteps clattered down the stairs. Fiona stood in the doorway, her face flushed with rage.

"Someone's had the cheek to come into my room and steal my script!" She yelled and stalked toward Gemma, who hid behind Grayson. "And I know who that slapper is!"

"Fi, language dear." Grayson drew Gemma out from behind him and kept his arm around her. "That's impossible. Gemma's been with me since breakfast. You must have misplaced it."

"It was on my bedside table when I came down to breakfast. It was gone when I went back up." Fiona spoke through clenched teeth. "Don't be such a bloody idiot, Gray."

Gemma laughed, secure in the circle of Grayson's arm. "Temper, darling. We don't want the local rags to hear you can't control yourself."

Fiona raised a finger in Gemma's face. "Is that a threat?"

The director drew up to his full height and glared down at Fiona. "Remember who runs this show, my dear, if you want to keep your role in it." Changing his mood in a heartbeat, Grayson plastered his charming smile back in place. "Take mine. I know this farce by heart." He held out his script; Fiona snatched it from his hand as he turned to the grouping watching the interplay. "Places, people. Let's take it from the top."

1:45 PM

After lunch, Simon made certain the dining room floor didn't need a sweep. His thoughts strayed to Kate and Ian, exploring Paris and then traveling by train south to Provence. What he wouldn't give to trade places with them. He missed France with an ache that reached into his fingers.

But this was Kate's time while he played the good brother, insisting that Nora and Maeve would step up to help out, and both were proving him right. Maeve and Agnes were preparing dinner; Nora and Callie had done the rooms in record time.

Nora recounted the cast members' tantrums that he'd missed when he was at the market. After he'd helped set up lunch, he'd stood in the doorway to watch the last of the morning rehearsal. The troupe had worked on what the director called blocking, their entrances and exact places on stage. It had seemed to go well, and the cast was now resting before their 2 PM rehearsal.

Simon checked the desk. Nora had answered all the emails and done the post. He stepped into the drawing room and surveyed the stage. Lamps were on tables; a coffee table stood on a rug rolled out in front of the sofa. Burt stood on a ladder, fiddling with a chandelier hung in place of the lodge's ceiling fixture. The thing was massive, with long curving brass arms. Each arm had a metal band running around the top that held a bulb. Burt affixed several glass prisms along a few of the bands and climbed down.

"Magnetic. Stand back and we'll give this a try." He held a remote in his hand and hit a button. The glass prisms fell to the ground.

Simon started, then leaned over and picked one up. The crystal had a flat metal disk at its top. "Not broken?" The pointed spear glittered in the light. "These look sharp."

"Shatterproof glass. They'll hit the table and scatter, but that's at the end as the stage is empty and the room falls apart." Burt stepped over to the fireplace and showed Simon a painting propped on the mantel. "When I get this rigged, it'll crash nicely to the ground, too." He pointed to the windows. "I still have to sort the curtains so they open and close on a repeater. And the phonograph will play the theme song, 'Always,' loudly and quickly to round out the climax."

"How will you get all those dangles back on after Saturday for Sunday's performance?" Never having been part of the backstage preparations for a play, Simon's interest was genuine.

"See this?" Burt pointed to a line that ran from the top of the fixture through a hook, along the ceiling and down the wall, only to disappear at the top of the left French door. "It's fixed outside on a winch, like a boat, with a dog stop to keep it from falling. I can raise and lower it to reattach the crystals. We used a similar device when the Community Theatre did *Phantom of the Opera*, and it worked like a charm."

Simon had never seen such animation in Burt. "So all these things can be repeated for Sunday night, then?"

"That's the beauty of—" A loud shriek from the second floor cut Burt off.

Simon raced toward the stairs. Where had that come from?

Nora appeared from her room. "What's going on?"

Several doors opened upstairs as Simon ran up. "I'll let you know." He reached the top landing and looked around. The door to the Shakespeare Suite banged open. Gemma Hartwell stood trembling in the doorway; tears streamed down her face.

"In here," she cried, pointing to the ornately carved Jacobean bed.

Grayson ran from his room next door, drying his hands on a towel. He drew the actress into his arms. "Darling, what's happened?"

By then, Helen, Poppy and Fiona had crowded the hallway and were gawking over the director's shoulder. The Dentons stood in their doorway, peering out anxiously. Simon brushed past Gemma and Grayson into the large corner suite, not seeing anything worth screaming about. If this was about a spider hanging in a corner …

He looked around the room: creamy upper walls, dark-paneled wainscoting, a large tapestry on one wall. The bed was neatly made up, its hangings and coverlet in the blue, green and vermilion crewel embroidery of flowers and animal shapes of the era.

Gemma shrugged off Grayson's arm. "On—the—pillow," she managed to get out between sobs.

Simon brushed aside the bed curtains and immediately saw the reason for the woman's distress. Laid in the center of the crisp, embroidered bolster at the head of the bed was the carcass of a light grey rabbit, its fluffy white underbelly a counterpoint to its angled, broken neck and the bloodied pulp of one mangled foot.

2:05 PM

Nora joined the group as Simon took charge.

"I'll get a garbage bag from the service closet," he said.

Nora pulled him aside. "Try not to touch it; use the plastic to envelop it." She saw the look he gave her and could almost read Simon's thoughts: "A bloody mystery Nora thinks she has to solve."

Nora took Gemma by the arm. The woman seemed rooted to the spot, sniffling. Helen peered inside the room. "There's an evil spirit amongst us," she pronounced. "This play is cursed!"

Grayson reacted instantly, snapping his towel. "Helen! Stop being a ghoul and lead the way downstairs. Back to work, everyone." He turned to Nora. "Please take Gemma to my room."

Gemma allowed Nora to help her into the Royal Suite, where she threw herself across the huge bed. Grayson tossed the damp towel into the bathroom sink and charged back out. "Five minutes to pull yourself together, Gemma, and I'll expect you at rehearsal." He stalked out of the room.

Nora grabbed the towel and ran the water to warm it. A large bottle of perfume from Illuminum, the same house the Duchess of Cambridge used, stood on the counter. Somehow, Nora doubted the director wore the scent "White Gardenia Petals." She noticed more feminine cosmetics spread out over the end of the counter.

She wished Declan were here to make sense of this malicious mischief. At least Sean was safe on the other side of the lodge. She'd left him sitting on a blanket on the floor of her room, surrounded by soft toys and his favorite plastic keys.

Nora handed Gemma the wet rag. The actress turned off the

waterworks and moaned a bit for Nora's benefit as she laid it across her forehead.

"Who would do such a rotten thing?" Gemma sniveled.

Nora sat on the side of the bed. "Someone's idea of a sick joke."

Gemma muttered, "Who knows?" And moaned again.

"Who knows what, Gemma?"

The actress remained silent. Nora's mind was in overdrive. Who *would* have committed such a perverted act and why? Perhaps Helen was right: Evil had entered Ramsey Lodge.

2:20 PM

Declan's walk had started with a ferry ride to Far Sawrey. He followed a gravel shore path and climbed a hill that gave him spectacular views of England's largest lake. The sun sparkled on Windermere's surface. Sailboats bobbed about, and powerboats decorously observed the newly reduced speed laws. The vista gave him a feeling of omnipotence. Freedom from work and stress encouraged him to smile at the other walkers he passed, as did the thought that when he returned, Nora would be waiting for him.

The night before, his mood had leapt from disappointment to great joy. His warm welcome had eliminated any awkwardness between Nora and him; the hours they spent together had been filled with playful discovery.

"I'm so glad you knocked on my door," he'd told her as they lay together in the early hours, her hair spread out across his chest. Had they slept? He couldn't remember, but he could still feel her touch on him. When she'd risen in the early hours to creep back downstairs before the baby woke, he'd moved to her side of the bed to lie in the warm spot she'd left behind.

Declan found the Cuckoo Brow Inn, south of Far Sawrey. They poured a good pint he enjoyed outside at a table, eating the sandwiches Callie had provided. Replaying last night, he ached for Nora as he brushed the crumbs off and continued his walk.

This wasn't the most challenging hike he'd ever undertaken but a reasonable one to start his week and clear his mind from the pressures of his usual investigations.

Working in the Criminal Investigation Department as a Detective Inspector, Declan enjoyed his squad and worked to develop a good team. While there were separate departments that investigated drugs, organized crime and even high-tech cyber crime, Declan thought of his unit as the regular working group for the crimes that affected Oxford's citizens: serious assaults, robberies, sexual offenses, even murder. He pursued all criminals with zeal borne out of his desire to outwit evil.

On his way back, Declan stopped at a gift shop on the quay and perused the postcard racks for the tackiest one he could find. CID's notice board displayed offerings sent from staff on holiday to tease those stuck at work. He chose one split into four views of the area with GREETINGS FROM CUMBRIA! splashed across the top. There was a view of Scafell Pike and a sunset over the lake for the top photos. The lower half featured Wordsworth's Dove Cottage, its gardens in full bloom, and lastly—the deciding factor for Declan—a shot inside The World of Beatrix Potter, with dozens of stuffed Peter Rabbits and Jemima Puddle-Ducks on display. Brilliant.

Then to bring a smile to the likes of Watkins, McAfee and the others toiling away, Declan scrawled across the back:

No crime, not missing you, glad you're not here. D

He addressed it and, after buying a stamp, stuck it into the red postbox on the corner. Mission accomplished.

Declan crossed the road to Ramsey Lodge, mood high. The

brown-stone Edwardian lodge looked attractive and well maintained; its white woodwork shone in the sunlight. Declan inhaled the spring air, wondering if he could get Nora away for a few hours tomorrow. Perhaps a trip to the Windermere Steamboat Museum? He wondered how far a ride it was to Sizergh Castle. Both would have facilities for buggies.

He opened the lodge door and paused on the step to check for mud on his hiking boots. An iron hedgehog, its back a stiff bristle brush, sat to one side for just this purpose, and as he worked on removing the clumps of dirt that clung to his boots, he heard Grayson Lange's bellowing voice.

" ... and I want to make it clear to whomever is responsible that I will not tolerate any more of these childish pranks. This ends here and *now.*" His voice shook with anger, then quickly changed tenor. "I'm quite prepared to overlook today's incidents in the interest of the play. Now if you'll turn your scripts to Act II ... "

Today's incidents? What was that about? Declan closed the door behind him. After being in the bright sun, he stood blinking for a minute in the darker hall.

Nora came downstairs leading Gemma Hartwell. He caught her serious expression and tried to ignore the rush to his groin. Gemma's face was red and blotchy. Declan raised an eyebrow in question at Nora, who stood beside him to watch Gemma's entrance into the drawing room. The actress was greeted with a loud burst of enthusiasm from Grayson.

"Here's our Elvira now! We're starting Act II, dear, so your entrance will be from those French doors outside. Fiona, you're sitting here when I make my entrance."

Fiona sat at the round table Burt had situated under the chandelier.

"Remember your direction is to greet me 'with a certain stiffness,' Fiona," the director instructed. "This morning you were much too friendly."

Declan enjoyed the glare Fiona shot Grayson, but the director ignored her as the rehearsal commenced. He and Nora turned as Simon came downstairs, carrying a small object wrapped in a green plastic bag.

Nora tugged Declan's sleeve. "We need to talk. In Simon's room," she commanded. "I have to get Sean."

Declan followed Simon to his kitchen and pulled out chairs.

"Don't ask." Simon placed his bundle on the table.

Nora returned with Sean and sat down with the baby on her lap. She explained the incident in detail, and Declan frowned.

"Not a nice thing to find on your pillow," he agreed, turning to Simon. "How did you get it into that bag?"

Simon rolled his eyes. "Miss Marple here had me pull the bag over the carcass and roll it into the bag, so no, I haven't touched it."

"Excellent." Declan caught Nora's eye and smiled. "Do you have a pen and any tape to seal it, Simon?"

Simon rummaged through a drawer and found a roll of masking tape and a marker. Sean reached for the bag but Nora distracted him with a set of plastic keys he promptly put in his mouth and chewed.

Declan sealed the bag and used more tape to wrap it mummy style. He signed and dated a last piece of tape and held the bundle out to Simon.

"What am I supposed to do with this?" Simon reluctantly took the rabbit.

"Have room in your freezer? Better to err on the side of keeping evidence, just in case there are more pranks." Declan flashed on the memory of the card he'd just posted and hoped he hadn't jinxed his holiday by writing about the lack of crime in the area.

"Don't forget Fiona's missing script," Nora said. "We should make a list of why this might be happening and who may be doing it."

Declan frowned, noting Simon gave her a similar look from his side of the table.

She looked from one man to the other. "What?"

"Let's not get carried away, Nora. It's enough I have a dead rabbit in my freezer." Simon sighed. "This has a childish quality about it."

"I agree." Declan noted the firm set of Nora's lips.

Nora was not to be mollified. "It might be childish, but what if these pranks escalate? No one working here would steal a script or kill a rabbit for kicks. I have a child on the premises, remember? Maybe Callie could look—"

"Nora, you will not involve that young woman in snooping in the guest rooms." Simon's firm pronouncement brooked no argument.

"It's an invasion of their privacy," Declan added. "And don't think I've forgotten your capacity for lying." He had to resist shaking his finger at her.

Nora buried her face in Sean's hair to hide her blush. "I only pretended that Oxford don was my uncle to talk to him."

Simon reacted before Declan could answer, widening his eyes. "What about telling the porter I was your husband?"

It was Declan's turn to widen his eyes. "You told someone Simon was your husband?"

Nora dismissed them both with a wave of her hand that Sean imitated with a shake of his keys. "You two get so upset over a little truth massage. Needs must, Agnes says."

Declan snorted. "You're unbelievable."

"Look who's talking," Nora threw back at him. "'Just call me Declan' to everyone, no hint of your detective title." Her green eyes flashed.

Declan couldn't decide whether to laugh or to be annoyed. "I'm on holiday," he reminded her. "But I'll keep my eye on things around here—and on you, Nora. Now if you'll excuse me, I need a shower."

7:25 PM

Nora turned on Sean's musical mobile and tiptoed away from his cot as his eyes fluttered. There was a soft knock at her door, and she raced to open it before Sean raised his head in curiosity.

Helen Mochrie stood in the hallway. Tonight's turban was purple. "Sorry to bother, but I think this must be yours." She held out Nora's blue robe.

"Where did you get this?" Nora kept her voice low and looked back at the empty hook on the side of the armoire where she typically hung her robe. A frisson of alarm ran through her. Had someone invaded her private space?

"I found it lying across my bed when I came out of the bathroom." Helen shrugged her shoulders and matched Nora's low voice. "How's that lad of yours?"

"Going to sleep, I hope." Nora couldn't tell if Helen was still in character or not, but she couldn't shake the fear someone had come into her room when Sean was napping. She tried to remember where she'd last left her robe.

"He seems to have a very mild disposition," Helen said. "Not mine. Even as a child he was given to—"

"—the most violent destructive tempers," Nora finished with delight. "That's from the play!" She explained her familiarity with the script.

Helen chuckled. "That may come in handy yet. I'm afraid staying in character is a habit I can't lose during a run." She pointed to the robe hanging over Nora's arm. "Now as to your robe, I suspect between pranks like Fiona's script and that ridiculous dead bunny, someone thinks this is a way to pay Grayson back."

Nora's brow furrowed. "Whatever for? I don't appreciate someone coming in here, especially when Sean might be here alone."

"I'm afraid Grayson's past is more checkered than he'd like to admit." Helen winked. "Try not to take it personally."

Nora looked at her sleeping child and decided that would be a very difficult thing to do.

Chapter Ten

"You'd better take that warning to heart … "
Ruth: Act 1, Scene 2

8:50 PM

Simon finished his pudding while Callie refilled coffee and tea. He watched Nora stir her tea. She'd bathed Sean and settled him for the night before she'd joined them for dinner but seemed preoccupied. Declan kept them entertained with stories of stupid criminals he'd dealt with, a counterpoint to the director's notes to his cast. While the cast members were engaged in listening to him, Nora quietly described how Helen had found her robe upstairs and the ugly feeling of her space being invaded with Sean captive in the room.

"There might be a key for that door," Simon suggested.

"Not safe to lock him in," Declan pointed out.

"Then what do I do?" Nora whispered. "I can't leave him alone knowing someone's been in there."

"I have an idea," Simon said and motioned Callie to the hallway. He had a brief conversation with her and returned to the table.

"All sorted. After clearing up, Callie will do her studying at Nora's desk until she's ready to turn in."

"A good solution, Simon," Declan said. "I doubt whoever's doing these pranks will go back to Nora's room, but why take a chance while we try to work out what's going on?"

"Which is why we need to make a list of who has a motive for these pranks and what they mean." Nora became insistent. "Helen thinks they're directed at Grayson."

Simon snorted. “Helen’s opinion isn’t one I’d bank on. Nothing’s been directed at him yet.”

“But it all bears keeping in mind,” Declan said. “Which is why you are to leave the snooping to the professional, Nora.”

Nora’s crossed arms told them what she thought of that idea.

Simon privately agreed with Declan to keep an eye on Nora, given her confounded need to put her nose where it didn’t belong. All right, she lived here and was in the midst of things, he could see that. But he had thought that when she’d become a mother, she’d lose the need to pry into everything. There was no question she was an excellent mum, but the second that baby was whisked away for a nap or to bed, she was up to her old tricks. And now that her space with the baby had been invaded, it would be tough to stop her.

He’d just put the last bite of pudding in his mouth when Grayson Lange rose and tapped his water glass with his knife.

“Listen to me, peons.” He waited for everyone’s full attention. “Today’s rehearsal went well, despite a few hiccups. Thank you for knowing your lines and working so hard. I was going to ask Nora to prompt for us, but it doesn’t seem necessary. Burt—” He nodded to Burt’s end of the table. “—the set looks amazing.”

A burst of applause from Helen had the others politely joining in.

The man knew how to grandstand, Simon thought grudgingly.

The director continued. “I’ve decided we’re going to sample the local pub, The Scarlet Wench. It’s just down the road, and I hear it has a fine selection of real ales and has even put up a welcoming banner in our honor. Everyone’s invited—you in the corner, too. First round’s on me.”

Chairs were pushed back, and Fiona and Gemma went upstairs to freshen up.

“Would you rather watch *Rebecca* with me in my room?” Helen asked the Dentons. "I have the new version, but I don't think Charles Dance is as handsome as Olivier."

"Delighted," Lydia beamed at Helen. "Rupert was never a pub man."

"I'd love a pint," Declan said, looking at Simon.

Simon caught on. "Nora, you and Declan take off. Callie and I can handle clearing up and the baby monitor, and Callie will stay with him until you get back."

Nora frowned. "Sure?" She thought back to the robe incident.

Simon was expansive. "Go ahead," he urged. "Sean sleeps well, and if he wakes, I've changed his nappy before and so has Callie." He pushed her toward the door. "Go and get your bag."

"Thanks, Simon." Declan clapped him on the shoulder. "Even though it's not been announced, I'll put my work hat on tonight."

10:45 PM

The noise inside The Scarlet Wench, coupled with the knowledge that someone had been in her room and the lawyer's visit next week, gave Nora twinges of a headache. Her usual compartmentalization seemed to be failing her. Was this really a helpful technique she'd developed to deal with stress or a way to erect walls to keep people out? Why hadn't she confided to Declan her fears over the lawyer's visit and the larger implications of the Pembrokes knowing about Sean? Simon knew, and she didn't mind that. Was she unconsciously keeping Declan at a distance from areas important to her?

She nursed her cider, watching Declan standing at the bar pretending to listen to the pub's owner, Daisy, as she expounded on the differences among various ales. He had one ear cocked to listen to the cast's conversation and observe their interactions. One of the things Nora liked best about Declan was that when they talked, he really listened to what she had to say. She could see this was a developed skill. Then why wasn't she ready to trust him?

Burt Marsh had downed a quick pint on Grayson's tab and bid the group goodnight. Nora decided he was polite, the height of an old-fashioned gentleman, but not a drinker. She wondered about the screening of *Rebecca* and wished she were snuggled in bed with Declan, watching the movie in his room with a big bowl of popcorn between them and her baby asleep for the rest of the night—and the activities that could follow. She mentally admonished herself for wanting to sleep with Declan again but drawing the line at taking him into her confidence. What kind of basis was that for a relationship?

Nora opened the door and stepped out to the side terrace, standing in the shadows under a hanging planter brimming with multicolored primroses. When she had a chance, she would bounce her fears about the Pembrokes off Declan. He would be the voice of reason. And she needed to be open and trusting with him.

"There you are." Declan joined her.

"Enough detecting?"

"I got what I was after—a look at the cast when they weren't on their guard."

"And what did the great and powerful detective find?" She moved into the circle of his arms.

He dipped his head and kissed her nose. "Fiona is definitely jealous of Gemma."

Nora laughed. "I could have told you that. Good thing I like having you around for more than detecting."

This time Declan's kiss was deeper.

"Absolutely not!" Fiona's voice broke them apart as the pub

door slammed open. "You've had too much, Grayson. That's why I took your keys."

"Incoming." Declan took Nora's hand, and they turned to watch the spectacle.

Grayson appeared in the doorway, his arm around Gemma, whose minidress sparkled in the dim light. "Give me those, Fiona."

Nora stayed with Declan on the patio, watching the interplay. Then Poppy appeared on the doorstep.

"You're all mad." Poppy flounced off. "I'm walking back."

Grayson snatched the keys from Fiona. Gemma screeched in laughter, and the duo trotted off to the silver Jag parked in the drive, facing out.

"Wait, Poppy." Fiona caught up to her, and the two women set off together on foot.

"I'd better stop him." Declan approached the car just as the director floored the Jag. It took off with a sharp squeal of tires, but instead of slowing down to turn onto the road, it slid at speed across the street and crashed into a brick retaining wall.

"Call 999!" Declan shouted and took off at a run.

Chapter Eleven

"… It's all part of some horrible plan … "
Ruth: Act ii, Scene i

11 PM

Simon stretched his back, pleased with the watercolour showing backpackers and tourists on the ferry. Nora's characters were hidden among expected items: Dove peeked out of the flap of a backpack; Tess lay along the wiper blade of a Range Rover; Skye sat atop luggage strapped to the roof of an ancient Ford wagon. The others were harder to spot, but children would have fun looking for them.

Maybe it was a good thing Maeve hadn't stayed tonight. He'd worked out the kinks in this illustration, and that gave him a sense of accomplishment. As he cleaned his brushes, he wondered what Maeve really thought of him. She had seemed so proactive in trying to gain his attention last year, but now that she had it, she seemed happy to be with him but didn't fall all over him. She was passionate in bed but cooler out of it, which was a good thing, he supposed. Maybe she felt she was maintaining her professionalism, but the romantic in him yearned for more. Time would tell.

He turned out the light in his studio just as his mobile rang. Nora had to shout over the sound of yelling and raised voices.

"Simon—there's been an accident at The Scarlet Wench." She succinctly described the Jaguar crashing into the brick wall. "There's an ambulance on the way for Gemma and Grayson. I'll be stuck here giving a statement to the police. Can you—"

"Relax. I just checked Sean half an hour ago, and he and Callie are both sound asleep. Are they badly hurt? Do you need me to come down there?"

She hesitated. "It's a madhouse with everyone giving their opinions. Gemma was knocked out at first, but she's awake and making a scene. Declan thinks Grayson's wrist is broken. Could you give Poppy and Fiona a lift to the lodge? They're arguing with Gemma about who should ride to the hospital with him."

"I'll be right there." He hung up and crossed the hall to Nora's room. Callie roused from atop Nora's bed when he opened the door, and Simon explained the situation.

"I'll stay right here," she promised.

As he ran to his car, Simon reflected that at least the accident hadn't happened at Ramsey Lodge.

11:15 PM

Nora was grateful when she saw Simon's car park down the road and Simon headed in her direction. The paramedics were checking Gemma, and Grayson was in the ambulance being treated after a Breathalyzer test. The crowd from the pub had dispersed once the local constable ascertained only Nora and Declan had actually witnessed the accident. Nora had described the incident, and Declan was finishing his statement while Fiona and Poppy crowded around the ambulance, arguing.

"I should ride with Grayson," Poppy insisted. "Gemma's wearing that stupid collar and won't be any help."

"You? Gray's a big boy, and Gemma hardly needs a babysitter."

Gemma wiped her face with the back of her hand and shouted, "You're just being mean because he's still not sleeping with you."

Nora bit her lip. Into the shocked silence, Simon spoke up.

"I'm here to give you all a ride back to the lodge, and then I'll go to the hospital and bring them both home."

Declan joined the group. "Thanks, Simon. Grayson and Gemma are both coherent, and once they're treated, they'll need that ride back to the lodge."

Fiona pushed Poppy aside. "I'll go with you, Simon. I have Gray's details, which they'll need." She shot a pointed look at Poppy and flounced away toward Simon's car, getting into the front passenger seat as he started the engine.

Nora followed with Declan, who put his arm over her shoulder. Poppy strode ahead of them, and the three piled into the back of Simon's Rover, cramped together.

"How hurt are they?" Simon asked Declan on the short ride to Ramsey Lodge.

"Gemma claims she lost consciousness briefly but seems fine. I'm pretty certain Grayson's wrist is broken."

"He had no business getting behind the wheel of that car," Fiona said. 'I tried to stop him."

"Miss Wonderful," Poppy whispered.

Fiona twisted around to glare at Poppy. "At least one of us tried to be responsible."

"Hey! I didn't get in the car with him, remember? I started to walk back with you, so don't get all high and mighty with me." Poppy crossed her arms.

Nora was thankful when they pulled up in front of Ramsey Lodge. Poppy ran upstairs as Simon and Fiona pulled away.

"I want to check on Sean and Callie," Nora said.

Declan nodded and went into Simon's kitchen. Nora cracked her bedroom door to find Callie leaving the bathroom.

"Sleeping like an angel." Callie rubbed sleep from her eyes. "How is everyone?"

Nora brought her up to speed. "It's close to midnight. Why don't you crash in Kate's bed for the rest of the night?"

"Sounds good. See you in the morning."

Nora crept over to the cot, where Sean slept peacefully. She took the monitor with her into Simon's kitchen, where Declan was on the phone, giving his credentials to the duty inspector at the Communications Center in Penrith. Once his Oxford rank was established, he passed on the details of the accident.

"We gave statements to the local constable, but here's the issue: The driver, who had clearly been drinking, insists that when he reached the road to turn, he tried to brake and his foot went straight to the floor. That's when the car shot across the road and into the wall."

Making them a cup of tea, Nora whirled around at this information. Declan held a finger up. "Yes, I agree the brake cables need to be checked. There have been a series of small incidents here revolving around this group of actors, and I'm concerned someone's carried things too far."

Nora brought their tea over to the table. A tiny part of her felt badly Declan had been pressed into service on his vacation as a chill passed through her. Most of her felt thankful he was on site.

Declan ended his call and sipped his tea. "They'll tow away the car tonight and get someone to look at it tomorrow."

Nora took Declan's hand. "What's going on here, Declan? Things are getting out of control. Grayson or Gemma could have been killed."

Declan's tone was grim. "I'm worried that's what someone's working up to."

Chapter Twelve

"Nothing in the world was further from my thoughts."
Charles: Act III, Scene I

Wednesday, 11th April

1:10 AM

In the Beatrix Potter Suite, Poppy Braeburn stood at the window, tracing images in the mist her breath left on the cool glass. Unable to sleep after seeing Grayson taken away in the ambulance, she pulled on thick socks and a pair of jogging bottoms under her flannel nightgown.

The fluttering in her stomach only worsened as time passed. The hiker staying at the lodge had seemed to take control of the situation quickly, a person used to being in command from the way he spoke to the police on site. It was all so bloody stupid: Grayson drinking too much, Gemma draped over him possessively, Fiona trying to insinuate herself as though she still had influence on Grayson's life. And calling him "Gray" in front of everyone, indicating she had a special relationship with him.

Had it really been only two days since she'd arrived, happy and upbeat to be part of this troupe? It seemed ages since Nora's baby had thrown up on her. Nora's look at the time, startled and embarrassed, had helped quell Poppy's spurt of annoyance. Poor thing couldn't help if he had had a bubble, happened to babies all the time. She remembered the infants at the New Age commune she'd lived in growing up. Everyone had pitched in raising each other's children. She'd been especially adept with the infants, and they'd all lived in each other's pockets like they were one big extended family.

Only they hadn't been. They had been drawn together by the adults' belief in pagan rituals, with Stonehenge and other outcroppings their cathedrals. Her head ached with the memory of years of following ley lines, like Christians searching for the Holy Grail. More like Monty Python, she thought ruefully, recalling people shouting names at them as their caravans would pass: New Agers, Druids, even witches; she'd been called it all.

Her parents called themselves pantheists and wore the name with a mantle of pride she had shed the minute she could. She'd grown up feeling her every emotion open to inspection from people who weren't her relatives, her every action interpreted as a sign from the moon or the stars, from God or the devil. They had been more like gypsies, with their line of beaten up vans and trailers, the sweet, burning-sage odor of weed permeating their clothes and linens.

But the communal spirit of the camps meant books and learning had also been shared, and she'd eagerly consumed them, exploring more on a topic when they'd stop near a library. She'd hold back begged coins for used books of her own. It had still come as an utter surprise to her parents that she had cast off their way of life for what she regarded as a sense of normalcy once she turned sixteen: school, a career, a set of boundaries.

Her parents reconciled themselves by telling the group she participated in experimental theatre and by choosing to believe she performed only in edgy projects. Their last meeting, two years ago when they'd come to see her perform as Eliza Doolittle in *Pygmalion,* had ended with awkward glances on their part. Her triumph that night had been a complete embarrassment to them. She hadn't bothered to track their movements after that and had no idea where they were encamped now.

Were those headlights coming down Glebe Road? She stood to attention, her body tense, but the vehicle continued past

Ramsey Lodge. The fluttering in her stomach returned and along with it, fear for Grayson's well-being. But even more than that fear was the panic that someone would find out she'd been in his room.

8:50 AM

Simon finished his breakfast and watched the assemblage surround Grayson Lange to sign his cast, displayed out of its sling for the activity. Maeve laughed and drew a smiley face after her name, her shiny hair swinging toward her face as she leaned over him. Even Burt signed his name with a flourish.

Simon should be sleepy but felt wired. Gemma had been released early on, the neck brace deemed unnecessary, with caution to watch for headaches and to rest as needed. He'd had to maintain a semblance of polite conversation with her and Fiona as they'd waited for Grayson's wrist to be set, worrying all the time how this would affect the play. He needed this play to come off as planned.

To his relief, Grayson had told them on the drive back that he planned to continue. "No reason not to. I'll add a line easily enough about Charles having had an accident prior to the action of the play and how his cast is a nuisance to his writing. I'm more worried about the other thing … " he caught Simon's eye. Declan had already told Simon of Grayson's insistence that his brakes had failed.

The women had sat in stony silence during the ride home. When Simon had looked in his rearview mirror upon the director's pronouncement, he had seen Gemma had fallen asleep but had met Fiona's dark eyes. She'd raised an eyebrow in question.

"I believe Declan has that all in hand," Simon had assured Grayson and had waited for a question from the back seat that had never come.

Now, as he finished breakfast at a round table in the dining room with Nora and Declan, he explained the director had suffered what the emergency doctor had called "a classic Colles fracture," which meant the cast would stop short of his elbow.

"He'll need follow-up next week with an orthopedist, but the fracture wasn't displaced, which they explained means he shouldn't lose any movement." Simon picked up Sean's plastic keys and jiggled them, to the baby's delight. He put them on the high-chair tray, and the baby immediately put them in his mouth. "He was damned fortunate he blew just this side of the limit or he'd have been arrested, too, for DUI."

"He seems in remarkable spirits, despite the pain and lack of sleep." Nora slathered orange marmalade on whole-wheat toast.

"He enjoys being the center of attention," Declan pointed out.

Simon leaned in and spoke quietly. "Fiona was a piece of work. She had all of his pertinent information and knew his insurance details. The nurse thought she was his wife."

"I wonder if they were ever married," Nora mused.

"Don't start." Declan pointed a finger to at Nora, and everyone laughed when Sean grabbed it and stuck it in his mouth.

"I'll bet he's taken a few painkillers; I know I would." Simon looked at his own left hand and grimaced at the devastating thought of what breaking a wrist might mean to his ability to draw and paint.

Declan's mobile rang, and he excused himself to take the call in the hallway. Simon looked over at the table. He thought the Dentons were curiously silent this morning.

"Look what I've run you up, Grayson," Poppy said. She'd fashioned a cover for his sling, complete with a pocket for his mobile phone. She helped him place his cast back in the sling and slid on the cover.

"Darling, it's absolutely lovely, whenever did you have time to do that?"

"When she was pining away for you last night, didn't you, sweet Poppy?" Gemma's face was pale this morning, but there was no mistaking the cut of her words.

Poppy blushed and looked at her lap.

"We shouldn't continue with the play," Helen pronounced. "It's bad karma."

Simon felt his insides clench at her remark.

"Nonsense!" Grayson declared. "I've already had a few ideas about how to work it into the script."

"We wouldn't be in this position if you hadn't let him drive off in that state." Fiona glared at Gemma.

"So now it's all my fault, and I wasn't even behind the wheel?" Gemma's voice rose. "You forget I have concussion. I'm going upstairs to get some aspirin."

"Poor you. Do us all a favor and make it cyanide," Fiona declared.

Grayson slapped the table with his good hand, making Sean startle, eyes wide. "You two, stop this incessant bickering. I won't have it, do you understand?"

Gemma ran for her room upstairs. Fiona shrugged her shoulders.

Declan returned and told Grayson he had to speak with him. The director took his time draining his teacup and let Poppy help him rise from the table. Declan caught Simon's eye and gave the slightest nod.

Simon heard Grayson's raised voice in the hallway reacting to the news. "Malicious intent!" After a minute, the director reappeared, face ashen. "I'll meet you all as planned at 9:30 for rehearsal. I think I'll have a bit of a lie down before then."

Poppy rushed to help him up the stairs, and the others followed. Declan sat down and answered Simon and Nora's look.

"Brake cables cut through. They're going over the car for prints but not hopeful. A puddle of brake fluid was found where his Jag was parked outside the pub."

Nora voiced Simon's first thought. "Someone tried to murder Grayson Lange."

9:28 AM

Nora drained the dregs of her tea after everyone else had vacated the dining room. The cast filed into the drawing room for rehearsal. Maeve chatted with Simon, helping him clear breakfast. She could hear Burt hammering in the drawing room, but Declan seemed to have disappeared.

She begrudgingly admired the director's tenacity to continue rehearsals in the face of obvious malice. Yet only a few days in the presence of his troupe had quickly removed any hero worship she might have had for the actors, between their petty squabbles and bickering and Grayson's manipulation of them all.

But this was serious stuff. How could she help Declan investigate this attempt on Grayson's life? She trusted Declan, of course, and she respected his tough police work. But he didn't know all she'd done. She'd spent years as a student in the theatre, had interviewed actors when she'd worked for *People and Places* magazine in the United States and then later in the United Kingdom. She knew what went on in their minds, what made them tick. And the danger was real.

As long as someone malicious was out there, she needed to do whatever she could to keep Sean safe. The thought occurred to her to send him away until the mystery was solved. Surely Val would help.

She bit her lip. No, she wouldn't overreact. She didn't want to frighten her baby or disrupt his routine. There was no reason to think he was the target of anything. For now, he would be safe with her.

Nora wiped Sean's face and took him out of the high chair, cuddling him. He still smelled like baby shampoo from last night's bath. She brought him into the kitchen for a quick visit with Agnes, whose face lit up. The child held out his arms to her, and Nora relinquished her hold. "If you've got him a minute, I could give Callie a hand."

"Go on, then. Me and the laddie are having a conversation, aren't we?" The cook tickled Sean under his chin, and he giggled in response. "She's upstairs already, quick worker that girl." Agnes leaned into Nora. "Told you things would go barmy with that group here. Too much to drink, broken wrists … "

Nora wondered how Agnes would react if she knew Grayson's brakes had been cut.

"Oh, Declan said to tell you he went for a little stroll about, needed to think."

Maeve came into the kitchen with a heavy tray she set down. "All set in there, just need to load the dishwasher."

"I'll do that," Nora offered and opened the washer door.

"I'll sweep, then, while Simon sets for lunch. Hello, Munchkin." Maeve pushed Sean's belly as she went back out, eliciting a chuckle.

Nora bit her lip at Maeve's appropriation of Simon's nickname for Sean. "She's being very helpful these days."

"Aye, she's sweeter. Must be getting honey somewhere." Agnes hummed. "I notice them disappearing into his studio when it's quiet. Inspecting his paintings, I imagine."

Nora looked up, but Agnes had walked over to the kitchen door and was showing Sean the budding magnolia.

Scraping dishes, Nora wondered where Declan had wandered off to, as she still needed to talk with him about the Pembrokes. Monday's meeting niggled at the back of her conscience, and she knew she had to address the situation before then.

Callie came down the back stairs with a load of damp towels and started the washer. Nora slammed the dishwasher shut; it wouldn't need to be run until after lunch. She'd promised Declan and Simon she wouldn't involve Callie in searching the cast's rooms, but she'd never said anything about herself.

Nora gathered a basket and shears from the shelf over the machines. "I'll just run up and see if there are any dead flowers to be removed from their arrangements," she told Agnes.

"I'm taking Sean to see the garden before he goes down for his nap." Agnes took her heavy sweater off a peg and draped it around both of them. "A spot of fresh air, laddie."

Nora helped her button it to keep it in place around them both. "He loves being outdoors. Thanks, Agnes." She kissed the baby's head and went up the back stairs to Poppy Braeburn's room. Callie left as Nora approached the door. "Leave it open, Callie. I'll freshen the flowers."

Nora entered the Potter Suite and made a beeline for the vase on the nightstand. She exchanged the water, cut the stems and threw a few wilted daisies into her basket. Then she gently shut the door and put her basket down, making a quick tour of the suite.

Poppy was neat, her clothing hung in the closet with care and with equal space between each hanger. Her few cosmetics stood arranged in a row along the bathroom counter. Felt slippers were aligned next to the bed; even her dresser drawers showed carefully folded items. It spoke to Nora of someone who had grown up with little and who valued what she owned, everything of good quality. Several pieces with labels stitched inside read: "*A Poppy Braeburn Original.*"

Nora got down on her hands and knees and lifted the white eyelet dust ruffle that hung around the bed. At first, she could only see the trundle bed, but as her eyes got used to the dark shadows, she picked out an object thrust near the head of the bed. She reached in and pulled out a large tin with pictures of the Twelve Days of Christmas. Turning it over, she read the label across the bottom: St. New English Cookie Assortment.

Nora opened the tin. Inside were photos, newspaper clippings and magazine articles, all carefully scissored. It took only a moment for Nora to realize the subject of each item was Grayson Lange. And was that a used disposable razor?

Now Nora understood why Poppy was so charming one second but became possessive of anything to do with the play. It all revolved around her infatuation with Grayson Lange.

She heard footsteps and quickly closed the tin and thrust it back under the bed in the same spot. By the time she reached the door and opened it, basket over her arm, Callie was reaching for the handle, a clean tub mat over her arm.

"Oh, Nora, didn't realize you were still in here."

"Didn't want to get in your way. What rooms have you finished?"

"This one and the Dentons' suite."

"Fine, I'll do theirs next." Entering the Morris Suite, Nora quickly perused Lydia and Rupert's room after dealing with their flowers. Their suite showed signs of habitation, but all their clothes were neatly hung. Both nightstands had books, and Nora noted their choices: Ian Rankin's newest police procedural would be Rupert's; she decided Alan Bradley's Flavia de Luce offering was more Lydia's style.

A framed photograph stood on the dresser and drew her close attention. Its highly polished silver frame indicated the care it received, and the photo showed a much-younger Lydia and Rupert. Between them stood a pretty, young woman with Rupert's lean frame and Lydia's porcelain skin and sweet smile.

The Dentons must have a daughter. Nora didn't recall either of them mentioning her. She'd Google that later today.

Callie was next door in the Lewis Carroll Suite. Fiona had left a few items of clothing draped over a chair, and the amount of makeup on her counter would supply Nora for a year, but she didn't see anything unusual at first glance and could hardly open drawers with Callie there making up the bed.

Nora changed the water from the vase and cut the stems down. She followed Callie to Gemma's room to repeat the process. In contrast to the other rooms, this one looked like someone had opened a suitcase and dumped the contents around.

"Not the tidiest person, is she?" Nora looked around as she cut stems. It would take more time than she had today to sort through anything unusual in this mess.

Callie made a face. "I'll set most of this to rights, and it will look the same again tomorrow. And she only slept in here last night for a few hours. A lot of her stuff is in the Royal Suite."

Nora remembered the pile of Gemma's perfume and cosmetics in Grayson's bathroom. "Helen's room done?"

Callie nodded. "Yes, but she asked for extra towels. That woman's plain weird."

Nora laughed. "She likes to stay in character. But then I've never met her out of character, so I've no idea what she's really like." A thought struck Nora. "Callie, you didn't by any chance leave my blue robe in Helen's room the other day?"

Callie frowned. "Why would I do that?"

Nora shook her head. "Not a clue. But she found it and returned it."

"That's even stranger. Maybe she liked the color and wanted it for a turban." Callie laughed and shrugged the matter off.

Nora accompanied Callie to the linen closet. They heard the washer buzz. "You want to put that load in the dryer? I'll take the towels to Helen's room."

"Sure thing." Callie skipped down the back stairs.

Nora piled up clean towels and pushed open the door to Helen Mochrie's room. She fixed the flowers and put her basket down. Inside the yellow room, the full flavor of Madame Arcati was on view. A vibrant, rose-patterned scarf was thrown over the table lamp; three turbans in a rainbow of colors stood lined up along the deep windowsill. The closet door stood open to reveal a violet broomstick skirt competing with a sapphire quilted jacket.

Nora placed the extra towels in the bathroom. She peeked into a round cosmetic case. A smattering of makeup, brushes and deodorant filled it. A thick, pungent odor came from a large bottle of musky cologne that stood on the counter, its heavy scent permeating the whole suite.

She quickly scanned the closet and under the bed. Not a dust bunny in sight. Nora reached for the top dresser drawer when a voice from the doorway stopped her hand in mid-flight.

"You wouldn't be about to open that drawer, Nora?" Declan Barnes stood in the doorway, his dark hair catching the sunlight pouring in the from the hallway skylight.

Nora snatched back her hand. "Just checking for dust." She ran her finger over the top and turned it toward him. "Clean as a whistle."

She saw him bite the side of his cheek to avoid a smile.
He crooked his finger and motioned her toward him. "Then you'll be able to leave and close the door behind you."

And he waited while she did just that.

Chapter Thirteen

"I was the victim of an aberration."
Charles: Act II, Scene I

10:12 AM

Declan led Nora down the back stairs. He could hear Sean banging on a pot in the kitchen. When Agnes had told Declan that Nora was upstairs, he'd instinctively known that the news that Grayson's brake cables had been cut had brought out the redhead's insatiable need to put her nose where it didn't belong. He stopped suddenly in the middle of the staircase and turned around. Nora was on the stair behind him; they were eye to eye, close enough for him to see the gold flecks in her green eyes and to catch her lemony scent.

"What?" She gave him a wide-eyed look.

He resisted the impulse to shake his finger at her again, remembering Sean's reaction the last time. He was not her father. "Don't pretend innocence with me, Nora." He lowered his voice so Agnes wouldn't hear them. "I know damn well you would have opened that drawer if I hadn't stopped you." To her credit, Nora looked down and didn't argue, which frustrated him even more. How could she have scruples one minute and none the next?

He grabbed her neck and pulled her toward him, kissing her firmly and letting go.

"What was that for?" Her eyes shined.

"Because you frustrate the hell out of me." He continued down the stairs.

"Then I should do that more often," she said briskly as they entered the kitchen.

Sean sat in a corner of the kitchen on an old rug and babbled away, hitting a pot with a wooden spoon, his back supported by a rounded cushion.

"There you two are." Agnes stood at the counter peeling a huge pile of carrots. "Simon sent Callie to the market."

"Upstairs is all done." Nora tucked a few stray hairs behind her ear.

Declan hoped his color wasn't as high as Nora's, but Agnes either didn't notice or chose not to comment. Christ, he felt like a schoolboy with back-stairs stolen kisses. He pulled himself into professional mode.

"I've spoken with Detective Sergeant Higgins in Kendal."

"We know him from last autumn," Nora said.

"He's in charge with Ian away. Anyway, he feels I need to let everyone on premises know about the brakes to be on alert for any other kind of sabotage."

"What brakes?" Agnes' eyes were as big as saucers.

Declan filled her in on the cut cables.

"And here's me thinking he had too much to drink." Agnes started viciously chopping the carrots.

"That, too," Nora murmured. "And I guess that blows your cover."

"I suppose," Declan agreed.

Nora frowned as she picked up Sean. "I'm going to put him down for his nap."

Declan watched her leave the kitchen, nuzzling Sean's head, her brow furrowed in thought.

Agnes put her hand on a plump hip. "You think this is more than pranks now, don't you? I tried to tell Nora this would come to no good."

"My instinct tells me this person is deadly serious, Agnes. We should all be on our guard."

CHAPTER THIRTEEN

10:15 AM

"And so there was nothing for it but to obey the beckoning finger of adventure and take to the road again. … "

At least Helen Mochrie had her lines down pat. Gemma would give the old bat that. She stood outside the French door on the patio, waiting for her entrance cue. She didn't appear until Scene 2 in Act 1, and as the actors droned on through the first séance scene, she wrapped her shawl tighter around her. There was a breeze off the lake that kept the morning air cool, although she had to admit it looked pretty enough. Boats made her seasick, and Gemma was happier to be on dry land, enjoying from a distance.

She yawned loudly. Not enough sleep last night after that stupid accident. Her neck felt a bit sore, but the Accident & Emergency doctor had assured her they hadn't been going fast enough for her to have sustained serious whiplash and had been stingy with the pain pills. She could kill for a fag, but Grayson didn't approve, and so she snuck them here and there when she could get away with it and could brush her teeth and use mouthwash. Those moments were more and more difficult to find, and soon she'd be a nonsmoker whether she wanted to give up cigarettes or not.

"Filthy habit," Grayson had pronounced soon after they'd met, and Gemma instinctively had known that if she wanted to wrest him away from Fiona, the smoking had to go. It was one of the many things she had done to suit him. Gemma wondered if this liaison would really further her career the way she'd hoped. Here she was, stuck in an old, musty house playing to the sheepherders, and Grayson acted like it was the West End.

A far cry from her beginnings, though, and wouldn't her old dad be chuffed to see her now, wearing fancy clothes and having men drool over her. Although he'd never laid a hand on her, Dad had always been a bit too much full of sex talk with her, especially when he'd had a few, which was fairly often. At least that had made her easy with her own body, although she used it more for attention than for actual sex. She wasn't promiscuous—she could count her lovers on her hands without repeating fingers, a rare occurrence in this modern age, she thought. Still, her mum had always complained about her dad's overfamiliarity.

"You treat her like a mate," she'd complained, and Gemma had agreed, but who else had he had, with her mum keeping the little family to itself, not making friends and suspicious of every neighbour's overture as gossip hunting. It had put a wedge between her and her mum, that was for sure, and now that her dad was dead, all that remained between mother and daughter was a cool distance and an occasional phone call.

Maybe that's why I look for attention, Gemma thought, and congratulated herself on the rare moment of insight. Getting Grayson Lange into her bed had proved less of a challenge than she'd thought. Her body easily distracted him. She didn't give a toss about the sex, although he was competent enough once she looked past his overblown ego.

Lately, he'd been complaining about her too-frequent headaches, which she knew meant she was stressed. "Bloody hypochondriac," he'd had the nerve to call her as they'd set off for Cumbria. With this accident, she had a perfect right to have a headache or two.

Now the tables had turned. With his plaster cast and painkillers on board, he wouldn't be bothering her nightly to prove his virility, and she might even get a few decent nights' sleep.

10:18 AM

Nora drew the blinds in Sean's alcove to darken it as his mobile tinkled away. He was getting better at falling asleep without rocking, and she allowed herself a discreet pat on the back for sticking to a schedule with him.

She sat at her desk and opened her laptop, minimizing the notes she'd been making for further story ideas. She slipped in some ear buds and hit her iTunes playlist, a mix of her U.K. and U.S. favorites. If Sean fussed, she didn't want to jump up. He had to learn to fall asleep on his own.

Nora knew Declan wouldn't catch the underlying significance of Grayson's brake cables being cut. In the play, that's exactly how the ghost of Condomine's first wife manages to kill his second. She would tell him, but she could already hear him calling it a coincidence. Perhaps, but it bore further looking into.

Everything seemed under control in the lodge, and she needed to steal a few minutes for herself. She opened a new browser window and started a Google search on Rupert Denton and Lydia Brown.

By the time Adele was rolling in the deep of her heartache, Nora had learned the couple's careers had started in Shakespearian theatre, where they'd met and married, then branched out to acting in popular plays and revivals independently, with a stint on a television soap opera where they had played lovers married to other partners. Their daughter had been named for their friend and mentor, Dame Maggie Smith, who still acted in the popular *Downton Abbey* series.

There was little mention of Maggie after their daughter's birth in 1983. By all accounts, they'd kept her out of the limelight except for one publicity photo Nora found as Maggie had neared her teens, attending opening night of her parents' performance in a revival of *The Lion in Winter*. It showed Rupert and Lydia dressed as Henry II and Eleanor of Aquitaine with the tall young woman between them, grinning shyly for the camera, awkward but lovely in her long gown.

Nora took a drink from her water bottle and rose to check on Sean. Fast asleep, clutching his bunny. His mouth worked a phantom nipple. What was it like to be brought up by parents who were actors? The rehearsals, late nights at the theatre, jostling for good parts would have been foreign to Maggie's normal schoolgirl friends. Had the Dentons been emotional at home with histrionic arguments and dramatic moments? Had Maggie's care been given over to a nanny all day long? Or perhaps just at night when the Dentons had been at the theatre? Had they strived for an ordinary childhood for their only child?

Nora thought about the warm and gracious couple she'd met. They seemed more likely to have been overprotective of their daughter, the kind who would try to give her a sense of normality, but this was nothing more than a hunch on her part.

The next mention of Maggie Denton came in an article in *Cheers!* magazine about her graduation in 2004 from the Royal Academy of Dramatic Art. The accompanying photo showed her wedged again between her famous parents, both older and graying but with proud smiles. The article described the couple as semiretired, taking parts in regional theatre where they could act together, and noted they had attended all of their daughter's performances at RADA as her career began its rise.

So Maggie had fallen under the influence of the theatre and had followed her parents into an acting career. Nora pulled up the website of her former employer, *People and Places* magazine, and clicked on the archives of their Notable pages. Nora had edited longer feature articles, not this page that contained snippets of information about births, death, marriages and other happenings in the lives of celebrities. She searched and found an article on Maggie Denton that described her death a scant two years before:

> Maggie Denton, 26, actress daughter of acting scions Rupert Denton and Lydia Brown, was found dead last week, a suspected overdose. Police are investigating, but initial reports suggest no evidence of foul play.

The photo showed Maggie dressed as Sarah in a touring production of Shaw's *Major Barbara*, her last role. In contrast to her blooming healthiness five years before, Maggie's face had been drawn and thinner. Grayson Lange had directed the play.

CHAPTER FOURTEEN

"This is a small village, you know, and gossip would be most undesirable."
Ruth: Act II, Scene 2

1:46 PM

Fiona Church brushed her dark hair into place. She leaned into the mirror in her bathroom, inspecting the shadows under her eyes. After the late night in the A&E waiting for Grayson and Gemma, she shouldn't be surprised. It didn't take much for lack of proper sleep to show itself on her face these days. She and Simon Ramsey had settled Gray in bed with his arm elevated on a pillow as his cast finished drying. He was sleepy, filled with pain pills. She'd fallen exhausted into bed once Gemma, thinking as usual only of herself, had gone into her own room without a backward glance after a mumbled "thanks for the ride" to Simon.

Simon Ramsey had turned out to be quite nice, not as snobby as she'd thought. They'd sat together in the waiting room as Grayson and Gemma had been treated. At first, she'd flipped silently through a few tattered magazines, but then he'd returned from the canteen with tea for both of them, and they'd started talking about his art. It had become obvious to Fiona that running Ramsey Lodge with his sister was a means to an end for Simon. He'd explained it had been their parents' business and they'd kept it going after their deaths, and that his sister had once been a set designer for London shows. He had become animated when he talked about his landscape paintings that were sold in an Oxford gallery, and he clearly enjoyed the diversion of the illustrations he did for Nora's children's books.

He'd been a good listener, too, asking Fiona about what drew her to acting in the first place.

"I always loved theatre and movies. I grew up in a big family, and my grandparents were big fans of classical theatre. They thought it part of our education to expose us to the classics and took us all twice a year. I went to movies with girlfriends, too. I'd sit there in the dark and imagine what it would be like to take on a new personality."

"It must be thrilling to transport yourself into someone entirely different from how you see yourself." Simon had smiled in understanding.

Then Gemma had been released and had ruined the mood, complaining about her neck, her head, losing precious sleep and about the state of Grayson's car.

"The whole front is absolutely ruined," she'd whined.

"Really smashed up." Fiona's cheerful agreement had earned her Gemma's narrowed frown.

"I'm sure it was very upsetting to see that brick wall coming at you." Simon had tried to placate troubled waters between the two women.

"Absolutely petrified! I was completely freaked out!" Gemma's blonde curls had bobbed as she agreed.

"Surprised you didn't wet yourself," Fiona had muttered.

Gemma had whirled on her with a nasty retort when Grayson had appeared in a wheelchair, and Gemma had rushed over to him instead.

Fiona had thought Gemma could certainly act when she wanted to, fussing over Gray as they'd helped him into the car, insisting she sit in the back with him to keep his cast in place. Yet once they had arrived back at Ramsey Lodge, it had been clear that the director didn't need three people to help him to bed, and Gemma had slid away to her own room.

CHAPTER FOURTEEN

Fiona patted on a touch of concealer under each eye, carefully blending, wishing life's cruelties could be erased as easily.

She didn't know why she'd been so shocked at Gemma's outburst about Grayson's relationship with Fiona right after the accident. It was typical of the bitch's behavior. Everyone in theatre circles knew about Fiona's past with Gray, although these people in the Lake District might not have—until Gemma had opened her mouth.

At the time of Fiona and Grayson's breakup, she'd given her friends the impression she'd been the one to end their affair. "Elephantine ego without the equipment to match," she'd sniggered to girlfriends, hiding the truth that it had been her own inability to receive pleasure that had put Grayson off.

In the beginning, she'd faked her way; easy enough to do and she was, after all, a skilled actress. She'd had no difficulties gratifying him. But Gray had seen through it and then had tried all the tricks in his book to give her pleasure.

"You're a tough nut to crack," he'd told her, and for a while it had seemed like a game and she'd loved him for trying. She *wanted* to feel pleasure, to fall off the cliff as described in the books she read. She tried everything she could to relax, but as she neared the precipice, she only got more and more anxious. Her lack of responsiveness to Grayson's efforts had exasperated him.

She'd kept him in the relationship for a while out of guilt, pouring out her childhood woes. She was lost as the second youngest of a large family, five noisy siblings all vying to be heard. She wasn't the baby, fussed over and doted on. Any opinion she had on a topic had been immediately quashed by an older brother or sister. Fiona felt defeated constantly by her own family, who called her willful and became hostile when she tried to insist she had a valid point of view. At times, she thought she'd been adopted, but with all those mouths to feed, why would they have adopted her and then gone on to have another? The ray of sunshine had been those twice-yearly theatre outings with her mother's parents, yet she'd been the only one to fall under the influence of the footlights.

"All I want is to feel safe," she'd pleaded to Gray, and the man had softened for a brief while.

But her clingy need for affection without the sexual attention he prided himself on had led to the demise of their relationship. "Go and suffer in silence, you frigid cow," he'd yelled at the height of their worst argument.

After that, by tacit agreement, she'd moved out without complaint or recrimination. Soon after, he'd taken up with Gemma. But his failure with her, or perhaps his easy abandonment of her, must have pricked his conscience because he'd kept her employed in his theatre troupe.

And she was whore enough in that aspect to have let him. She only felt alive when she wore another's clothes and spoke words written by someone else. It occurred to Fiona at that moment that Gray must think she still loved him. It would fit his ego. The thought brought a wicked smile to her face.

She washed her hands and wiped them on a clean hand towel. One thing about Simon and this place: They didn't stint on fresh towels and comfortable beds, and the food was quite good. She'd have to tell her new friend Simon Ramsey how she felt about his hospitality.

Fiona left her room and hurried around the hall to get to rehearsal. She didn't want to be late again and give Gemma fodder for comments. She ran for the stairs.

1:55 PM

Simon sat at the registration desk, checking online registrations. Every time the landline rang, he hoped it wasn't Kate. When she'd called from Paris, she'd told him he should text any important messages or questions. Surely, with Declan's help, this mess at the lodge would be sorted out soon enough and he wouldn't have to contact her. This was one time in her life she deserved not to worry about Ramsey Lodge.

He could hear desultory murmurs from the cast coming from the drawing room. Grayson hadn't emerged yet from his room where he'd skipped lunch to have a nap. Declan and Nora still sat at their table, playing with Sean and a stack of blocks. That little romance seemed to be chugging along well. Simon gave Declan full points for accepting the baby as part of Nora's life. With Callie helping Agnes prepare dinner, he took a deep breath. He gave a thought to Maeve coming over and realized how much he looked forward to being alone with her.

His neck stiffened when a female cried out; then he heard bumping at the head of the stairs. He ran from the desk and found Fiona sitting in the middle of the stairway, one hand clasping the rail tightly, face white with fear. Declan ran in from the dining room and helped Simon check Fiona over before helping her to her feet.

"What happened to the light?" Simon noticed the head of the stairs was in shadow.

Fiona rubbed her lower leg. "I was in a rush and didn't notice. Then I felt something and tripped."

By now Poppy, Bert, Helen and the Dentons were clustered in the hall at the bottom of the stairs. Agnes and Callie poked their heads out of the kitchen. Nora called up, "You need a first aid kit or a doctor?"

"Let me see your leg, please." Declan's firm voice made Fiona thrust her leg out.

He raised her slacks and examined her leg and ankle, then took out his mobile and shot a few pictures of what even Simon could see was a very fine red line along the front of Fiona's leg.

"Best get this documented before it fades." Declan pulled down Fiona's pants leg. "No kit needed." He asked Fiona directly, "Do you want to be seen by a doctor?"

She shook her head. "Absolutely not. We know who put that light out." She glared down at Gemma.

Gemma yelled, "Bitch!"

Grayson Lange appeared at the head of the stairs, cradling his arm. "Can't a person get a nap in this place?"

"Stay right there." Declan's authoritative voice stopped Grayson in his tracks. "And the rest of you, quiet please." He ran up the rest of the stairs and stopped near the top, kneeling down to examine the first step.

Simon had an awful feeling in the pit of his stomach. Not another accident, and on the lodge's premises this time. He could see the future of Ramsey Lodge disappearing before his eyes. What if Fiona had fallen all the way down? She could have been killed.

"Nora, get me a bag, please," Declan called down. "Any kind will do." He snapped photos of the stairs.

The group at the bottom of the stairs was anything but silent, asking questions of Fiona all at once.

"Is the lass all right?" asked Bert.

"Did you get hurt, dear?" from the Dentons.

"Probably too much private sipping in her room after lunch." Gemma laughed.

"Spoken like a true trollop." Fiona stood and tried bearing weight on her sore leg.

Gemma opened her mouth to yell again, but Helen grabbed an arm to silence her.

Nora returned with a clean garbage bag and the same roll of tape Simon had given Declan for the dead bunny. She passed them to Simon, who handed them up to Declan.

By now, Grayson Lange's patience had worn thin. "Would someone please tell me what's going on here?"

"One moment." Declan reached down and drew out a handkerchief. Simon saw him wiggle something out of one side of the woodwork; then he appeared to wind it around in a circle. He dropped the handkerchief-wrapped bundle into the bag and used the tape to seal the bag. He wrote across the tape and stood up. He had everyone's attention. "You can go down now, Grayson."

"Who put you in charge?" Gemma demanded from the hallway as Grayson started down the stairs, holding onto the railing.

Simon dreaded what he knew would be the end to Declan's anonymity. He helped Fiona work her way gingerly down the stairs, aided by Nora. Grayson followed behind them.

Declan waited until everyone safely reached the hall. "I'm here on holiday, but in Oxford I'm a detective inspector."

"A bloody copper in our midst!" Gemma shouted.

"Shut up, you idiot." Poppy punched Gemma in the arm. "He's got a right to go away same as anyone else."

"The point is—" Declan's voice rose above them all. "—it appears fishing line has been deliberately strung across the top step from a nail set low, then wound around the newel post."

There were gasps from below, but it was Helen's voice that spoke out. "Just like in the play—cut brake cables and a fall downstairs."

2:12 PM

Nora trooped after Declan and Simon into Simon's kitchen.

Nora knew Helen saw it, too. Someone was using the play to orchestrate these events. She ought to feel vindicated, but instead all she felt was a clammy fear.

"Declan, I have to tell you something important. The Dentons had a daughter who committed suicide two years ago after appearing in a play that Grayson directed."

Declan stowed the bundle in the freezer next to the stiff corpse of the dead bunny. His face was grim. "I'll put in a call to Kendal right now." His comment addressed Simon.

Nora tugged at his sleeve as he took out his mobile. "Did you hear me? These incidents are all tied into this play and to Grayson Lange. In the play, there are falls and a car accident that kills Ruth from cut brakes and—"

"Who's Ruth?" Simon filled a plastic bag with ice for Fiona's leg.

"Damn, no coverage now," Declan said.

"Ruth is Condomine's current wife, whom Fiona plays, but that's not what matters."

"None of it matters, Nora." Declan's face was suffused with anger. "First, you're meddling in the guests' rooms, and now you're seeing connections from old history where none exist."

"You were snooping in their rooms?" Simon's brow furrowed in annoyance. "I thought we had a clear understanding—"

"And I thought I was dealing with two men with brains in their heads instead of in another part of their anatomy." She rushed from the room and into her own before she said something ruder. Shaking with anger, she gathered Sean from his cot, where she had unceremoniously dumped him to be safe when Fiona had fallen.

He mewed when he saw her, on the verge of tears, and she picked him up.

"Shush, lovey," she soothed. "Couldn't leave you alone in your high chair, you silly goose. You're fine," she explained as she changed his nappy. But was everything fine? What kind of monster had been set loose on Ramsey Lodge?

Nora felt her throat tighten. She needed to be away from this place that had always seemed like a haven. Putting a jumper and hat on Sean, she pulled on a jacket and grabbed her mobile. She fastened Sean into his buggy and pushed him hurriedly through the dining room toward the front door.

In the drawing room, she saw Grayson Lange in the middle of a circle of his troupe, a hushed discussion taking place among them. He moved his puffy fingers to exercise them as Fiona held the ice bag to her lower leg and Gemma hung on Grayson's good arm.

"Darling, that could have been me that fell." Nora heard Gemma's raised voice as she opened the front door. With Gemma, it was all about her, Nora thought, bumping the buggy down the steps. Sean crowed with delight and banged his feet on the buggy's edge. She turned toward the quay and her favorite lakeside bench. She had to get away from these toxic people and whoever hunted them. Why had she ever thought them to be such models of humanity to admire? With the exception of possibly the Dentons and Burt Marsh, the others were a fractious, backstabbing bunch of misfits.

She thought back over the incidents as she walked. A missing script was one thing, a dead bunny a sick prank, but cut brake lines and falls downstairs were an entirely different matter. What if she had been the one to trip on the fishing line? What if Sean had been in her arms or strapped to her chest? She couldn't bear to think of it.

The incidents weren't directed at just one person, so what did that mean? Did someone want to send a message to or really hurt the cast of *Blithe Spirit*?

Nora mulled this over as she reached the bench and sat down, looking out over Windermere. A line of geese screeched overhead, and she watched a pair of swans glide by. The geese distracted Sean, and he babbled happily while Nora took out her phone and called Val. As it rang, she saw an unmarked car pull up the drive at Ramsey Lodge and recognized Detective Sergeant Higgins as he hurried inside.

"How's our favorite detective?" Val's warm alto soothed Nora instantly.

"He's fine, just fine." Nora was too upset to gush.

"Any action?"

"That's not why I'm calling." Neatly sidestepping that for the moment, Nora plunged into an explanation of the events of the past few days.

When she stopped her recitation, Val's voice grew thoughtful. "Yankee, should I come and take Sean back here for a few days? For that matter, why don't you just bring him here and stay yourself?"

"I can't do that, Val. I'm supposed to be helping Simon, remember? He's going to have it tough once word gets out about all of this. People are superstitious in small towns, and lodge business is sure to suffer."

"Just a second." There were voices in the background. "Let me call you right back. We're not done here." Val rang off.

Nora looked at Sean. His strawberry-blonde hair shone in the sunlight, and he cooed as the swans glided closer. She remembered feeling an instinctual and immediate love from the first moment she had held him in her arms and had counted he had the right number of fingers and toes. The protective mask she wore at times fell off unequivocally with Sean, revealing an honest and deep love she knew would never fade.

With a start, she realized this must be what Muriel Pembroke had felt at one time for Paul. Whatever the cause of their eventual estrangement, there was a time when what she felt right now, this very second, was what that mother had felt for her son, too.

Nora's mobile rang and she answered right away. "Val? Yes, please do come and get Sean. I can't leave Simon right now, but I don't want the baby at Ramsey Lodge a minute longer."

"I'm still not sure you should stay with a maniac on the loose," Val argued.

"If you take Sean, I'll be free to help find out what's going on here."

"You mean our delicious detective isn't on the case?"

"Oh, he's on the case all right. Only he can't see the forest for the trees."

"Do I detect a little friction between the lovebirds at Ramsey Lodge?" Val's snicker had Nora smiling.

"Let's say a momentary glitch I'm quite sure will be fixed as soon as I convince him I have something real to contribute."

"Oh, Yankee, you have got your work cut out for you. I'll get to you tomorrow. But as I recall from my dealings with our dear detective, I seem to remember a stubborn streak almost as wide as yours."

CHAPTER FIFTEEN

"Well, of all the filthy low-down tricks ... !"
Elvira: Act II, Scene 3

2:30 PM

When Declan came downstairs to the drawing room, he found the cast in a desultory rehearsal. Only the Dentons, sitting on chairs watching the scene unfold before them, appeared animated. Gemma and Fiona battled with each other and with Grayson in a match of Coward wit that had no one laughing.

Even Helen's usual high spirits lagged, her bright turquoise turban slightly askew as she adjusted her scarves and waited for her cue. Burt stood by the fireplace, working at rigging a vase to fall during the climax of the play.

Poppy hung in the doorway, intent on her iPad. When she glanced over her shoulder and saw Declan, she slammed the cover shut.

"Back to work?" He pointed to Fiona and Grayson, the two walking wounded.

"The show must go on and all that rot." She shrugged, apparently unfazed, and moved off to sit in a chair in the back row, where she reopened her iPad.

Not a talkative one, Declan decided, or was talking reserved for Grayson Lange?

Simon came in from the kitchen, his frown lines deepened. "Agnes is getting a migraine; Callie drove her home. All this stress. Thank goodness dinner is sorted and Maeve comes in tonight. And here's more trouble."

They watched Detective Sergeant Higgins enter the Lodge.

"Sergeant, good of you to come." Declan shook the policeman's hand, as did Simon, although Declan picked up on Simon's reluctance. Last autumn, Simon had had his own dealings with Higgins.

"Major conference on in Manchester, and we're down to a skeleton staff for emergencies." Higgins drew out his notebook. "I've had a look at the forensics report on that car. No fingerprints found." He turned to Simon. "Why don't you show me this evidence you have, and I'll get your statement?"

"Anything to get that bloody rabbit out of my freezer," Simon said.

"You'll do background checks on that lot?" Declan inclined his head in the direction of the drawing room.

Simon's face paled. "I guess there's no getting around that."

"Not unless you think Callie or Agnes have developed a sudden mad streak," Declan said. "The answers lie with the cast. When the reports come in, could I have a copy?"

"Certainly, Inspector," Higgins said. "The chief is happy to have your assistance."

Declan clapped the man on the shoulder. "We'll get it sorted. In the meantime, I might take a quick walk, as I think we've had today's drama."

Simon motioned for Higgins to follow him. "I certainly hope so."

2:40 PM

Poppy sat through the dreary rehearsal from her perch on the back row of chairs. She was surprised at the way the Dentons watched, as if it were the first time they'd seen this scene. This was the boring part, between her entrances and exits. Once she'd marked up her script, she had little to do when she wasn't on stage. She fiddled with her iPad. It was really amazing what could be found online these days. Images and old photos galore.

Maybe after dinner, she'd start the final fittings for the costumes if Grayson agreed. Then she could work on any needed alterations in her downtime instead of enduring this mind-numbing tedium. The only thing of the slightest interest to her was watching Grayson as he moved around the stage, trying his lines in various deliveries, coaxing the others to sit taller or move more gracefully.

Poppy watched Fiona milk her sore leg for all it was worth, stopping to adjust her ice pack. Bloody cow should have hit her face instead. Poppy stifled a snicker as an image rose in her imagination of Fiona with her face blown up in bright colors like an Oompa Loompa from *Willie Wonka*. How fitting for someone who'd had Grayson in her grasp and had let him go.

As for Gemma, if she had to listen to that tart's loud giggle much longer, she'd go seriously bonkers. Poppy selected the images she wanted and hit "share" to Grayson Lange's Traveling Theatre Troupe's Facebook page.

2:43 PM

Nora stowed her mobile. She saw Declan searching for her on the quay. He wore his hiking gear, shorts with thick socks and boots, which allowed her to examine his muscled calves. She remembered the feel of those legs wrapped up in hers, and her pulse quickened. Her feelings toward the detective changed from minute to minute. How could he annoy her so much in one moment and then make her heart beat faster the next?

She waved, and he joined her.

"There you are." He knelt down to Sean's eye level. "Enjoying those swans, mate?"

Points to Declan. "He gets very excited when they swim close to us," Nora said.

"One day we'll take you to the shore and let you feed them, all right?" He spoke directly to the child. "Just have to watch they can't nip you."

"He'd love that. I haven't wanted to get too close on my own." She met Declan's probing gaze. In the bright light, his grey eyes had an aqua glow. The annoyance between them fell away.

"The two of us can surely handle it, if you're ready."

Nora's heartbeat thudded in her ears. *I'm more than ready*, she wanted to say. Instead, her breath caught in her throat, and she nodded. He got up and sat next to her.

A goose swooped overhead. Sean cried out happily and stretched his arms up, breaking the tension of the moment. Both adults laughed, but Nora's worry for Sean returned.

"Val's coming tomorrow to take Sean to Oxford for a few days."

"Good idea." He stroked her shoulder. "Maybe you should go, too."

"I can't leave Simon." Nora smiled at him. "Besides, you're here, not in Oxford."

Declan sighed. "Nora, I admit I don't want to send you away. So far, the incidents seem directed at the cast, but what if that changed?" His lips brushed her hair. "Just having me on site won't guarantee your safety."

It meant the world to her that he cared for her and the baby. "I saw Higgins arrive." Nora wrinkled her nose. "I imagine Simon can't wait for that bunny to be out of his freezer."

"Higgins will be here a while to go over everything with Simon—how the troupe came to be here, all the incidents—or

I wouldn't think about leaving you to take a quick hike." He placed his arm along the back of the bench. "Agnes has gone home with a migraine. Callie drove her home."

"Callie's off tonight, anyway, with Maeve in." Nora buttoned Sean's sweater and sat back. "Where are you headed?"

"Maybe just to Miller Ground, too late to do more. There's a front coming in, so before it—" He examined her. "Unless you're afraid even with Higgins here. I don't have to go."

"No, you should go," she protested. "If we get rain, you can't walk in a downpour. And it *is* supposed to be your holiday."

"It's not the only reason I came here." His thigh brushed hers, and he lightly touched her shoulder.

She tilted into him, feeling his breath across the top of her head as he spoke about the intelligence checks Higgins would carry out. She inhaled his scent, woody with a hint of something like spiced honey. If she could just freeze this moment.

She didn't want to renew the tension between them right now, but somehow she had to convince him that Maggie Denton's death was important and especially that the play had something to do with what was happening at Ramsey Lodge.

"This is a beautiful place," he said, a low voice in her ear. "I can see why you'd want to live here."

"It's one of the loveliest places I've ever seen," she agreed, taking in the lapis water. She noted the edges of the fleecy, white clouds to the west had taken on grey edges. It would surely rain tonight. "But it's losing its gloss for me lately." She remembered she hadn't told Declan about the solicitor. She was about to do so when he spoke.

"Do you ever miss Oxford?"

Was that hope in his voice or was it her imagination? She decided to let the issue of Mr. Daniel Kemp drop for now. They'd had enough to deal with for one day. She thought of Oxford's golden spires and the glow of its ancient buildings in the afternoon light. "Sometimes," she admitted.

And they left it at that for the moment.

CHAPTER SIXTEEN

"I feel as though something tremendous had taken place."
Madame Arcati: Act 1, Scene 2

3:30 PM

Declan eyed a large outcropping up ahead to the right and noted a flat rock that would make a good seat. He stepped off the trail and sat down, leaning back against taller rocks behind him. Stretching his legs, he paused his iPod, dropping his ear buds around his neck. It seemed almost sacrilegious to have Pink Floyd's *The Division Bell* thumping in his ears when he was surrounded by so much nature, but the album reminded him of his late teens, when it hit the top of the charts. The craggy fells across the lake looked purple in spots. He could see pathways cut into them leading to sparkling tarns. The breeze was light, and he closed his eyes and let the afternoon sun warm his face.

He would never have taken this brief hike and left Nora and Sean alone at the lodge unless it was timed with DS Higgins being on site. When he had found out Nora was sending Sean to Oxford, he had felt it was the right decision. It meant she would be relieved of one worry—and that meant she would up her snooping, which he didn't want to encourage.

He'd learned in the past that she had good instincts, but what was happening at Ramsey Lodge was difficult to figure out. He had to admit he agreed with her that the mystery revolved around this particular group of people. Whether that had anything to do with the death of the Dentons' daughter remained to be seen. As for the actual play being somehow tied in, he doubted that. Still, the last thing he wanted was for Nora to be in any kind of danger. Part of him hoped she, too, would go to Oxford with Val. That would be a sad irony—Nora in Oxford when he had finally made it to Cumbria to be with her.

Something else was bothering Nora. He had sensed it as they'd talked. And how did she feel about him? It was another reason to leave her with her own thoughts for this brief time. He hoped that by coming here he'd shown her that he wasn't put off by her child. That was easy, for the little boy was certainly a charmer. She would share what was bothering her when she was ready. He'd have to trust her on that. He hoped Higgins' intelligence checks would reveal someone he could point to as the culprit, and then this would all die down—and he could focus on the real reason for his stay at Ramsey Lodge.

He opened his eyes. This was a huge change from the bustle of Oxford, which had its own beauty with its deep sense of academic tradition and history. Lately, he'd been thinking about change in all its forms. He knew he could never stop being a detective—it was too much a part of him and was how he felt most alive—but could he see himself policing in a place other than the Thames Valley Police?

This area had its share of crime. Just look at last autumn's murders, when Keith Clarendon and two others had been killed. There was crime in every village and city in the world, so he wasn't necessarily tied to Oxford to do his job.

No, it was more a question of what he wanted out of life besides his work. He saw death too often to take life for granted. He'd realized for some time that his existence was lacking something … or someone.

Declan reached into the pocket of his fleece for the apple he'd taken from the fruit bowl at Ramsey Lodge. He rubbed it across his leg, polishing it until the red and green shone, a habit that took him back to his father. He bit into the skin, the juice running into his mouth, its tart-sweet fragrance filling his nostrils, reminding him of the apple tree that had stood in the garden of his family home. His parents' marriage stood out like a talisman, a goal he wanted to fulfill in his own life.

A group of middle-aged hikers approached, chatting in what sounded like German. He nodded as they passed, and they saluted him, waved and carried on. One couple in the rear stopped to take a photograph, the woman focusing her camera over the vista spread before them. They had to be in their late forties or early fifties, he estimated from wide streaks of grey at their temples, with the well-defined leg muscles of long-time walkers.

As he watched, the man's arm came up to the woman's shoulder in a tender and familiar gesture. They waved gaily to him as they walked on, calling out "guten Tag!" as they came abreast of his rock. Declan envied their easy camaraderie. The man's arm dropped to his side, and the woman held his hand as they passed. Declan missed that feeling of being part of a couple, one half of a whole.

His brief marriage to Anne had fallen apart because she hadn't been able to tolerate the demands and uneven hours of his job. Nora wouldn't be like that. If anything, he'd have to hold her back from getting too involved in his work. She also had her son and her writing to pursue. He didn't think he'd ever get tired of being with her. Declan finished his apple and wrapped the core in a napkin, tucked it into his pocket and started to whistle "High Hopes" from the Floyd album. The clouds were gathering, and he could see far off to the west that grey tendrils of rain were already coming down. Better start back to Nora and the lodge. He hoped Higgins had finished taking statements from the cast. The interruption to rehearsals would not have gone over well with Grayson.

Declan removed his left boot and adjusted the toe of his

sock where the seam had begun to rub. Thoughts of Nora in all her guises filled his mind: Nora annoyed at him when they disagreed, green eyes flashing with stubbornness; Nora's face softened with tenderness when she held her son; Nora looking him right in the eye, then closing hers in ecstasy as they made love. A voracious reader, Declan remembered a couple of lines he thought might belong to Hemingway:

"Death no longer lingers in the mind. Fear no longer clouds your heart. Only passion for living, and for loving, become your sole reality."

Declan retied the shoe and took one last look around the spot, committing it to memory and thinking, "This is the place where I've decided whom I need to spend the rest of my life with, wherever that might be."

Chapter Seventeen

"She's beginning to show her hand."
Ruth: Act II, Scene 3

5:40 PM

Maeve Addams turned the dial to preheat the oven. Agnes had left clear instructions to bake the lasagna on low heat and then raise it near the end to brown the cheese. Rain spattered against the kitchen windows. She felt glad to be in the warmth of the lodge and to know she wasn't leaving it tonight. She glanced at Nora, feeding Sean in his high chair.

"He really loves that baby rice." Maeve tucked her shiny bob behind her ear, watching Nora deftly spoon in the mush.

Nora agreed. "It will be fun to see how he likes fruits next."

A gust of wind rattled the back door, distracting Sean, who paused eating with his little mouth open in a wide "O" of surprise.

"It's all right, lovey, just wind," Nora assured him, scooping the last spoonful into his open mouth.

Maeve had to hand it to Nora. She'd risen to the role of single parent, and it was easy to see she was a good mother. She watched Nora wipe the baby's face and hands, then hand him two empty plastic cups to bang on his tray.

"Those will keep him happy a while. How can I help?" Nora rinsed the cloth in the sink.

Maeve consulted Agnes' note. "The salad's made, and the bowl of meatballs and sausages need to be reheated closer to dinner. All that's left is making garlic bread, but nothing right now. Thanks for asking, though."

Maeve met Nora's eye so the other woman would know she

was sincere. They'd gotten off to a rocky start when Nora first moved into Ramsey Lodge. Sheer jealousy on Maeve's part, truth be told. Mooning over Simon Ramsey for ages had taught Maeve that despite using every trick in her book of wiles, a hard sell was not for Simon.

Time had changed things, and Simon had lost that hangdog look he'd had around Nora. That was when Maeve had decided to change her game by stepping back from the personal push and upping her sheer indispensability to the lodge. She'd developed her own relationships with their suppliers, pleasing Simon with deals and with her interest. On her own initiative, she'd repainted the front door and had asked the Barnum girls to wax the woodwork until it had shone in the lead-up to Kate's wedding. She'd found Kate and Ian the caterer for their wedding reception and had acted as organizer to keep everything flowing smoothly on the special day. A funny thing had happened when Maeve had plunged into her work: She'd fallen in love with Ramsey Lodge.

Simon had noticed her interest early on, and one evening, he'd invited her to see the albums his parents kept, detailing the restoration work they'd done throughout the years. She had been impressed and had confided over a glass of wine that she felt captivated by the historic building. One glass of wine had led to them finishing the bottle. Things had gone along just fine after that, despite the hectic time surrounding Kate's wedding, and by tacit agreement, neither of them had pushed to be together every night. Yet. Maeve had learned that less was sometimes more in certain situations.

Now, as Maeve looked Nora in the eye, she didn't see a rival as much as a woman she knew Simon respected—but wasn't romancing—and that made all the difference.

"Why don't you give Sean his bath and spend a little time with him before he goes to sleep for the night?" Maeve's manner was gracious.

6:45 PM

Nora enjoyed bathing her baby. Sean sat in his bath seat and squealed when she poured warm water over his head to wash away the no-tears shampoo. He slapped his hands up and down in the water, watching the droplets fly and giggling. Had there ever been a happier baby?

Her father would have loved this little guy. She missed him with an ache in her heart. He'd have been so proud of his grandson. Her sense of loss made her cringe at the knowledge her baby had another set of grandparents who didn't even know of his existence, a piece of their son in this perfect child. She knew the time had come to tell the Pembrokes they had a grandchild—no matter what their solicitor might have in store for her.

"Let's watch the water go out." She pulled the drain and Sean watched the water spiral down and out until she lifted him out of the tub, wrapping him in a warm towel and hugging him closely to her.

Dressed in pyjamas, hair dry and standing up like an orange halo, Sean played with blocks on the floor as Nora changed for dinner. Then she sat him in the middle of her bed, where he chewed on his rabbit's ear and watched her intently as she packed a bag for him and refilled his nappy bag.

It would be the first time she had been away from her baby. The thought of being separated from him felt awful, but he was safer away from Ramsey Lodge just now. Nora chewed her lip as Sean leaned back against the pillows supporting him, his eyes drowsy.

Another huge gust of wind rattled her window; the rain picked up in intensity, and she almost missed the gentle tap at her door. Nora opened it to find Declan, hair slicked back from a shower.

He saw the sleepy baby and whispered: "Maeve says dinner in ten."

Nora opened the door. "Come in. You don't have to whisper. I'll put him to bed. I have to help Maeve with garlic bread."

"Done." He grinned at her wide-eyed look. "I'm pretty good in the kitchen."

Nora lifted the heavy-eyed baby and carried him to his cot. "Your talents extend far beyond detecting." She laid Sean on his back and turned on his mobile, tucking his rabbit in his arm and tiptoeing away.

Declan pointed to Sean's packed bag. "Just for him?"

"Yes." She knew Sean would be fine with Val, and it wouldn't be a bad thing for the two for them to have a few days apart. She picked up the baby monitor.

He held up his hands in a gesture of resignation. "Don't mean to push." He sat on the side of her bed and patted the mattress. "Join me for a sec."

"Go to bed with you?" She sat down next to him.

"Yes, but I expect the young man should be fast asleep first, and maybe after dinner instead of before."

She smiled. The idea of sneaking away to Declan's room again sounded wonderful.

He took her hand and held it between his. "What's bothering you?"

"You mean besides leaving my child for the first time and a maniac loose at the lodge?"

Declan cleared his throat. "I'm not pressuring you, am I?"

"Oh, Declan, it's not you at all." She pulled him to her and kissed him. It was time to tell him why she was worried. She didn't want him thinking it was because of him. She explained about the call from the lawyer and how her only meeting with the Pembrokes had been less than pleasant. "Things between us weren't good before Paul died. I probably wouldn't have ever met them if that plane hadn't gone down. I've kept putting off telling them about Sean."

He stroked her hair. "I'm sorry this so tough on you."

"I know what I need to do. I'm having difficulty with how it will change everything."

Declan pulled her closer and kissed the top of her head. "You'll figure it out. I have enormous faith in you." He stood up. "Now let's eat. I've been promised a fantastic pudding."

Chapter Eighteen

"Jealousy causes people the have the most curious delusions."
Charles: Act II, Scene 3

7:30 PM

Simon watched the cast at the long table tuck into dinner. Burt and Helen ate with gusto, Poppy dug in and Fiona had stopped complaining about her leg. Gemma cut up Grayson's sausages and meatballs for him. The Dentons held everyone's attention as they ate, describing how when they'd played *The Lion in Winter* on stage, they'd called Katharine Hepburn for pointers. Beside him, Nora stiffened at the mention of the movie, her fork halfway to her mouth. Simon wondered what that was about.

He took a deep breath and tried to release the knot of tension between his shoulder blades. He prayed the person responsible for the accidents had tired of these deadly actions. Maybe having to talk to DS Higgins today would be enough of a warning to put the person off his or her game. Simon glanced at the animated faces and wondered who would be capable of arranging these incidents but more importantly, *why*. Was it someone who wanted the production to fail? Or was there a more personal reason?

Simon felt a hand on his thigh and shifted his eyes to Maeve. A tiny smile played across her lips as she appeared totally focused on Declan's enthusiastic description of Oxford's historic Covered Market. Simon dropped his hand to his lap and squeezed her fingers, then picked up his garlic bread.

"Excellent bread, Declan. Maeve said you gave her a hand. Thanks for that."

"I'm a dab hand in the kitchen—not sure Nora believes me," Declan said.

The lights flickered but held. Outside, the wind howled, and the rain picked up. Just what Simon needed now, lights to go out in a storm. Thank goodness Ramsey Lodge had a huge generator, all oiled up and ready to go in an emergency. Simon pushed away the prickling at the back of his neck, put his fork down and took out his mobile.

"Think I'll check the forecast. This storm is really hanging around." Simon brought up the app for the local weather. His face fell. "Looks like this will last all night." Right before dinner, he had filled his bath with water in case they needed to flush toilets. Now he was happy he'd listened to his father's voice in his head and taken that precaution.

"Good thing you went on a walk today, Declan." Nora looked out the window at the driving rain.

Simon thought Nora's appetite was off tonight as he watched Maeve reach for another meatball. That woman could eat what she wanted, and nothing spoiled her slim frame. He pictured her long legs wrapped around him and shifted in his seat. He'd check that generator after dinner. The last thing he needed was to get out of a warm bed in the middle of a rainy night.

8:45 PM

Grayson Lange sat with the others in the library and flexed his fingers. His cast felt tight, his fingers puffy; the rain made his wrist ache even more. He took off the sling and laid his hand along the armrest of his chair.

Poppy jumped up, grabbed a pillow off the window seat, and used it to prop up Grayson's arm. "You need to elevate that hand if you want the puffiness to go down."

"Better listen to Nurse Nancy." Gemma flipped the pages of a glossy fashion magazine.

Poppy's cheeks reddened, and she returned to her post at the window seat, looking out at the weather.

Grayson knew Poppy was right; the A&E doc had said much the same thing. The glow from the painkiller he'd swallowed before dinner was still there, but he knew it would only give him a few hours of relief. He'd take another at bedtime. He watched Helen and the Dentons playing cards at a corner table. Declan and Nora had their heads together on a sofa, and the Ramsey fellow and his girl were finishing in the kitchen. A dreary night all around.

"Gemma?" He touched her shoulder. She'd been checking her iPhone but turned to him, and her eyes took a second to focus. Too much wine again. He held in a sigh. Gemma was becoming high maintenance. Once this production ended, he'd start driving a wedge between them. It would have to be done with finesse. She had to think she was the one ending the relationship or there would be drama-queen scenes.

"Yes, darling?" Gemma took another sip of wine and seemed surprised to find the glass almost empty.

"I think I'll have one of your sleeping pills tonight." He watched with satisfaction as she frowned. "My wrist is killing me with this rain." He thought he got his pained expression just right.

"Of course," she said. "But then I'll have to sleep in my own room. They make you snore."

"Absolutely," he soothed her. "My little star needs her beauty rest." He poured Gemma more wine, and as she raised her glass, he caught Fiona's eye.

Fiona turned toward him and discreetly raised her magazine. He was the only one who saw her put a finger into her mouth with a gagging motion.

"Bloody hell!" Gemma's voice cut across everyone's conversation. She held out her phone to Grayson. "Just look at what's on our troupe's Facebook page."

He screwed up his eyes to see a soft-porn picture of Gemma, wearing a skimpy, see-through bra and thong, looking right at the camera with a wink. "Where the hell is that from?" Grayson asked.

Gemma had the grace to blush. "It was in *Razzle* before I made it on stage."

Fiona laughed. "I didn't know you used your bedroom skills on stage, too."

Grayson knew he'd made a huge mistake by putting Fiona and Gemma in the same show, but neither seemed to care about their obnoxious behavior in front of others.

"Slut—" Gemma hissed. Her fingers flew over the buttons on her phone. Then a wide smile spread across her face as she held out her phone toward Fiona. "Ha! Seems I'm not the only one with a photo she'd like to forget."

"Let me see—" Fiona grabbed Gemma's phone and looked at the image that had Gemma so satisfied. "But how? Who?" She sputtered.

"Oh, for God's sake, give me that," Grayson commanded. Fiona mutely handed him the phone. The troupe's timeline was graced with a photo obviously taken years earlier, showing Fiona drunkenly holding up a lamp post in front of a pub just after being sick, mascara running down her face.

"This is absurd!" Grayson's voice shouted above the howl of the wind. "I want this childish behavior to stop this minute!"

Poppy spoke up. "Grayson, could I start final fittings tonight? It might be, er, a distraction … "

Helen raised her head. "Yes, let's do that! I can't wait to see my outfit. You did get my measurements, dear?"

Poppy nodded. "Yes, and I brought the costumes in your sizes, but there might be fine tuning or hemming. I won't know until you try them on."

Grayson banged his good hand on the armrest. "Capital idea, Poppy. Why don't you start with Helen?"

Poppy ran upstairs, returning with her sewing box and a striped caftan in garish purple, red and gold.

Helen clapped her hands. "I'll just slip into the drawing room and throw this on."

Simon and Maeve came into the library with a tray of drinks as Helen returned, attired in the flowing gown. "How do I look, Grayson?"

His reply was drowned out by the thump of the front door blowing open as a huge gust of wind hit the front of the lodge. Grayson watched as Simon and Declan ran to the hall to deal with the door. They were gone a few minutes, and when they returned, Grayson immediately knew from their faces that something was wrong. Water dripped off them both. Simon had his mobile out.

"It's wild out there." Declan grabbed a napkin and wiped water from his face. "The road's flooded, and we saw flashing lights and barriers on the quay."

Simon brushed wet hair off his head and faced the crowd with his mobile in hand. "The entire area's flooded, and several bridges have been breached. Even the road at the front is closed. Burt, you'll have to stay here tonight."

Excited talk broke out among the group. Grayson waited to see who would give up their bed. He certainly wouldn't be giving up his. He turned to Fiona. "Fi, dear, will you share with Poppy for a night and give your room to Burt?"

Fiona's face darkened at the suggestion, her eyes narrowed in anger.

Nora pointed out, "We piled the last furniture from the drawing room on Kate's bed today when all the props were unpacked, so that's not an option any longer."

Declan spoke up. "Nonsense, the cast should have their own accommodations. Burt can have my room. I'll bunk with Simon."

"I don't think so, Declan." Maeve was firm. "That spot is taken."

"Declan will share with *me* tonight," Nora declared.

Grayson was amused to see it was the women who settled things.

Helen hooted with glee. "Romance on the premises!" she announced. There was a smattering of laughter from the others.

The lights flickered and went out.

9:20 PM

Nora waited for the noise of the generator to kick in as her eyes grew used to the dark and she listened to the baby monitor; luckily, it ran on batteries. All quiet in the nursery. But no generator noise. "Who's got a lighter?"

Burt produced one and flicked it on. "Take this."

Nora made her way into the dining room, followed by Maeve. She lit a candle from one of the tables, then the two women grabbed a tray and gathered up all the table candles, using the lit one to light the others. Maeve brought one back into the library and used it to light the way for the others as they filed back into the dining room and retook their seats. Simon brought up the rear with Declan, one balancing the drinks tray and the other carrying bottles of sherry and brandy.

"I'll be right back," Nora said and used a candle to check on

Sean. The baby slept on, oblivious to the howling wind and rain. She opened a bottom drawer and brought out a winter baby sleeping bag and unzipped it. Leaning over the cot, she carefully laid him inside of it and pulled his arms through, then zipped it closed. Sean stirred but didn't wake. The two layers would keep him warm once the heat in the lodge started to fade.

She used the candle to light a larger one she kept in a dish on her desk for its scent, and soon, a mild scent of juniper and cardamom filled the air. Nora moved the candle away from the wall to a safer spot right in the center of her desk and placed the dish on a slate coaster.

Nora left her door ajar and saw a torch waving toward her. Declan met her at the door carrying a pottery bowl filled with ice.

"Mmmm, smells like a G and T in here," he said, sniffing the air. "Sean all right?"

"Asleep and warm."

He held out the bowl. "Stand his formula in this in your fridge overnight. If we keep the door closed, it should be fine for the night."

Nora took the bowl and did as he suggested, pleased at his thoughtfulness. "Why isn't the generator on?"

"Simon can't get the bloody thing to start up. He thinks the diesel's fouled."

Nora gave an involuntary shiver. "Declan, what's happening here?"

He reached out to brush a tendril of hair over her shoulder. "Don't know, Nora, but Val won't be able to get through, so Sean won't be able to leave tomorrow."

9:25 PM

Simon asked Burt to check the generator, and Declan tagged along, holding the torch as the older man checked the oil and inspected the engine. It started and sputtered out several times. They checked the fuel filter, and Burt grimaced.

"Buggered," Burt pronounced. "Maybe water in the fuel supply? No way to get it fixed tonight."

"Bloody hell." Simon blew out a hard breath. No power tonight. He thought quickly and handed both men kitchen trays. "Follow me, troops."

The three men made their way carefully to the basement, where Kate stored tall hurricane lamps she used at Christmas. Burt and Declan carried them back up, balanced on the trays, and Simon followed with a carton of large, fat refill candles in one hand propped against his chest. His other hand held the handle of a large cooler.

In the kitchen, Simon put his carton and cooler down and transferred a bag of ice from the freezer into a huge bowl he placed in the fridge. "This should help keep the temp cool in here if we don't open it." He dragged the cooler into a corner out of the way and took out two more bags of ice. Burt held the torch while Declan and Simon filled the cooler with a mixture of juices and drinks for the next day.

"Burt, grab a few of those Ramsey Lodge matchbooks we give out," Simon instructed when the caravan reached the hall.

Declan distributed to each cast member a candle-filled hurricane lamp, and Burt followed, lighting each candle and giving each person a matchbook to take upstairs. Simon brought the bottles of brandy and sherry over to the table. Maeve and Nora handed out glasses, which clinked loudly as they worked their way around the table.

There were several hurricanes left. "Declan, would you and Burt put these in the upper hall? There are more torches in the bottom drawer of the registration desk." Simon thanked them as the men left to add light to the hallway and upper floor.

"Sorry for the inconvenience." Simon opened bottles and offered them around. He tried to keep his tone light. What the hell else could go wrong? He shuddered at the thought of more fishing line in the dim hallways. "There are extra blankets in your cupboards, and I suggest you put them on your beds. It will get chilly later without the heat on."

"Then I'll pile mine on! Sherry, Simon." Helen pronounced. "Settles the spirits. They're in their element in this weather. Can't you hear them walking around?"

The French doors across the hall rattled, giving credence to her statement.

Gemma laughed. "Helen, you're bonkers, you do know that?" She held out her glass. "Brandy for me, Simon, and fill it up."

"Yes, do fill it up," Fiona sniped. "Like you really need more alcohol."

Helen held up her hands and waved them around. "Hush, you two, you're upsetting the spirits."

Simon distributed drinks, threading his way between chairs at the table.

Grayson took a brandy. "Just a small one. Probably best not to drink too much with those painkillers on board."

Fiona sniffed and looked away, biting her lip. Simon had the distinct impression she'd seen the director consume more than a small brandy with his pills. She waved the bottles away. "None for me, thanks."

"It's an adventure." Poppy's voice was high and excitable. "I'm not sewing so I'll have a brandy, please."

"Brandy for me, too." Rupert patted Simon on the back.

"Can't order the weather, Simon, not your fault."

"Sherry would be nice," Lydia said.

Nora and Declan each took a sherry as Simon sat down and Maeve poured him one. He picked up on the look that passed between Nora and Declan.

"Val won't be able to get through." Nora sipped her sherry and explained to Simon and Maeve that Val was to have taken Sean back to Oxford for a few days.

Simon hid his surprise and tamped down the flash of betrayal he felt on hearing the news. He couldn't blame Nora for wanting her child off the premises with everything that had happened this week. If he could just keep the incidents away from the press, things might be saved by positive publicity from the play.

"Knowing Val, she'll get here eventually." Maeve put her hand on Simon's arm and looked him in the eye. "Things will look much better in daylight."

Simon covered her hand with his, grateful she understood his mood. "I sincerely hope so."

Chapter Nineteen

"This is quite definitely one of the most frustrating nights I have ever spent."
Ruth: Act III, Scene 2

10:50 PM

Declan helped Burt and Simon fill containers with water from Simon's bath. He complimented Simon on his foresight. They used scrubbing buckets from the kitchen and plastic tubs from Kate's workshop and even raided Agnes' larder for her largest plastic bowls.

"I don't want to be around when Agnes sees we've used these." Simon grimaced.

"She can always bleach them," Burt retorted.

They trudged upstairs and left a water-filled bucket or bowl in each bathroom for flushing.

Maeve followed in their wake with a rag and wiped sloshed water off the stairs. "We don't need any more slipping on stairs tonight."

Even in the dim light, Declan could see the consternation on Simon's face.

"Don't even think like that, Maeve." Simon's exasperation was evident in his voice.

Declan couldn't blame Simon for being cross. The possibility that the generator motor had been deliberately sabotaged dashed all thoughts of the perpetrator stopping. Simon must have the same questions Declan had: Who was behind these incidents, and why? The lousy weather added to the menacing feeling, and from the weather report Declan saw on Simon's mobile, it looked like one of the worst rainstorms in Cumbrian history. The fact that there was still a signal for the mobile towers was bloody amazing.

Simon lent Burt a tee shirt and joggers to sleep in, and he had extra toothbrushes on hand. Sporadic conversation settled over the dining room table, and the once boisterous group huddled over their drinks as driving rain hit the windows and hurled small stones against them. The wind moaned and whined around corners and crevices in the old building, and at times, gusts screeched. Everyone jumped as a burst of thunder clapped overhead.

"Elements afoot," Helen pronounced. "They can reach 'almost hurricane velocity.'"

"Act 1, Scene 2," Fiona intoned, and Poppy giggled.

"Get over yourself, Helen," Gemma said.

"It never hurts to know one's lines backwards and forwards," Helen said. "Something only a true professional understands."

Lydia stood. "Time to retire."

Rupert pushed his chair back. "I quite agree."

Declan couldn't blame the couple for wanting to escape the carping of the others. "I'll help with a torch as you go up."

"We might as well all go up." Grayson stood and marched ahead of them all, cradling his arm. Each person carried a lit hurricane lamp and matches. Declan and Simon followed with extra unlit candles and torches to light the stairs, Simon behind Lange, the Dentons and Burt, with Declan bringing up the rear behind the women.

"I wonder if I can read by this light," Poppy mused, trailing behind Gemma and Fiona with Helen. "I doubt I'll sleep with all this noise."

"Do you want me to stay up with you?" Helen asked as they reached the top of the stairs.

Behind them, Declan saw the younger woman consider the offer.

"The spirits will keep you safe," Helen added.

"It's okay, thanks, I'll be fine," Poppy demurred and shut her door with a bang.

Helen shrugged and winked at Declan. No spirit company for Poppy, Declan chuckled to himself. In his room, he packed up his kit and a clean set of clothes for the morning and threw it all in his rucksack. Burt came in with a fresh stack of towels and his borrowed clothing. They could hear Simon helping to settle everyone in their rooms.

"Comfortable bed." Declan added his robe and a pair of shorts to the sack and closed it.

"As long as no one up here snores, I'll be fine." Burt took the towels into the bathroom and ducked his head back out. "Thanks for the bed. Beats a sofa in the library."

Declan descended the stairs using a torch. A flash of lightning lit up the front hall and cast the drawing room into quick relief, the props and furniture on the stage ghost-like in the shadows. He could almost see Elvira Condomine rise from the sofa, and with a shiver, he turned and walked through the dining room. Helen was getting to him.

He passed Simon's closed door and entered Nora's room. She emerged from the bathroom in a nightgown, carrying a candle-lit lamp with her hair brushed out and flowing. In the blurry candlelight, she looked like a Pre-Raphaelite model, and he watched her glide toward him, her lemony scent reaching him before she did.

He put his rucksack on the floor and held his arms out. Sean whimpered just when she stepped into the circle of his arms. He hugged her tightly, feeling her outline through her nightgown. As their lips met, Sean howled, and Nora stiffened.

He released her. "I'll just use the bathroom."

"And I'll get Sean settled."

Declan brushed his teeth, listening to Nora trying to shush the crying baby. He looked at his reflection in the mirror. Face it, old chap: This is not the night for wild sexual exploits.

11:35 PM

Alone in Declan's bed, Burt listened to the various noises coming from the other rooms as people settled down for the night. He thought of what Estelle would have made of the *Blithe Spirit* cast. He could hear her response as clearly as if she lay beside him: "They're all bonkers, and as for that Helen—thinking she can talk to ghosts!"

How barren his life had become with Estelle gone. Long, lonely days stretched ahead of him. They'd never been blessed with children, and when he'd brought up adoption, Estelle had told him, "God didn't mean us to be parents. Our students will be our children; we must be each other's best friend and companion." It had worked when they were teaching and in retirement when they'd spent time in the community theatre side by side. His own family was long gone, and Estelle's one sister had emigrated to Australia thirty years ago. Except for her occasional call or card, the phone stayed quiet.

He read a lot, but there was only so much time to be passed reading, and then his eyes hurt and he had to take a break. He went to trivia night at The Scarlet Wench but wasn't a drinker beyond a pint or two. He had little interest in television, although he did have a fondness for *Inspector Morse* repeats.

Morse: Now there was a man who used his brain, something Burt admired. The sense Burt made of science, Morse had made of crime. Detecting was a science as much as an art, a study of human foibles and urges. Burt enjoyed each novel and then the television series. Too bad that Colin Dexter had tired of Morse and had killed him off. Probably spent his royalties and residuals sitting in the Randolph Hotel bar. That had been a sad day, closing the cover on the last book in the series. He watched the new series now, with Morse's sidekick Lewis promoted to inspector and taking Morse's place. At least the show had the good sense to use the same actor to play Lewis, although Burt hadn't made up his mind yet about the ascetic young man who played the new sergeant.

Burt sighed and turned onto his side. Where was sleep when he yearned for it? He should have drunk a double brandy to keep his mind from wandering. This was his future: the occasional trivia night at the pub and waiting for the next episode of *Lewis*.

11:59 PM

It was one of the longest hours to date in Nora's brief experience with motherhood. She felt frayed around the edges, tired, tense and on edge.

Even after a dry nappy, Sean wouldn't go back to sleep. Nora had heard the bed creak earlier when Declan had climbed in. This *would* be one of the nights Sean didn't sleep through. She topped him off with a few ounces of water, which didn't satisfy him. Declan heard him still fussing after a while and murmured "Good night, then."

Rocking Sean in her chair, Nora looked down. In the candlelight, the baby's eyes locked on hers. *Not in my room you're not*, she felt him message her. Then she chided herself. He was an infant, a few months old, and here she was putting her ideas onto him. Guilt, indecision, take your pick.

After a few minutes, Declan's breathing became even. Perhaps for the best, she thought with more than a tinge of disappointment, but what was she expecting? She didn't want her time with Declan to be spent holding her breath while listening for the baby—or worse, trying to keep quiet to avoid waking him. She groaned and let her head fall against the back of the chair. The timing was all off. But when would it be right?

The whole week had become a disaster, with accidents and falls culminating in this storm and the malfunctioning generator, which could have been fouled at any time for its next use. That also pointed to someone trying to harm the lodge's reputation, yet it could have been done recently. Could the generator have been tinkered with to throw people off track and add to the general confusion? But who can really predict weather? Maybe it was just broken, a case of being filled with bad fuel?

All the other incidents were clearly directed at the cast. A dead bunny on Gemma's pillow and cut brake lines on Grayson's car—now no hot water or electric or heat. Could Helen be right about the ghosts of *Blithe Spirit* invading this production for some unknown reason?

Nora glanced toward the bed and listened to Declan's rhythmic breathing. She felt reassured he was there, nearby at the very least. She shook her head, wishing she had her notebook handy. It narrowed things down a bit if she eliminated the missing script and the generator, which could just be down to happenstance. But the deliberate happenings were all directed at cast members. And then there were those postings of unflattering photos of Gemma and Fiona at the same time. It had to be connected somehow. She thought back to the candlelit table and the faces glowing in the light, sipping brandy or sherry. Who among them would have a reason to do this? Could it be more than one person?

She looked down and saw Sean had finally drifted back to sleep. Perhaps the noise of the wind and rain had affected him more than she'd thought, little fellow, and a wave of tenderness for her baby rushed over her. Placing him carefully in his cot, she blew out the candle and tiptoed to her bed.

Declan lay spread out across the middle of the bed on his side, one arm flung up across the pillows. Just like a man, she thought, slipping off her robe.

"Declan?" she whispered. She lifted the covers and slid in next to him, turning her back to fit in, curling into him and letting his body warm her. He wore a pair of shorts and she could feel his strong chest against her back through her nightgown. For a moment she considered taking her gown off. But perhaps worry over the maniac among them had robbed him of his ardor. Doubtful, she thought, smiling in the darkness at the memory of their night together.

Declan shifted in his sleep and one arm dropped over her, trapping her against him. She snuggled closer, her eyes drooping. It had been a long while since she'd shared her bed. She didn't think she'd sleep, not with the wind and the rain, not with his firmness against her back. Yet she felt her eyes heavy with sleep, and she knew her son wouldn't care in the morning that he'd kept her up late.

CHAPTER TWENTY

"It's considered vulgar to say 'dead' where I come from."
Elvira: Act 1, Scene 2

Thursday, 12th April

6:12 AM

Wild shrieks from upstairs woke Nora and Declan.

"Stay here." Declan threw on his robe and ran out of the room.

Nora heard footsteps running upstairs and a general commotion. She put on her robe and grabbed Sean from his cot. Still fast asleep, he stirred in her arms as she rushed into the hallway. Maeve stood in Simon's door, wearing one of his soccer shirts.

"What's happened?" Maeve rubbed her eyes, her shiny bob askew.

"I'm going to see."

"Give Sean to me." Maeve held out her arms for the sleeping baby.

"If he wakes, his formula's in my fridge—"

"Just go!"

Nora took off as fast as her slippers would let her run through the dining room and up the stairs, still lit in the weak morning light by several dying hurricanes. Someone sobbed, and voices were raised.

"Everyone, please stand back." Declan's authoritative voice rang over the gabble.

Nora pushed past the guests standing around Gemma's doorway and met Simon on the threshold. His face was white. She looked inside to see Declan at the side of the bed, going through the motions of feeling for a pulse on the body of Gemma Hartwell.

Nora sucked in a breath. Declan stood and shook his head. The still figure lay among the sumptuous trappings of the Shakespeare Suite, a blonde Ophelia with a serene expression, her hair fanned out on her pillow. Nora felt she'd stumbled down Alice's rabbit hole into a surreal nightmare.

Declan closed the door behind him and faced the people lining the hall. "I'm afraid there's no chance of resuscitation."

"Are you certain?" Grayson moved to brush past him.

Declan put out a restraining arm. "Without question. She's been dead for hours." There were gasps at his pronouncement.

Rupert had his arm around Lydia, who cried softly into her husband's chest. He raised his head. "It was Lydia who found her and screamed.

"I knew it—I knew there was evil here," Helen whispered.

Fiona reeled around and would have pushed the old woman if Nora hadn't stepped between them.

"Shut up! Just shut up, will you!" Fiona burst into tears and ran into her room, slamming the door.

"Actually, I'm going to ask all of you to return to your rooms now and get dressed, then gather in the dining room until I can talk with each of you separately." Declan's tone brooked no argument.

Burt and Helen immediately turned to do as he'd asked, with Poppy following behind. Grayson stood looking at the closed door and Declan's implacable face.

"Quite right. Come, dear, let's get you to lie down for a few moments." Rupert guided Lydia next door to their room and gently shut the door.

"Simon, we need to lock this room after I open the windows. It will keep the body cooler." Declan stood in front of the door, arms crossed, as Simon ran downstairs to get the key.

"Why do you get to go back in there and I can't?" Grayson pressed.

Nora knew the answer to that: because Declan had already been in the room, and the less the crime scene was disturbed by outsiders, the better. The director's eyes hollowed, and he seemed to distance himself as Declan explained and then asked his own question.

"Was Gemma with you at all last night, Grayson?"

The man roused himself to answer. "No, I took a painkiller along with one of her sleeping pills after that brandy … she couldn't handle my snoring when I'm out like that and wanted to sleep in her own room."

Nora caught Declan's eye and nodded, remembering the overheard conversation between Grayson and Gemma the night before.

Declan persisted. "You didn't see her at all after you came upstairs?"

"She helped me undress, then tucked me into bed and went to her own room." His face paled. "I didn't think it would be the last time I'd see her alive."

The man seemed sincerely distressed, but Nora reminded herself that she was dealing with a group of people who were used to wearing mantles of expression that were not genuine at all.

"You mean you might have been nicer to her?" Declan's sharp tone surprised Nora, but he had years of interviewing experience that taught him to read between the spoken lines.

Grayson looked up. "I don't know what you mean. I'm going to take your advice and get dressed." He turned on his heel and shut his door just as Simon returned with the key.

"Could you tell how she died?" Simon held out the key.

Declan shook his head. "Not yet." He entered the room and opened the windows, looking around the suite as he carefully trod where he'd been before. "Rain's coming in a bit. And there's a large candle lying on the floor near the foot of the bed. Get me a few plastic bags, would you, Simon? And I could use some towels to protect your carpet."

Nora ran to the linen closet for a stack of towels while Simon retrieved plastic bags from the closet behind the stairs. Declan took them all, tucking the bags into his robe pocket. He laid a bag flat, then used several towels to pad the floor under each open window in turn, but he kept one towel back.

The daylight was stronger, and in the doorway, Nora stood next to Simon and watched Declan step closer to the bed and lean in to inspect Gemma's body. He lifted one eyelid. "Petechiae," he muttered.

He used one end of the towel to lift Gemma's hair and inspect her neck. Keeping his hand covered by the towel, he lifted the pillow next to her and sniffed both sides, inspecting it carefully. He took one of the plastic bags from his pocket and kept the towel around the pillow, shoved them both into the bag and closed it. He laid it by the door.

Next, he looked carefully around the room before stooping to use the inside of a second plastic bag to wrap around the candle on the floor. He left the room and locked the door.

Nora wanted to ask his thoughts but kept silent. He was the professional. He'd share his ideas when he could, but from years of reading mysteries, she knew petechiae meant a lack of oxygen.

Declan pocketed the key. "I need to do this the right way. Let's get dressed so I can start interviews once I call it in to Kendal Station."

"You'll get a stronger mobile signal to if you go out on the terrace," Simon offered. "Poor woman. This is horrific."

Nora admired Simon's sadness. With Gemma's death, the play couldn't go on. Away went the financial security he'd hoped it would provide, but his first instinct was to rue the loss of life.

Declan nodded. "I'll tape and sign these bags." He clapped Simon on the back.

Nora followed the men downstairs. Poor Gemma and poor Simon, too. A death on the premises of Ramsey Lodge—and of a celebrated actress? The press would have a field day. She ordered her thoughts as they headed down the hall. If Gemma's death seemed to be from natural causes, Declan wouldn't have bagged evidence. A chill ran through her as they stopped at Simon's door, which stood open. Her sense of unreality lifted and with it came clarity of purpose.

Maeve had brought in Sean's high chair and played with him with his blocks. Maeve rose when she saw them in the doorway. "What's happened?

Sean hooted when he saw Nora and raised his arms to be picked up. "Hello, lovey." Maeve must have changed his nappy when he woke, for he felt dry and warm.

Simon explained and Maeve brought one hand to her mouth to hold back her gasp. "Simon—how awful!"

"Maeve, would you mind keeping an eye on Sean a while longer?" Nora nuzzled the baby. The stakes had definitely been raised.

"Of course. There's not much else I can do right now."

Nora turned to Declan. "You'll need someone to take notes after breakfast as you interview." She held up a hand as Declan and Simon both started to protest. "I'm the writer and have my own shorthand; it makes sense." Besides, this way she would be privy to what was said and draw her own conclusions. She still believed her years of working with celebrities gave her something to offer: a perspective Declan couldn't possibly have.

"It really does, Declan." Maeve's support clinched the deal, and Nora flashed her a brief smile of thanks. "Simon, we can bring Sean into the dining room after we're dressed. And put out cereal and fruit and even juice for anyone who wants to eat."

"I can boil water on the gas stove and make tea." Simon looked at Nora. "We won't let that baby out of our sight."

"That's settled then." Before Declan could protest, Nora left to get dressed.

Declan followed her in and sorted out the clothes he'd packed. "I suppose I could use the help," he allowed.

She flashed him a smile, than ran into the bathroom to brush her teeth. She eyed Declan's open kit, a tan leather bag softened from years of use. Spying a familiar Penhaligon's bottle with its rounded stopper, she lifted it and sniffed. Opus 1870 gave her a rush of the peppery, woody cedar scent he used. It steadied her in the midst of this bizarre morning. She dropped it back in the bag and came out to grab clean clothes. Declan had his jeans on and threw her a brief smile.

Nora paused, bra and panties in hand. Now what? Go into the bathroom to get dressed when they'd already been intimate? Then she realized Gemma was upstairs, dead, and this was not the time to stand on ceremony with someone who'd already seen all her jiggly bits and scars. She pulled her nightgown over her head and turned away to fasten her bra and pull on clean panties, hoping her pregnancy pounds really did make her look as sexy as Declan had intimated. She peeked over her shoulder to see Declan occupied with his shirt buttons. With goose bumps from the coolness, she hurriedly slid into her jeans and pulled on a tee shirt and then a sweater for layering to ward off the chill. By the time she turned around, Declan had added a fleece to his shirt and was on his way into the bathroom to brush his teeth.

While he was in the bathroom, Nora went to her desk for her notebook. She realized her hands were trembling. There was a dead woman at Ramsey Lodge, right here in this house she called home. Would she ever feel safe here again?

She thought of Gemma's family, who would soon be getting the painful news of her death, dealing with the loss of their daughter—or sister, if she had siblings. The thought made

Nora remember the call to the Pembrokes she'd been avoiding. Though it weighed heavily on her conscience now, she wouldn't be able to reach them with the flooding. This wasn't the right time at all. It would have to wait.

Nora neatly pushed their call back into the to-do compartment of her mind. She had to concentrate on the task at hand. While she was happy she could finally help Declan on a case, her overriding need was to find the murderer before he or she could strike again while her baby was in the house.

CHAPTER TWENTY-ONE

"The whole experience has unhinged me."
Charles: Act 1, Scene 2

7:50 AM

Simon sat woodenly in his kitchen. This was a terrible tragedy, an awful happening—a dead actress from a play he had a financial stake in, right here on his property.

Nora came in, squeezed his shoulder and left with Sean. Declan followed her and took Sean's high chair. Maeve came out of the bedroom, warmly dressed, and guided Simon into the kitchen. "Time to do something useful, Si."

He shook himself out of his stupor. He was still the owner of Ramsey Lodge and had responsibilities. He led the way to the lodge kitchen and put water on to boil while Maeve arranged muffins on a tray.

He refilled the fruit bowl, quickly opening the fridge to extract grapes; he was pleased it was still cool. The bag of ice he'd added last night was half gone, the melted water caught in the bowl he'd stacked it in. At least one thing was going right. The juice and milk were fine in the cooler, too. With any luck, the electric would come back on soon. He glanced out the kitchen window. Was it his imagination or was the rain slowing down?

He brought juice and glasses into the dining room and added them to the sideboard. It would be help-yourself today if anyone even felt like eating. His thoughts strayed to that poor woman upstairs. Gemma had looked beautiful even dead—like a wax figure. Declan hadn't confirmed it yet, but Simon doubted her death was natural after he'd watched Declan bag that pillow, although maybe he was just being cautious. She could have died from an overdose of something she took, maybe helped herself to Grayson's pain pills? He felt a pang of guilt if the brandy he'd offered after all the wine she'd drunk had contributed to her death. A natural death could happen anywhere and at any time, but she was awfully young for something like a heart attack, unless she'd been into cocaine. Great, drugs on site, or if not … Simon shuddered to think what would happen to business at Ramsey Lodge if Gemma Hartwell had been murdered. Selfish, totally selfish. A woman was dead, regardless of the cause, and here he was thinking of how it would affect his trade.

He followed Maeve into the dining room, where Nora sat by Sean, giving him his breakfast, notebook next to her at the ready. Declan came in from the terrace and draped his wet anorak across the back of an empty chair. Simon didn't envy him the job of cooling Nora's enthusiasm while trying to conduct an investigation. She'd be right in the midst of it all until it was cleared up, especially with Sean here. Simon looked at Declan's face and was suddenly certain Gemma had been murdered.

"I got through out there, but the signal is in and out." Declan plopped into a chair next to Nora.

"What did they say?" Simon steeled himself for the answer.

The detective had everyone's attention. "First, the weather. Cumbria is flooded. A bridge has collapsed on the A596 near Workington, and a policeman died."

Maeve gasped, and Nora shook her head as Declan continued. "There are widespread power cuts, and the police surgeon can't get here until the water recedes." He pushed his wet hair off his forehead. "I'm in charge and no one leaves the lodge. Not as if they could. That should all go over well." He wiped water off the back of his neck with a paper napkin. "The only good news is that the electric is starting to come back in this area, and Windermere and Bowness should be back today."

"What about ... " Nora gestured upstairs.

"We're to leave her in situ, and I'll call back later for an update on the police surgeon and the forensic team."

What more can go on? Simon asked the question he knew was in all their minds. "How did she die, Declan?"

"I can't be certain. She has broken blood vessels in her eyes, a sign of asphyxia, and her pillow had smears of lipstick and scent. My impression? She was smothered as she slept."

"And if she took a sleeping pill after all that alcohol, anyone could have gotten into her room without waking her," Nora pointed out.

Declan nodded briskly. "In the meantime, Simon, gather everyone around the table where we can keep an eye on them. I'll start interviews individually in the drawing room."

Maeve brought cereal and juice over to their table. "Better get something inside you. I'm going to see if I can check on Agnes." She took her mobile out of her pocket. "Can I borrow your anorak?"

Declan nodded. "Just keep her and Callie away, and don't tell them what's happened."

Maeve took his damp jacket. "I won't, but they'll hear soon enough."

Simon grimaced. "There's no way Val can get here today, Nora."

She gave him a brief smile. "Not your fault. None of this is, Simon. I'll try to reach Val later."

"She'll have heard about the flood on the news," Simon pointed out.

Nora took Sean's plastic keys and shook them. He made a grab and immediately started to chew on them.

Simon saw worry line her face. This was horrific, and so much more than a loss of business was on the line. "Declan, we need to find out who's responsible before another night passes."

8:20 AM

Declan watched the cast sit morosely around their table as he brought them up to speed on the situation. Simon carried in a pot of tea and poured a cup. He served it to Lydia after telling the others to help themselves. The woman had herself in control, although her eyes were still red. Rupert had his arm around her shoulders.

"Please remain in the dining room after eating," Declan said as chairs scraped back. Burt and Fiona went to the sideboard. Poppy poured tea for Grayson and herself. Helen sat quietly, nibbling a hangnail, accepting tea from Fiona.

Declan described the severity of the flooding. "I'm to head up the investigation in the absence of local Criminal Investigation Department. That means a statement from each of you."

Grayson started to protest but clapped his mouth shut when Declan added: "I believe Gemma was murdered."

A ripple of shock ran across the faces ranged around the table. Helen's cup rattled in her saucer, and she put her hands in her lap.

"I'd like to start with you, Mrs. Denton, after you've had your tea." Declan saw Rupert trace soothing circles on Lydia's back.

Lydia stood. "No, let's get this over with." Rupert stood to join her.

"Just Mrs. Denton for now, please," Declan clarified, and Rupert reluctantly sat back down.

Maeve took Nora's place at their table. Nora nodded her thanks and picked up her notebook and Lydia's teacup. Declan took Lydia's arm and walked her into the drawing room.

"Why's she allowed to leave the room?" Poppy protested, pointing to Nora.

"Nora's taking interview notes." Declan's tone was curt.

He heard Fiona as they walked out. "Pipe down, Poppy. You'll just have to stick it out here like the rest of us."

Declan arranged a few folding chairs into a circle. Nora put Lydia's tea on an empty chair beside her.

"Drink some of that. I hope it has plenty of sugar in it." Declan's tone was kind. These would be some of the most unusual interviews he'd ever conducted.

Lydia obliged and smiled wanly at the detective.

"Why don't you start by describing your movements after you went upstairs last night, Mrs. Denton?" Declan nodded to Nora, who opened her notebook. He watched as she wrote Lydia's name and the date and time across the top line.

"Please, call me Lydia." She described their bedtime routine. "We shared an orange and talked for a while. I wanted to read, but Rupert thought it might hurt my eyes. I put the extra blanket on our bed, and we put the candle in the bathroom and settled down to sleep." She reached for her tea.

"Did you sleep well?" he asked.

"Oh, yes. Rupert got up to use the bathroom around 3—old bladders, you know. I felt him leave the bed, so I went, too, and then we both went back to sleep."

"Did you hear any noises from Gemma's room?"

"No. I woke about 6, my usual time, and saw our candle was ready to go out."

Declan nodded encouragement; Nora noted times and actions as Lydia continued.

"It was starting to get light but I worry so about Rupert falling, so I went into the hall to get another candle from the extras Simon left on the table at the head of the stairs. Such a nice young man, so thoughtful." Lydia sighed.

Declan knew she was getting to the part of the morning she'd rather not remember.

"I saw Gemma's door was ajar. I worried she'd been sick, so I went in. She was lying there, so still … " She looked up at Declan and Nora. "At first, I thought she was asleep, but there was enough light coming in the window as I got closer to see she wasn't moving, didn't seem to be breathing. And then I touched her; she was so *cold* and I—" Lydia started to cry.

This was where he had to keep her talking. "You didn't touch anything after you called out?"

"No, just her hand." Lydia wiped her eyes with a crumpled tissue. "Rupert got to me first, and I told him I thought Gemma was dead, and he took me out into the hall. And then you got there," she finished with a gulp.

"What made you think she'd been sick?"

"Because she'd been quite drunk last night, hadn't she?" She sniffled into her tissue.

Even as she patted Lydia's knee, Nora caught his eye and raised a reproachful eyebrow. It reminded him to bring up Lydia's daughter.

Declan waited for Lydia to compose herself before asking: "Lydia, I understand you and Rupert had a daughter."

Lydia's head came up. "Maggie, our lovely girl," she whispered.

"She was in a production with Grayson Lange," Declan prompted.

"*Major Barbara*; Shaw, you know. She played Sarah." Lydia's lip trembled.

Declan waited for her to go on. Nora shifted in her seat, and he feared she would barge in and throw questions at the woman. But Declan knew the value of silence.

"They—she fell in love with him. Once the show was over, so was their affair. Maggie stopped eating, lost her drive. She wouldn't listen to reason or see a doctor." Her voice hardened. "He was her first big love, and he tossed her away like a used tissue. She wasn't worldly. It did her in, in the end." Lydia twisted her tissue into shreds.

More silence. More sips of tea. Then Declan ventured a statement.

"Yet you and Rupert agreed to work with him."

Lydia's shoulders slumped. "I didn't want to, but Rupert had this idea Grayson should know the heartache he caused. It became almost an obsession. Besides, parts for the two of us don't come along so often … " her voice trailed off. "Rupert felt Grayson owed us those roles, you see."

"Lydia," Declan asked, softening his voice, "did Rupert cut Grayson's brake cables?"

The woman's head snapped up. "No! Rupert is a gentle man. He wanted Grayson to understand how we'd suffered. Having us around must be hard on him, but he never referred to Maggie when we auditioned, and so we didn't, either."

"Did Rupert want the play to flop?"

Lydia looked horrified. "NO! Rupert just wanted an opportunity to let loose on Grayson at some point."

There were raised voices from the dining room, and from across the hall they heard Rupert's ringing tone: "You were responsible for her death, and now you have another life on your conscience!"

Nora said, "I think he already has … "

Chapter Twenty-Two

"You ought to be ashamed."
Elvira: Act III, Scene 2

8:50 AM

Grayson Lange felt Rupert's hot breath on his face as the man's bony fingers reached for his throat. He shrank back as Simon grabbed the older man's shoulders and restrained him before Rupert could throttle him.

"I never—I don't know what you're talking about." Grayson cowered in his seat, his eyes darting down the table, seeking reassurance from those remaining.

Simon pulled Rupert's arms down and held them firmly. He watched the rest of the room react to the man's outburst. Helen stood up. Burt looked at his plate, an awkward witness to the scene. Fiona put her head in her hands. At the corner table, Maeve played with Sean and pretended not to notice. Only Poppy gave Grayson the warm look he craved and moved into Gemma's seat.

"Settle down, Rupert." Simon guided the man into a corner of the dining room.

Grayson rolled his eyes as the detective arrived with Nora and Lydia close behind.

"You don't understand." Rupert didn't fight Simon's restraint. "He killed our daughter, and he probably killed that girl upstairs."

Grayson stood and threw his napkin down. "I don't have to stay and listen to this."

"I'm afraid you do," Declan said.

Grayson plopped back into his chair to communicate his annoyance. He was happy to see Rupert's hands were shaking.

Poppy leaned over to whisper to him. "Let it go, Gray, don't make it worse."

Declan stepped forward. "Why don't you come into the drawing room now, Mr. Denton?" He took the man's elbow, and Nora followed them out.

Grayson saw Lydia clench her hands. She wouldn't sit at the same table with him at this moment.

Simon guided her over to his own chair in the corner by the child and Maeve. "Lydia, why don't you keep Sean happy, and Maeve will get you a hot cuppa?"

Maeve was already rising. Comely lass, that one, Grayson thought, admiring her. Lydia sat down and reached out to rub the baby's arm. Sean responded with a toothless smile and squeal that diffused the strained scene. Bless the child for being a distraction.

Grayson finally let out his breath. He leaned back in his chair. What a bunch of histrionic hams.

8:58 AM

Nora flipped to a fresh page in her notebook as Rupert took the seat his wife had vacated. The man had lost his color; his hands still trembled. He rubbed his face briskly and leaned forward, long arms dangling between his legs. Nora felt a rush of great pity for him.

"Some gallant knight." His voice was husky with pain. "I should have gone for a punch in the face."

"Then I'd have to bring an assault charge against you, Mr. Denton." Declan's smile was wry and loosened the man up. "Take a deep breath. I expect you've been wanting to do that for a long time."

"Almost two years, actually," Rupert acknowledged. "I know what you're thinking: Is he the one caused that bloody accident, made him break his wrist?" He shook his head. "Believe me, if I were stronger, it wouldn't be his wrist I'd break."

Declan shook his head. "You don't need to be saying things like that, Rupert."

Rupert met his gaze. "I couldn't help it. I really believe he killed my Maggie."

Declan nodded. "Your wife told us the story. I'm very sorry."

Nora felt a pang of sorrow for the man's loss. It upset the balance of nature for a parent to lose a child. She reached out to touch the man's arm, thinking of the pain the Pembrokes must have endured when Paul died. Rupert gave her a grateful look and patted her hand before she dropped it to return to her notes.

"Just to clarify," Declan asked. "Was there ever any suggestion Grayson had anything to do with your daughter's overdose?"

"No, she died by her own hand, full of sorrow, poor thing. Whether it was accidental, trying to block out her pain, or true suicide we'll never know." Rupert's fire returned. "But he's as culpable as if he'd held the water to her lips to wash those pills down."

"I understand. Let's go over a few points." Declan gave Nora a subtle look to be certain she was getting all this in her notes. "If you feel such anger toward Grayson, why agree to be in this play?"

Rupert's eye glowed. "He owed us those roles. And I wanted to make him squirm every time he saw us. I wanted to confront him, tell him what I thought of him, face to face."

This matched Lydia's account. Nora put an asterisk next to his response. She had enormous difficulty imagining this frail, emotional man capable of plotting and carrying out the events of the past few days. If Grayson were the object of his wrath, why arrange for Fiona to fall or put a dead bunny on Gemma's pillow? Unless those were meant to disrupt the play. But then why kill Gemma? Nora thought Rupert would be more the type who would warn the young woman to stay away from the director.

Declan's thoughts must have run along the same line. "What did you think of Grayson's relationship with Gemma Hartwell?"

Rupert sighed. "Morals are so different these days. I'm hardly one to sit in judgment on that score." He shook his head. "Mostly I felt sorry for her, because when Grayson tired of her, he'd throw her away and be on to his next conquest."

Yes, but now Grayson didn't have to go through that upset, Nora thought. Gemma was conveniently out of his world. Lydia's words about Maggie came back to her: "He tossed her away like a used tissue."

Nora turned to the last page of her notebook where she'd listed everyone's name and possible motives. She circled Grayson's name. Could Grayson Lange be the type of person who would cause his own accident to deflect attention, just to get rid of a lover he'd tired of? After all, Gemma was in the car that night with him. Nora warmed to her theme. He could have cut those brakes, not meaning to crash hard enough to break his wrist. It was an interesting thought. She added "Maggie Denton" next to his name.

She realized with a start that her attention had wandered from the interview, but it seemed Rupert's description of last evening matched his wife's.

"I got up to use the loo once. Didn't look at the time, but I expect Lydia might know. Fell right back to sleep until I heard her shouting."

"So you didn't realize your wife had got out of bed?" Declan asked.

"We both get up at night. I don't always wake." Rupert shrugged. "Lydia would never hurt a fly. She's a gentle soul."

Nora made her notations. Interesting that Lydia had described Rupert in exactly the same way.

10:15 AM

Declan watched Poppy Braeburn flounce back into the dining room. There was more here than met the eye with that young woman. Remembering her furtiveness with her iPad, he suspected Poppy was responsible for posting those unflattering photos of Fiona and Gemma.

The young woman insisted she was a heavy sleeper and hadn't heard anything until Lydia's shouting woke her.

"I'm the farthest away on the other side of the lodge," she pointed out.

When she'd gone, Nora shared her suspicion that the actress had an old-fashioned crush on Grayson Lange. She seemed awfully certain, and Declan had the distinct feeling Nora knew more than she said.

"And you would know that how?" he asked.

Nora blushed. "My experience with theatre people and celebrities."

"I don't want to know." He didn't need the details of Nora's snooping to confirm what he'd seen with his own eyes when he escorted Rupert back. Poppy had moved to fill Gemma's seat before the chair was cold. Would she try to fill the void in his private life as well?

"I should check on how Maeve's getting along with Sean." Nora stood.

Declan rubbed the back of his neck and stood for a moment before mounting the stage and walking to the windows. Anxious to change the subject from how she knew about Poppy's infatuation? "Please bring Fiona in when you come back."

The rain had slowed to a desolate drizzle, the sky filled with grey clouds. There were no cars out yet, which meant the roads were still flooded. The moment the water receded enough to let a car pass, he knew police would be out inspecting damage in the area. Soon after, he hoped they could get through to Ramsey Lodge for Gemma's body. And Val could come for Sean. Maybe he should reconsider letting Nora stay at the lodge. But then, he knew Nora well enough to know he couldn't change her mind once it was made up.

He checked his watch. Too soon to call Kendal station again. The car crash was already in the hands of the local police. Could he have prevented Gemma's death if he'd investigated Fiona's fall more thoroughly? He'd left details of all the incidents with Kendal, and DS Higgins had been out to investigate. He'd even frozen the bloody carcass of a dead bunny. What more could he have done?

He heard footsteps, and Nora joined him at the window. "Fiona's in the loo; she'll be here in a moment."

"Sean all right?"

"Went right down for a nap. Maeve will keep watch. No one will get past her. I have the monitor at the desk, too. Put fresh batteries in it and in the base and left his baby sleeping bag on to ward off the chill."

Declan rubbed her arms briskly. "Not exactly the week either of us anticipated."

Nora looked up at him. "But you'll figure it out."

He had the feeling she had been about to say "we" but had stopped herself.

"Here I am, ready for my grilling from the great and powerful Barnes." Fiona Church stood in the doorway.

She moved lithely to a chair and carefully draped herself across it. Despite everything, Fiona had dressed with care in a blue pantsuit with crisp creases and had pinned up her hair in a sleek French twist. Were these people ever "off?"

Declan started his questioning, and Nora flipped to a clean page. He took Fiona over her movements last night.

"It was biting cold. I took my makeup off and found the extra blanket and got right under the covers."

Declan nodded. "Did you hear anything after that?"

"No, nothing. I usually sleep very well without using anything."

Declan watched her fingers curl and her eyes stray to the side and knew this wasn't the truth.

"So no pills, but how many of us really sleep through the night?"

Fiona shrugged. "Heard those two next door. The loo flushed a few times. That's it. My room is tucked away in a corner."

"Did you know Gemma Hartwell before this play?" Changing tactics might shake her composure.

Fiona paused. Trying to decide how much can be found out if she lies, Declan decided.

"Certainly I knew *of* her," she admitted. "Ours is really a small world."

"You weren't friends, then."

"Hardly." She examined her nails.

"Did you know the Dentons?" He watched her facial expression.

"I knew them by reputation, but we'd never worked together."

Very careful answers. Smart woman. "What did you make of their daughter's death?"

"A tragedy of course, but nothing Grayson was responsible for, the way Rupert believes."

Nora interjected: "You were with Grayson when Maggie died, weren't you?"

Fiona had the grace to blush. "We were an item for a while. It might have been during that time. I can't remember."

Declan raised his eyebrows at Nora to desist. She bent her head over her notebook, duly chastened. Small community, yet Fiona couldn't recall when Maggie Denton had died? Declan doubted Fiona's memory lapse but left it alone for now.

"Going back to Gemma. Can you think of any reason why someone would murder her?"

Fiona raised her head then to glare at him. "Don't forget I was almost killed, too, Mr. Detective." Fiona's brown eyes widened. "I could have broken my neck falling down those stairs. And Grayson's lucky he only broke a wrist in the accident."

"I notice you don't mention Gemma could have been hurt more seriously in the car accident." Declan leaned forward into her space. "But you and Grayson survived, and it's Gemma who's dead now."

There was a moment of silence between them. Fiona stared defiantly at him.

"Are you certain there isn't something you know about these incidents, Miss Church?"

"Really, I have no idea who's responsible." She lifted one shoulder eloquently. "Just that it had to be someone who either knew Gemma well or had done their homework."

"Why do you say that?" He felt Nora raise her head at this remark.

"Because of that dead rabbit on her pillow. Gemma's real name was Bunny Sipling."

The minute Fiona left the room, Nora turned to Declan.

"That's what Gemma meant." Nora explained what the actress had said right after the rabbit had been found on her pillow. "'Who knows?' She meant her real name."

"Easy enough to find out if you Googled her or looked her up on Wikipedia," Declan pointed out.

"Yes, but someone went to the trouble of doing that, so that prank was specifically meant to alarm her; it wasn't a random event."

Declan had to agree with Nora's assessment. Soon she'd be wanting to sit for her sergeant's exams if he wasn't careful. Helen Mochrie entered the room, gliding over to them, her long skirt flowing around her ankles. Today's turban was purple with turquoise stripes and a row of silver discs along her forehead.

"Please have a seat, Ms. Mochrie." Declan pointed to the chair beside him.

"Mrs. Still miss my dear Archie, but you can call me Helen."

For a moment, Helen seemed almost normal, and Declan realized it had taken Gemma's murder to shake her out of character.

He took her through the same questions about her evening routine and sleep.

"Oh, yes, I heard footsteps all night long." She nodded, setting the metal discs swaying. "I sleep with one ear open, always."

After everyone else protesting they hadn't heard a thing, Declan was momentarily disconcerted. He caught Nora's eye and saw her bite her lip to stifle a laugh at his raised eyebrows.

"Was there any way you could tell where these footsteps came from, or when?"

"Let's see." Helen looked into the distance. "There were some around 2 AM, then at the other end of the house around 3-ish, some toilet flushing with those, then more after 6." She looked directly at him. "But those last must have been Lydia going to get candles, because I heard those steps pass my door to the head of the stairs and then head back toward her room. A few moments later, the screaming started."

Declan immediately alerted. The 2 AM footsteps were the important ones.

Helen looked pleasantly at them both. "Is that what you wanted?"

"You do have good hearing." Declan hoped the compliment would jog her to remember more. "That first set, near 2 AM, could you tell where they came from?"

Helen closed her eyes in thought; the image of Madame Arcati going into a trance was hard to dispel. Declan looked sideways at Nora, who winked at him.

Helen sighed. "No, no good. Can't tell where they came from, just that they didn't pass my door."

"That's still very good, Helen, thank you." Declan wrapped up the interview by asking about her background in relation to the others.

"No, I've never worked with any of this cast before." She fluttered her hands. "But we're an incestuous bunch—we all know *of* each other."

"So I'm told." Declan smiled back at her. He was aware of Nora flipping to the back of her notebook and drawing lines. "How long have you known Grayson Lange?"

Helen's tinkling laugh brought Declan and Nora to attention. "Why, all his life, dear Inspector. I'm his mother."

11:20 AM

Helen wished she had a camera to record the surprised looks on both faces before her. Really, the delivery of that line was one of her best performances. She sat back, delighted with a job well done.

"His mother?" Nora squeaked. "But he calls you Helen."

Helen nodded. "My rule. When we work together, I don't want anyone thinking, 'She only has that role because she's his mum.' Better all around. I've always used my maiden name on stage."

The detective composed himself. “Why didn’t you tell us this before?”

“There wasn’t any reason I should have.” Helen felt placid and comfortable. “I knew he wouldn’t want me fussing over him when he broke his wrist. He had all those women to do that. He was never a mummy’s boy.” She hoped she had managed to keep the distaste out of her voice. He was still her flesh and blood. “He was a daring child. I was on a first-name basis with the casualty staff. He was fickle then, too, completely unaware of the feelings of others.”

Declan asked, “Do you work together often?”

Helen considered this. “If there’s a role I want, we do. Whose idea do you think it was for Gray to start this traveling troupe?” She sat back in satisfaction as they exchanged puzzled glances. Nora was making copious notes, flipping back and forth in her notebook. Let them document what they wanted.

Declan cleared his throat. “I’ll bite. Why did you suggest Lange’s Traveling Theatre Troupe?”

“It’s obvious he’s never going to be the next Olivier, darling. His notices were lukewarm at best. But the boy craves to be the center of attention. What started as confidence and assertiveness when he was a child had led to a certain ruthlessness I’ve ceased to admire. He’s a much better director than he ever was an actor. He adores telling people what to do.”

“That’s an honest evaluation,” Declan noted.

“I’m a pragmatist, Inspector. It doesn’t pay to wear blinkers about people we love when it come to their faults and vices.” Another great delivery. She did so love still being able to surprise people at her age.

CHAPTER TWENTY-THREE

"I long ago came to the conclusion that nothing has ever been definitely proved about anything."
Madame Arcati: Act 1, Scene 2

12:15 PM

Maeve accompanied Simon to the lodge kitchen to prepare lunch for the petulant crew who were griping to each other in the dining room. The cast was on edge. The Dentons sat at the round table with Maeve, playing with Sean, until Nora took him to her room for his lunch bottle. Maeve watched the Dentons move to the end of the long table, sitting stiffly and ignoring Grayson, until Burt engaged them in low conversation. Through the window, Maeve could see Declan's head as he tried to get through to the Kendal Police Station now that the rain had stopped.

"Maybe food will be a distraction. Their grumbling is getting to me," Maeve complained. "Can you believe those bitches, Fiona and Poppy? First it was Fiona and Gemma scrapping, but now Poppy's taking her place." She opened the freezer and quickly withdrew three chickens, slamming the door. "We can roast these for dinner with carrots and potatoes tonight. Have to feed the howling masses." She threw the chickens into the sink to defrost.

Simon came up behind her and wrapped his arms around her waist. His mood seemed to lighten as the rain receded. Maeve couldn't handle a gloomy Simon along with those annoying women.

"Maybe they're irritable because they didn't have the same kind of night we had." He nibbled her earlobe.

Maeve swatted him away, glad they'd had those few hours together in the middle of this mess. "Help me figure out what to feed these awful people. They remind me of cranky children."

Simon perused the pantry. "There's always beans on toast."

"Be serious. We can do tuna and egg salad. There's a bowl of hard-boiled eggs." She opened the fridge and handed Simon the eggs, mayonnaise and celery. "And take these berries, Si. They'll spoil if we don't use them soon."

"Thank goodness for gas." Simon turned on one of the ovens to warm the bread.

Maeve washed and diced celery for the salads. "I hope Declan can make sense of things soon. I hate having a dead body upstairs. And knowing we're feeding a murderer makes my skin crawl."

"I know." He peeled the eggs. "I keep trying to pretend this isn't happening."

"Poor darling. You don't seem to be having much luck." Despite the improvement in his mood, she saw the strain on his face. This couldn't end well. Once news got around, business at the lodge was certain to suffer, and Simon would feel responsible. She added celery seed to the egg salad. Unless the publicity could actually help? In her opinion, people were basically ghouls.

Maeve watched Simon flake pungent tuna with a fork. "Simon, when this is all over and Kate is back, I think we should have a holiday together." His response would tell her a multitude of things. Would he warm to the idea or push her away?

Simon looked up. "Where to?"

She pretended to mull it over. She knew exactly where Simon would want to go. "I've never been to Provence. I could practice my French." She was rewarded with a brilliant smile.

"Something to hold onto, then. It's a date."

12:30 PM

With Sean's bottle finished, Nora sat in her chair, turning the pages of a nursery rhyme book. He reached his pudgy fingers out to touch the page as she read "Little Miss Muffet" aloud. She couldn't help connecting poor Miss Muffet with Gemma and wondered if the actress had struggled or cried out when that pillow had come down across her face.

Nora squeezed her baby closer as she finished the rhyme. Sean, content to rattle and chew on his keys, made noises she echoed at times. Soon he would start speaking. What would be his first word? The events of the past few days had kept her mind from dwelling on Daniel Kemp's forthcoming visit, but now she wondered again what his purpose could be. While she'd decided to call the Pembrokes before he arrived, with Gemma dead, now hardly seemed like the right time. But maybe this was exactly when she *should* call, before news of the murder went national. If only the weather would just cooperate.

While she waited for that, there were more important things to consider, like finding out who had murdered Gemma Hartwell. Nora had a lot on her plate but couldn't lose sight of the fact a killer was among them at Ramsey Lodge, just rooms away from where she sat with her precious child.

She pictured the list at the back of her notebook and the lines connecting people. It was an incestuous group; she agreed with Helen on that. Gemma and Fiona had both slept with Grayson, and Poppy wanted to; his mother was here, as were the parents of his former lover who had died of a broken heart after he'd moved on. It all revolved around Grayson Lange.

With a start, she realized her snooping in the guest rooms

earlier this week had not included the director's suite, something she needed to rectify.

12:40 PM

Declan entered the dining room, where Maeve and Simon were passing bowls of salads and warmed bread down the long table. The upper end of the table ignored him; only the Dentons smiled at him, and Burt gave a curt nod. He was used to that when he wore his detective's hat. The round corner table was empty.

"Where's Nora?" he asked Simon.

"Spending time with Sean. I haven't called her yet."

"I'll do it." Declan walked the short distance to tap on Nora's door. No answer. Maybe she was still feeding Sean in the alcove? He walked into the room, softly calling her name in case she was trying to get the baby to sleep, although it seemed early for his afternoon nap.

Her chair was empty. Declan looked into the cot. Sean had rolled onto his side and was happily chewing the ear of his favorite rabbit. When he recognized Declan, he crowed and held his arms out to be picked up.

Declan picked the baby up, chuffed the child recognized him. He looked at Nora's bathroom door. It stood open and empty. He took the baby into the dining room and installed him in his high chair.

"All set?" Simon asked. He and Maeve were seated with filled plates, and Maeve handed Sean a teething rusk.

With a sinking feeling that quickly turned to burning rage, Declan knew exactly where he'd find Nora. "I'll be right back."

12:50 PM

Nora knew her time was limited and quickly inspected Grayson Lange's room. The Royal Suite looked less regal in the weak light, and she threw open the heavy drapes to see well. Where to start?

The closet revealed tweedy jackets with suede elbow patches and pants slung over hangers. Collared shirts and a stack of marled jumpers were thrown on the top shelf. She patted pockets, inhaling a scent that reminded her of a men's fine haberdashery: oak, beeswax, leather and myrrh. She flashed on a memory at age eight, sitting on the dock with her father when he'd been banished from their summer cottage to smoke his pipe. Legs dangling from the itchy wood, bare feet browned from days on the beach, Nora had idolized her dad. She ached with longing for him and for Sean to know him; John Tierney would have been a wonderful grandfather. She seemed to be dwelling on him these past days.

She closed the closet door softly to rifle through the dresser drawers. A boxer man, knits and silks thrown together in a jumble. Tees and socks. Nothing remarkable, nothing personal.

On the bedside table, his fancy watch was tossed on top of a well-thumbed paperback of *The Picture of Dorian Gray.* The top drawer revealed a bottle of lubricant lying under a recent issue of *Mayfair*, Britain's answer to *Penthouse.* Typical. Moving into the bathroom, she noted most of Gemma's cosmetics were still spread out across the counter, along with the bottle of painkillers Grayson had been taking since his accident. Nora read the label: Co-Codamol 30/500, 1 or 2 every 4-6 hrs pain. An added label cautioned driving and warned of constipation and/or dizziness as common side effects. Thirty pills had been dispensed. Nora spilled those remaining into her hand and counted. Nineteen left. That meant he'd been taking two every six hours or so, a number she supposed was reasonable with a fresh fracture.

"Busted." Declan's quiet voice from the doorway startled Nora. She jerked her hand, spilling the pills all over the counter and floor.

She bent down to retrieve them as her cheeks flamed. "I counted his pills to see if he could have given any to Gemma," she whispered. She stood and scooped the remaining pills off the counter back into the bottle, taking care to remove a thread from a cotton towel.

Declan's whispered voice was sharp. "And you would be doing *what* that would be helpful? Since you've successfully managed to put your fingerprints on that bottle, we'll have no way of knowing if someone else tampered with them." His low sound made his anger all the more menacing.

Nora's mouth fell open. "Apparently nothing." She closed the bottle with a snap. "Nineteen left, about the right number." She replaced the bottle where she'd found it and tried to leave the bathroom but Declan blocked the doorway.

"Yet you felt it was reasonable to snoop in his room because—"

"Because Grayson's at the heart of this, Declan." Nora's tone was insistent.

"So despite having a trained detective on hand, you felt it was reasonable to destroy evidence while leaving your child alone, I might mention, with a killer in the house? Just to satisfy your curiosity?"

Nora could see he was fighting to keep his voice quiet. He turned back into the bedroom. She looked down, her face hot with shame as she stepped past him. "I'm sorry, Declan, truly I am. But it wasn't to satisfy idle curiosity. There's a killer here, and we're no closer to finding him. And because my child *is* here, then yes, I feel justified in doing anything I can to find that person." She left the room before he could answer and hurried down the stairs, hoping Declan would close the door the way she'd found it.

12:56 PM

Poppy tried not to preen from her new place at Grayson's side. Lunch was dull to the point of stultifying, people eating for sustenance, not with pleasure, pushing food around their plates. Awkward silences, too. Not much talking except "Pass the bread, please." The old man shoveled in his food, she noticed. Burt must be happy to have someone else cook for him, lonely git. Even cold salads look like a treat when you live alone. She felt a streak of sympathy for Burt and hoped she never became like him.

She wanted to ask Grayson if she should work on the costumes, then brought herself up short. Would the play even go on without Gemma? Her role as Elvira was the lead. Poppy didn't want to be the one to ask the question.

She picked at her egg salad and fruit and tried to beam whenever she caught Grayson's eye. The play simply had to continue. She needed to be in his presence, to show him she was indispensable in any way he could want or imagine. Then she had a brilliant thought that provided the perfect solution.

This would be her mission over the next few hours, dead body upstairs growing fusty and warm or not: she needed to convince Grayson he should keep the performances going—and even more so, that it was his idea that *she* replace Gemma. Nora could do her role of the maid, Edith. Nora knew the play and had acting experience, and Edith was only in a few scenes. She'd have to be cagey and lull him into a conversation she could manipulate.

"Fiona, could you please pass the fruit bowl?" Helen was exceedingly polite, and Poppy thought she might have dropped out of character.

Fiona acquiesced without comment. The Dentons hunched together at the end of the table near Burt.

"Fruit, dear?" Lydia encouraged Rupert to eat. The man's gauntness had suddenly become apparent.

Poppy had thought of him as slim, but now he looked like an Ichabod Crane impersonator, his eyes sunken into his face, his hands shaking below bony wrists as he reached for an apple. God, she hoped she never got to be that pathetic. She thought about her tin of clippings and all the exhaustive research she'd done on Grayson. What was his favorite game? "Grayson?"

"Yes, Poppet?" Grayson slathered butter on a piece of country bread, his pupils dilated.

Good, painkillers on board would make him easier to manage. "Would you like to play Scrabble after lunch?"

"I'll play, too." Helen gave Poppy a sly smile, insinuating herself into the situation.

Poppy had the idea the old broad didn't want her to be alone with Gray. How absurd—she was old enough to be his mother.

A broad grin broke across the director's face. "Capitol idea."

CHAPTER TWENTY-FOUR

"Was I ever unkind to you when you were alive?"
Charles: Act 1, Scene 2

1:55 PM

Lunch at the corner table had never been so quiet, Declan decided while watching Nora pick at her food. He'd calmed down, but she wasn't getting off lightly.

Maeve tried to get Simon to chat about the sights Kate and Ian would see in Paris. From her conversation, it appeared the couple might be planning a trip to southern France. But Simon seemed morose and suddenly interrupted Maeve, leaning in to ask Declan a question.

"Were the morning interviews—useful?" Simon's brow was furrowed.

"I wish I had a solution, Simon, but nothing hangs together yet." Declan knew Simon was worried about the murder and the lodge's reputation.

Nora didn't take part in the conversation. Guilty conscience or sulking? Either way, he let her be. He'd been furious with her. She didn't realize she was jeopardizing the case. She hadn't even asked him if he'd got through to Kendal. He couldn't condone her snooping when it interfered in the proper way things should be done. There was a reason for procedure. Besides, she could be putting herself in danger. She didn't understand the volatility of their situation: a closed environment, no electricity, people getting on each other's nerves, and everyone eyeing each other with wariness and suspicion.

He wanted to resolve this for Simon, too. He didn't envy the man, trying to run a business with a killer on the premises. Declan had never felt so pressured to bring a case to a quick close.

When it seemed everyone had finished eating, he stood up. “Thank you for your patience this morning.” Declan’s voice was naturally commanding, and everyone turned in his direction. “I’ve spoken to Kendal, and they hope to have a duty police surgeon here later this afternoon, or they’ll ask the pathologist to do the honors since he lives in Windermere. In the meantime, please continue to use only the downstairs bathrooms until your rooms have been cleared.” He deliberately didn’t glance at Nora. “You may also use the library or stay in the dining room. Burt, you’re up next.”

Conversation broke out around the long table. Nora cleaned off Sean’s face and lifted him out of the high chair. “I’ll just change him and get my notebook.” She didn’t meet his eyes. She left the room carrying the baby, who waved gaily at the table. Lydia reached out to tickle Sean’s leg as he passed.

“Let’s clear lunch, Maeve.” Simon pushed back his chair. Maeve nodded, squeezed Declan’s arm as she passed by him and grabbed a large tray from the serving table.

No one was more surprised than Declan when Fiona spoke up.

“Actually, I’ll help in the kitchen.” Fiona rose from her place. “If I don’t move around, I’ll start to grow roots in that chair.” She gave a weak smile and looked to Declan for permission.

“That’s fine.” He motioned to Burt, who followed him into the drawing room. By unspoken agreement, the two men walked over to the set of French doors and out onto the terrace while they waited for Nora. The clouds had cleared to the north, and Declan could see a few patches of returning blue sky in that direction.

“Be all over by tomorrow,” Burt pronounced.

“Kendal says a couple of rivers to the north broke their banks.”

Declan appraised the man standing next to him. Early seventies, he decided. He knew the man's wife had died a few months before and didn't envy him spending the rest of his days in a solitary existence. Burt Marsh didn't strike Declan as the kind of man who would be comfortable browsing SinglesOverSixty.co.uk. This play must have been a welcome diversion for the widower.

"Expect the Scotland trains all cancelled," Burt said.

Nora joined them on the patio, notebook and pen in hand. She refused to look Declan in the eye. Still pissed off at being caught? His heart softened. He had been in the right, but maybe he'd spoken too harshly. He would find a way to set things right with her later.

"I hope we get the electric back before dark." She looked out over the lake.

"All set to begin?" Declan kept his voice level.

Nora finally looked at him, chin raised. "Sean's in his high chair in the kitchen with Maeve, and would you believe it? Fiona Church is peeling potatoes."

They walked inside, and Declan shut the door against the breeze. They took seats, and Nora flipped her notebook open.

"Burt, can you tell me your movements yesterday evening?"

Burt looked him right in the eye. "You mean after you left me in your bedroom?" His dry tone was not lost on Declan.

"Yes. Hear any noises, anyone moving around during the night?"

"No, I was out like a light."

"And you didn't get up to use the bathroom all night?"

"Oh. Well." Burt's face broke out in a rare smile. "Caught me out then." He tapped his navel. "Prostate a bit big at my age. Got up to the loo once."

"You don't know the time?"

"Nah, before any light, middle of night I'd say."

"When you were up, you didn't hear any footsteps?" Declan persisted.

"Not until dawn. Must have been Lydia Denton going out to the hall. *Then* I heard her shrieking all right."

2:45 PM

The baby cooed when he spied Nora entering the kitchen on a break between interviews. He waved his keys at her in delight as she picked him up and snuggled him.

"He's been jabbering away." Maeve handed a colander of peeled carrots to an aproned Fiona, who started to slice them into circles.

"We're trying to get him to say 'Mum' but he hasn't cooperated." Simon ran the water to fill the pan of peeled and cut potatoes.

"You know your way around a kitchen, Fiona." Nora watched her deft use of the chef's knife.

Fiona gave Nora a hollow smile. Purple circles under her eyes showed the strain of the last few days. At least one person seemed moved by Gemma's death, and the most unlikely one, to boot.

"I worked in a Thai place in Soho between acting gigs," Fiona said.

"Yum," Maeve pronounced. "I bet you ate well."

"It sounds like a lot of work," Nora said.

"Yes to both of you: a ton of work but I never went hungry." Fiona wiped her hands on the apron and picked up another carrot.

"Do you have any tricks to quickly defrost frozen chickens?" Simon turned over the unwrapped chickens, sitting in water in the deep sink.

"Without a microwave? Afraid not."

"Then I'm afraid dinner will be late tonight." Simon wiggled a giblet packet, trying to work it out of the cavity of one of the chickens.

Nora left them discussing the meal and carried Sean into her room. She checked his nappy. "Still dry in there, mister." She gave him a good long cuddle and laid the baby in his cot, turning on his mobile. "Sleep tight." She handed him his bunny and walked away before he could protest.

She paused to run a brush through her hair and clipped it back in a low ponytail. God, she hoped the electricity would come back on before dark. No bath or shower if it didn't. Besides the lack of hot water and heat, she didn't fancy lying in the dark with Gemma's body upstairs.

Nora mentally reviewed the interviews. So far, the only thing of interest had been the footsteps Helen insisted she'd heard, something no one else acknowledged. Did that mean they were heavier sleepers or liars? Or was Helen mistaken? She might have taken her Madame Arcati role a bit too far, inventing footsteps in the middle of the night.

Of course, there was also the bombshell that Helen was Grayson's mother, but Nora didn't see how that provided a motive to murder Gemma. There had to be something else they were missing, some piece of the puzzle just out of their reach.

She bit her lip as she walked back toward the dining room. Declan probably wouldn't appreciate her use of the plural when it came to the case. She hated the friction between them, but too bad if it prickled like a thorn and made him uneasy. She had a vested interest in finding the killer under their roof with her child there, and he didn't seem to get that. She knew the play was wrapped up in this somehow.

Grayson hadn't made an announcement yet, but she assumed the play would be canceled. How could it possibly go on without Gemma?

She had a glimmer of an idea.

A quick look inside the library showed her Poppy and Helen, an unlikely duo, had moved on from their Scrabble game and were playing cards with Burt. The Dentons sat in chairs near the fireplace, reading books from the lodge's shelves.

Grayson was sitting in the drawing room next to Declan when she took her place.

"Who won your Scrabble game?"

"I did." The director's tone was such that she should never have expected a different outcome.

"If we can get started." Declan took control of the interview. He took Grayson through his actions the previous evening once again.

Nora pointedly ignored him and started a new page. She had to keep her ears peeled; this might be the most important interview they did all day.

Grayson's tone was languorous and stiff; Nora suspected he'd topped up his pills after lunch.

"I told you this before. I went to my room, and Gemma helped me undress. She gave me a sleeping pill that I washed down with two of my painkillers. Then she helped me in the bathroom and into bed." Tears filled his eyes.

Nora hoped the emotion was genuine. The couple had been intimate, and the woman had died a horrible death. Then again, if Grayson was her killer, it was good to remember the bottom line: He was still a trained actor, no matter how poor his notices had been.

"How did she die?" Grayson's tone was softer.

Declan raised an eyebrow and caught Nora's look. If Grayson wasn't her killer, he wouldn't have the details of smothering Declan had shared with her. Or was this merely a good dodge? She wondered how Declan would answer.

"I'd only be guessing. We have to wait for the duty police surgeon."

Grayson shook his head, and Nora marveled at Declan's perception with his next question.

"Were you perhaps thinking of Maggie Denton, afraid Gemma took her own life?"

Grayson's face darkened; he spoke slowly. "I had no idea Maggie Denton was suicidal—" He accompanied his protest with a glance across the hall to the library where the young woman's parents sat reading. "I still think it was a tragic accident." He bowed his head.

Nora caught Declan's eye and tilted her head toward the door. He nodded, and she got up and slid the drawing room pocket doors closed. If this wasn't real sorrow, Grayson was a better actor than she'd credited.

"You seemed cool enough about it this morning when Rupert accused you," Declan reminded him.

"Bluster for the parents. Hard enough having them around as a constant reminder." He drew himself up and rested his cast along the back of the chair next to him.

"Then why give them the roles?" Declan was persistent.

Nora paused in her note-taking to catch the director's demeanor as he answered.

"Didn't seem fair to rule them out just because of Maggie. Maybe I felt I owed it to them, fair enough. Small price to pay after what they've been through." He wiggled a finger at Declan. "Not because I was at fault. Besides, I knew they'd do a damn fine job in the play." He gave an elaborate shrug.

Nora decided Grayson Lange was definitely a narcissist. It was all about him. He and Gemma had been a better match than she'd originally thought.

4:05 PM

Simon helped Maeve finish setting up for dinner in the dining room.

"The chickens will be ready to go into the oven in plenty of time." Maeve put fresh napkins beside each plate.

"We'll roast the living daylights out of them," Simon agreed. "The only casualties so far have been the ice cream and sherbet, had to throw those out. Any ideas for pudding?"

"Taken care of." Maeve's voice had an imperious lilt. "I defrosted Agnes' secret supply."

Simon put salt and pepper pots down the middle of the table next to the freshly filled hurricane lamps they'd need tonight. "Agnes has a secret supply?"

"Yup. She keeps two different kinds of cake all baked and frozen. I took out the almond one, and it will be perfect by the time we need it. We can spoon those berries we've had macerating in wine over it." She tucked her brown hair behind an ear. "God, I'd kill for a hot shower."

Simon winced. "Please, no reference to killing."

"Sorry."

Across the hall, he noticed Poppy Braeburn sleeping on the prop sofa. "Why don't you take a nap?"

"Why don't you join me?" she countered.

"Thanks, but Declan said the duty police surgeon will be here shortly, and I need to be on hand." He saw disappointment cross Maeve's face and disappear. "Go and have a lie down."

"You can wake me," she said over her shoulder as she left the room.

"Deal."

Simon put his hands into his pockets and stood in the drawing room doorway, careful not to disturb Poppy. Once Declan released them from the room, the Dentons headed for the patio, braving the breeze in their sweaters, holding hands and talking. Helen roamed about, deadheading the surviving flowers in the planters and boxes spread around the patio and railings. Everyone was getting restless, cooped up inside, and Simon couldn't blame them.

He went into the library to check on the others, ever mindful of his role as host. He'd felt a crush of responsibility on his chest, weighing him down since Gemma had been found. The car accident had been bad enough, but murder? He'd go seriously crazy if this wasn't sorted soon. There was no doubt the play had to be canceled. He'd never make his money back. And he'd promised Provence to Maeve, but could he even afford it?

Grayson Lange and Burt Marsh sat in the chairs by the fireplace vacated by the Dentons. Burt flipped through a nature magazine. Grayson dozed, an open book across his chest, his cast propped on a pillow on the arm of the chair, the swollen fingers poking out. It must be painful. The director would have to be an incredible actor to throw suspicion off himself by deliberately causing his own accident as part of a plan to kill Gemma. Simon didn't think Grayson was quite that good or that smart.

He caught Burt's eye and made motions of a drink. Burt nodded, put his magazine down and silently joined him.

The two men went into the kitchen, where Simon pulled two beers from the cooler. Simon opened them, and they knocked cans. He took a long pull. He opened the back door and stepped outside to survey the damage from the wind. Burt joined him on the threshold.

"Mostly twigs and branches to clean up once it dries out a bit." Burt looked around.

Simon checked the herb patch near the door. "Agnes won't be happy if her favorite rosemary bush bites the dust." Mud strangled the lower branches of the large plant.

"Those things are stronger than you'd think. We can flush the mud off." Burt drained his can. "Thanks for that."

Simon had his head down, inspecting the bush, when Burt's change in tone alerted him.

"Simon, look—"

Simon thought Burt saw the police van making its way up the road. Instead, Burt pointed up the fell, where light gleamed in a few houses. There was a sharp *thunk*, and then the microwave started beeping as lights came on all over Ramsey Lodge.

4:10 PM

Nora's eyes popped open when the lights came on. She jumped up to check on Sean and was surprised to see Declan rise from the other side of the bed. Once the interviews were over, she'd felt exhausted and crept into bed. Declan must have lain down after she'd fallen asleep.

Sean slept on. She turned out the light in his alcove. The heat would build up soon, and she could bathe him tonight. But how should she act with Declan? She knew she'd disappointed him, but she had her reasons, although she had to admit that sometimes she didn't stop to think things through.

Declan yawned and slapped his leg. "Lights, finally."

"And all that brings—heat, hot showers and clean hair." She didn't say "and shaved legs" aloud. Normalcy then. After all, couples disagreed at times.

"I'm going to brush my teeth."

"I'm right behind you. And then I know what I'm going to do before Sean wakes."

Declan drew her into an embrace as he passed her. He bent down and nuzzled her neck. "What's that?"

"Start to transcribe those interviews."

"Good idea." Declan made as if to slap her rump, but she scooted out of the way, and he shut the bathroom door.

Nora turned on her laptop. The reassuring whirling soon led to Pages opening on her Mac. She clicked open her inbox; nothing that couldn't wait, although she was surprised there wasn't one from Val. She dashed off a quick note to her:

> Lights back on at RL. Will be in touch tomorrow. Xoxo Nora

Opening her notebook, she started to transcribe the notes into her word processor. She realized she could whip right through since they were mostly negatives. Only Helen Mochrie had given them those unexplained footsteps.

"Your turn." Declan left the bathroom door open.

Nora didn't look up from her laptop. "Want to jump in the shower?"

"Is that an invitation?"

She turned around. Declan's hair was mussed and his eyes still heavy-lidded from sleep. She felt weak in her middle. Forgiven, then.

There was a soft knock on the door, followed by Simon's voice. "Declan, pathologist's here with the crime scene investigation team."

Nora laughed. "I'll take a rain check."

CHAPTER TWENTY-FIVE

"At the first sign or trouble they run out on you—
like rats leaving a sinking ship."
Mrs. Bradman: Act II, Scene 3

4:45 PM

Declan stood in the doorway of the Shakespeare Suite, watching the pathologist conduct his examination. The duty police surgeon's road remained flooded. Dr. Milo Foreman lived closer and had agreed to come in.

Simon had told Declan that Milo enjoyed cooking, and it didn't take a detective to see he also liked eating his efforts. The man's general demeanor was cheerful, even at a murder scene, and he'd insisted Declan call him by his first name. Declan studied him with interest. The pathologist whistled as he probed Gemma's grey, mottled body, took her liver temperature and put plastic bags over each hand. He had an appalling but necessary job. Declan didn't know if he could do it. He preferred to speak for the dead ones. His goal was to find out who had committed this unspeakable act against Gemma Hartwell.

Milo stood up from Gemma's bedside, turned off his voice recorder and stripped the gloves from his meaty hands. The rotund man paused to jot notes into a tiny leather notebook and motioned to the crime scene investigator standing just inside the door.

"Your turn." The tech had already videotaped the scene from the door and now moved into the room in his white suit to take a panorama of pictures of the body in the bed before settling down to gather evidence. "And don't forget that pillow," Milo added, taking off his paper suit and crumpling it with his gloves into the bag the CSI had set up at the door. "They want to be called a 'CSI' now, you know, not a SOCO. American television influence."

Declan cleared his throat. "What can you tell me?"

"Based on the rigor and what you've told me about the time she was last seen, I'd say she died between midnight and 6 AM."

The timeframe was exactly what Declan already knew. "Anything else?" He knew medical examiners were notoriously slow about deciding on time of death and tried not to let his impatience show.

"Opening the windows to lower the room temperature was helpful, in terms of slowing the body's disintegration. Can't tell about drugs yet, of course. That takes longer than the bloody shows on television would have you believe, but I expect even in Oxford you've learned that." The man raised bushy eyebrows and guided Declan away from the doorway. "Saw the petechiae you mentioned. We'll give that pillow a thorough going over. Have to check the hyoid bone on postmortem for strangulation, but at first glance I'd agree it appears she was smothered while deeply asleep. No signs of fighting but bagged her hands just the same."

"What about the other rooms? These people need somewhere to sleep tonight. I've kept them out of their rooms all day."

"Higgins has more of the team arriving shortly with the mortuary van. We'll get it sorted for them to sleep tucked up tidily in their beds tonight." They halted at the head of the stairs. "Though I wonder how many of them will close their eyes knowing one of them is a murderer."

Declan's throat tightened. He might need to provoke a confrontation to bring this case to its resolution. But to do that he needed more information than he had right now. Where and how was he going to find that within this closed cast?

5:30 PM

Nora had finished the transcription when Sean woke for his dinner. She moved his high chair into the kitchen to avoid seeing the crime scene techs but heard them moving steadily throughout the rooms upstairs. She spooned up baby rice that Sean ate greedily.

Maeve and Simon bustled between stove and sink, rubbing the chickens with herbs and lavender, stuffing them with cut lemons. Simon put the chickens, carrots and potatoes in the oven to roast. Their wet hair showed they had both had showers, and Nora felt envious and incredibly dirty. Cold-water sponge bathing didn't do the job.

"Never thought a simple shower could improve my mood so easily." Maeve set a timer.

Nora cleaned off the baby's mouth and wiped his hands and tray.

Simon looked up from putting biscuit mix into a bowl. "Plenty of time to bathe the baby before dinner, Nora. We'll eat as usual after 7."

She didn't need to be told twice and grabbed Sean from his high chair. Declan could bring it into the dining room later for her. Nora ran warm water in the tub and undressed the baby in a room that had warmed up. She tested the water temp before lowering Sean into it. He giggled and splashed while she washed him and his hair. She let him play for a few minutes in his bath seat, using a cup to pour warm water over his back to avoid a chill.

Declan tapped on the door and sat on the closed toilet. "Enjoys his bath, doesn't he?"

Nora opened the drain and the baby watched the water swirl away, pointing and making gibberish noises.

"Give him to me." Declan picked up the bath towel. Nora lifted the squiggling, wet baby out of his bath seat and into Declan's firm grasp, wrapping him in the large towel. She played peek-a-boo a few times with the edge of the towel until Sean's chuckles had them all laughing.

Nora sat back on her haunches, watching the large man swipe at the baby's hair and rub him briskly. Who knew the sight of a large man and a little child—her child—could be so stirring? Nora's heart lurched with emotion, and she stood up and enclosed the two of them in a quick hug.

"That is a very sexy picture, DI Barnes." Nora drew back to search his eyes.

"Hold that thought." He addressed the baby. "Let's put your pyjamas on, young man, and let your mum take a quick shower." Without waiting for a reply, Declan walked out with the baby, leaving Nora to shower on her own. She wondered if he'd ever put on a nappy. He'd figure it out.

The hot water felt luxurious to her, and she washed her lank hair twice. She shaved her legs, too, and sighed with delight when she stepped out of the shower and wrapped herself in a towel. She rubbed her wet hair and dried off, then slipped into the bedroom to dress, the air cool on her damp skin.

"And this little piggy stayed home," she heard from the alcove, with Sean's responding giggle. Oh, to be a fly on the wall with a camera right now. Nora slid into clean jeans and a silky shirt and was looking for her favorite opal earrings when the two most important men in her life rounded the corner.

Declan held Sean out for inspection. "How did we do, Mum?" The baby's hair was combed all wrong but he had a warm sleeper on and clutched his keys, reaching his flannel-clad arms out to her. Her throat constricted in a moment of pure joy: no sex, no promises of a future, just the man she was falling in love with holding her perfect child in his arms, a happy smile on both their faces.

8:40 PM

Nora decided she couldn't eat another bite and put her fork down. Nervous energy; she was surprised she'd had any appetite with her plan. Simon had closed the dining room doors at the start of dinner to avoid everyone seeing Gemma's body carried out in a black bag. They slid open, and Declan rose to meet the sergeant from Kendal.

"If I could bother you for a moment." Detective Sergeant Higgins introduced himself.

Nora watched all heads swivel to the detective.

"My team has finished with your rooms, and they are released for your use." A murmur ran like a ripple around the long table. "I need to review your statements, kindly taken by DI Barnes."

Nora walked across the room and handed Higgins a thumb drive. Nora knew him from the previous autumn and the Clarendon murders. She stood next to Grayson, out of the way.

"Thank you, Miss Tierney. These will be typed up officially, and you'll be asked to sign them, probably tomorrow afternoon." Declan whispered in Higgins' ear. "Mr. Marsh? You're allowed to return to your own home if you can safely navigate the road. But no one else is allowed to check out of Ramsey Lodge for the time being."

Nora watched Grayson stir at this pronouncement. "No one would think of checking out, Sergeant. We have a play to put on."

Stunned silence met the director's statement.

"That's up to you, sir. Goodnight." Higgins left, and a buzz of talk rose in the room as soon as he disappeared.

"Grayson, this is carrying things too far." Rupert's indignation matched his high color. "We should cancel the play immediately." His wife nodded her agreement.

Helen took on a lecturing tone. "Grayson, your behaviour is reprehensible. I did not rai—expect this level of apathy." Tonight she'd left off a turban, and the short white curls hugging her head bobbled. "A cast member has been *murdered,* under your watch."

Fiona shook her head. "You're buggered, Gray, face it."

"Grayson, really—where are your feelings for Gemma?" Lydia shook her head.

Fiona's was the dry voice of reason. "I think you're missing a cast member, Gray."

Nora spoke up. "I'll do it. I played Elvira in college. I know the part by heart." Declan would not be happy with her; she couldn't look at him.

Grayson roared with laughter. "See, we have our new Elvira right here!" He stood and threw his good arm around Nora's shoulder. "Good girl, Nora, rescuing us all."

Nora watched the others' reactions. Trust them to go over the top. Some of their points were valid, but she had her own reasons for insinuating herself into their midst.

She met Declan's blazing eyes and had the grace to blush. She knew he wouldn't be happy with her impulsive offer, but being actively involved in the play would not only help Simon, it would let her go undercover to find the murderer.

Poppy looked ready to explode. "I would think you'd cast a known entity with real acting experience as your star, not some pathetic wannabe."

Maeve found a sudden interest in the pattern of the tablecloth. Only Burt seemed amused by the situation.

"Really, Nora? You feel qualified to step into a professional production with all of your … " Fiona gestured towards the baby's high chair, "*other* responsibilities?"

"Absolutely not." Declan's voice rang out. Simon looked helplessly between him and Nora.

"This is my decision, for lots of reasons." Nora's emphatic statement implored Declan to understand. Instead he looked seriously angry.

"It's revolting." Rupert stood and threw his napkin down. He clenched his hands into fists at his sides.

Lydia stood up and put a restraining hand on her husband's arm. "Find yourself another Dr. and Mrs. Bradman while you're at it."

The couple stood and stalked to the doorway.

Grayson stood, too. "Now, everyone, simmer down and take your seats. Lydia, Rupert, come back here. I *am* thinking of Gemma. She was the consummate professional."

Fiona coughed and took a sip of water.

Nora watched Grayson ratchet up his charm as everyone sat back down. She retook her seat at the table, avoiding Declan's glare while the director worked his magic.

"That old saying 'the show must go on' has a long history behind it. Why, it was Noel Coward himself who coined that very phrase, and here we are putting on one of his best-loved plays. We must continue that tradition and keep the faith that Gemma would want us to continue—and dedicate the show to her memory."

"I suppose we shouldn't disappoint our fans," Helen allowed. "We could make an announcement at the opening that the play is dedicated to Gemma."

Beside Nora, Simon groaned. Lydia and Rupert shook their heads in disgust.

Grayson continued. "There have been tickets sold and props rented. Think of Simon and his business. Who wants to be responsible for canceling on our gracious host who's gone out of his way during these most trying times?"

Nora saw the Dentons' discomfort; they looked down at their plates.

Grayson's tone toughened. "And may I just remind you all? Each of you has signed contracts."

"That seals it." Fiona turned to look at Simon. "Is there any pudding?"

CHAPTER TWENTY-SIX

"My patience is being stretched to its uttermost."
Ruth: Act II, Scene 3

9:35 PM

Declan conferred with Burt Marsh at the front door, controlling his anger with Nora. He had to remain professional. Simon offered to drive Burt home in his old Range Rover and left to retrieve it from the car park. The SUV's high-clearance and four-wheel drive would let him navigate any remaining water and mud.

"Why don't you come back late morning if you can get through—unless you want a cooked breakfast." Declan remembered the man's status. "By then, whether or not the play continues will have been decided."

"I'll either be packing props or finishing the set." Burt didn't seem to care either way.

Declan clapped the man on the back. Simon pulled up to the doorway and tooted the horn. "See you tomorrow," Declan said, then waved to Simon and closed the door, standing there for a moment to gather his thoughts. He could hear the chatter from the others, clustered in the library, discussing whether or not the play should go on. Grayson had gone up to bed soon after dinner, pleading pain in his wrist and giving them a long-suffering, wistful look as Poppy helped him upstairs. For him, it was all decided.

Declan needed to get things back on an even keel with Nora. He was not happy about her stepping into the play but acknowledged that having someone closer to the company could be helpful. He also knew from his own experience with Nora that she was stubborn and independent and would rarely back down once her mind was made up. He'd have to work doubly hard to protect her. He didn't like this at all.

He found her in the kitchen, working on dinner cleanup with Maeve, the baby monitor on the counter. Amazing how those two had become chummy. When he'd been here last autumn, his impression had been that the two women barely tolerated each other. Yet now they seemed easy in each other's company, going out of their way to be helpful and work in concert. He'd noticed how protective Maeve had been of Sean, too. Maybe that was the clue to the thaw.

Declan leaned against the doorframe and watched them wipe counters and dry pans, chatting over the noise of the dishwasher. Maeve saw him out of the corner of her eye.

"Spying on us, Declan?"

Nora wheeled around.

Declan pushed off the wall and approached Nora. He stopped in front of her and resisted the urge to scoop her up in his arms in front of Maeve. "We need to sort a few things out. Step into my parlour." He opened the kitchen door and stepped outside.

"I know what you're going to say." Nora raised her hands as she joined him. "But you have to see if I'm in the thick of things, we're more likely to find out who's behind all of this."

"That's what I came in to tell you. I reluctantly agree with you." Was he putting the case above his common sense? But he had to find the murderer.

"You do?" Her eyebrows rose to her hairline.

"I do. Unfortunately. But that means the minute—no, the *second* you see or hear anything useful, you let me know immediately." He already regretted his decision.

"Absolutely. Without question. You're the boss." Nora threw her arms around his neck and dragged him down for a kiss before they went back inside.

Maeve gathered damp tea towels and threw them into the washer. "I was going to put the kettle on, all right?"

"Perfect." Nora's beaming smile made Declan's heart swell. He had another thought and counted off on his fingers. "One, Sean is asleep; two, Burt doesn't need my bed tonight; and three, you have the baby monitor in case he stirs or anyone goes anywhere near your room." He watched conflicting emotions pass over her face as she considered leaving the baby alone. Maybe this wasn't the most realistic expectation.

"Hey, is this where the party is?"

Everyone turned at the sound of the new voice.

"Val!" Nora ran to hug her best friend.

Declan turned a wry expression into a welcoming smile.

9:50 PM

Nora couldn't stop tears of relief from coming into her eyes. Finally, Val was here. Sean would be safe once he left for Oxford. Besides, she missed Val's calming presence more than she wanted to admit. She wiped away her tears and smiled at her friend.

As she set up tea in the kitchen, Maeve emptied the last of Agnes' shortbread onto a plate while Val explained how she got to Ramsey Lodge. They pulled up stools and sat around the large island.

"We heard about the floods. Sophie lives in Manchester. I drove there yesterday in the co-op's Vauxhall van and waited to hear when the roads were open."

"Sophie? I've been hearing that name a lot recently." Nora bit her lip when her teasing made a shadow cross Val's face and her friend averted her golden eyes. Was it too soon to think Val would look for romance? Just because she was seeing everything and everyone through rose-colored glasses didn't mean Val was in the same place.

But the shadow turned into an unusual blush as Val shrugged. "Too early to tell, and we don't live around the corner from each other. Tough to carry on a relationship long distance."

"Tell me about it." Declan had everyone laughing.

"How are things here? Are you coming with me, Nora?" Val flashed those outrageous eyes at Nora, but Declan answered first.

"I'm afraid not." He put his arm around Nora's shoulders. "Nora's going to fill in for the dead cast member so the play can go on as planned."

"What?" Val's golden eyes opened wide in surprise.

Nora shifted on her stool. She explained the drama of the past few days. Val's eyes grew even larger at the news of Gemma's death and Grayson's insistence that the play continue. "So we know there's a killer on the premises."

"And you've decided you're going to unmask him or her?" Val turned to Declan. "The assistant of your dreams, right?"

Nora widened her eyes at Val. "You're not helping, my friend."

Val ignored her. "All I know is I get my godson to myself. You won't have him here as long as there's a killer on the loose—and a mystery to poke your nose into."

Nora gave Val a friendly shove. Declan spoke up, "I'm actually not totally convinced Nora's staying here is the best idea." His voice remained calm and even. "But I understand why Nora wants to help, and I've cautiously agreed to it."

Nora gave him her best steely glare. "Every child needs time with his godmother—alone." Even as she said it, she realized she'd never been away from Sean for more than a few hours of writing time when Callie took over. But for his safety, she had to let him go with Val. And she'd be busy rehearsing, getting up to speed on the play. "I'm staying, and he's going."

The kitchen door swung open. Simon had deep hollows under his eyes but brightened when he saw Val.

"Just what I need—tea and Val Rogan." Simon gave Val a hearty hug. "You made it through—good to see you."

"No problems getting Burt home?" Nora asked.

"Lots of standing water here and there, but the roads are passable." Simon blew on his tea.

"You look exhausted." Val fluffed her dark, pixie-cut hair. "You must all need a good night's uneventful sleep."

"That's assuming tonight stays quiet." Nora twisted her mug around in circles.

"And that's our cue, Si." Maeve picked up her mug. "Bring your tea."

"Where am I sleeping?" Val asked.

10:15 PM

Declan furrowed his brow and sipped at his tea, at first intending to let Nora handle this one. Theoretically, Val could have his bed, and he could sleep with Nora. But that left Sean right there, overhearing their every noise. And it left Val upstairs, where a killer was sleeping. Bloody hell of a time to develop a conscience.

"Let's see." Nora hesitated, looking between her lover and her best friend. "Gemma's room is still a crime scene, and I wouldn't want you there, anyway—"

"You sleep with Nora," Declan interjected. "I should remain upstairs to tamp down any criminal behavior." He saw the grateful look Nora threw him.

Val slid off her stool. "I don't want to come between the two of you."

"You won't." Declan said. "A killer took care of that. Nora, can I have a word?"

"And that's *my* cue to get my overnight bag. Thanks, Declan. See you in your room, Nora." Val slipped out.

Declan stood and gathered his thoughts. He was putting Nora's safety at stake to solve his case, and it wasn't an easy feeling. He felt angry with himself as he looked into Nora's eyes. He saw a hint of stubbornness but also great tenderness. She spoke with a beseeching urgency.

"You're waffling on our agreement, aren't you? I *have* to go undercover, Declan. Simon can't afford to have the play cancelled—I owe him that. And I can't let a murderer go free."

"That's *my* job," he pointed out but had a sinking feeling it wouldn't matter what he said to Nora. Some part of her wanted—needed—to be involved in helping him.

"No one else can get that close right now but me; you must see that. You're the copper, the filth to these people. I'm just the gal who at least knows the lines, and they can laud it over me about how good they are. They might let their guard down, and I'll see or hear something useful. And I know how these people are. I can read them better than anyone else here."

Her pleading made sense, but he'd be damned if he'd tell her that. "If something happens to you, I'll never forgive myself."

"Nothing's going to happen to me," she insisted. She turned her face up for a kiss and closed her eyes.

"It damn well better not." He left her standing there with her eyes closed, waiting for a kiss that wasn't happening, at least not tonight.

"Unfair," she called down the hall.

10:45 PM

Nora drew on her nightgown and checked Sean one last time. Val came out of the bathroom wearing pajamas covered in barking dogs and joined her at the foot of the cot. The baby hugged his bunny, his lips pursed and little fists closed. It would be difficult to pack him off with Val, but his safety had to be her primary concern right now.

"He's grown so much in just three weeks," Val said. She'd been visiting Nora every few weeks since Sean's birth.

Nora wondered if Val's frequent visits to Cumbria always included stopovers in Manchester. Val would tell her more about Sophie when she was ready. "Take that side." Nora pointed to the left side of the bed nearest the door. "If Sean wakes, I can slip out easier." She wanted to lie where Declan had slept, hoping to imprint him on her or soak up some of his scent. She would especially miss him tonight now that they were working together. She understood his annoyance at her door was based on his fear he'd made a bad decision. The important thing to remember was that she'd earned his respect.

Val slid under the covers and propped herself up on pillows, ready for a chat. "So tell me, how's the detective's meat and two veg?"

Nora colored. "Don't be crude." She threw a pillow at Val, who ducked. The pillow went flying off the bed onto the floor.

"Just teasing you." Val kept her laughter low but clearly enjoyed Nora's discomfort.

Nora got out of bed and retrieved the pillow. "Knowing you has made me lose any vestige of New England reserve left in my genes."

Val sat up straighter, her voice rising. "Don't tell me you haven't shagged him yet?"

"Shh." Nora pointed to the alcove and slipped back under the covers. "We slept together the first night he was here and again last night, too, but just to sleep with Sean right there." She pointed to the alcove. "And I'm not going into details except to say: brilliant."

"Yankee, I'm ever so sorry I'm the one in your bed tonight." Val tried not to giggle.

Nora hit an emotional wall. Val's grin faded when she burst into tears, and Val threw her arms around her friend.

"Yankee, what's wrong?"

"I've heard from the Pembrokes' solicitor. He's coming here Monday." She reached for a tissue and blew her nose.

"Muriel and Harvey?" Val made a face. "Those two—what do they want from you?"

"I don't know." Nora sniffed. "They're settling Paul's estate, and there are papers I have to sign."

"They probably want a release from any responsibility for my godson."

"That's just it, Val. I never told them, remember?" Nora gulped. "I wanted to tell them before that man arrives, but then there was the accident and then the flood and then Gemma died … " She held back a fresh onslaught of tears.

"Those two were so stiff and cold at Paul's memorial. Do you really want them in your life and in Sean's?"

"Not really. But he *is* their grandson."

Val tilted her head to one side. "You're quite sure of that?"

Nora swatted her. "Of course I'm sure. Just look at Paul's eyebrows in Sean's face." She threw her damp tissue at the wastebasket and missed. "Anyway, I hadn't been with anyone else for over two years when I got pregnant."

"Just asking." Val considered this. "Is Paul's name on his birth certificate?"

"Yes. When the registrar came to me that first day, I couldn't think of any reason not to give Sean dual citizenship because Paul truly is Sean's father. Was."

"Sperm donor, at least. Yankee, I think you're well and truly suckered then." Val grabbed another tissue and handed it to Nora, who laughed instead.

"I hate that the Pembrokes blame me for keeping Paul from them, when he's the one who never wanted to go down to Cornwall."

Val shrugged. "Maybe they don't know that and it's time you told them."

"And they were in mourning for their only child. They were just as upset as I was that day. I've been horrid to them."

"Don't go all gooey on me. I'm the one who had to keep that woman away from you when she launched herself at you. You could have been united in your grief."

Val made good sense, but in Nora's mind an image flashed of Rupert lunging for Grayson out of desperation and grief. Muriel must have been feeling those same emotions. "Maybe I've done them a disservice. I didn't even try to get to know them."

Val snuggled down and turned out the light at her side of the bed. "You'll have plenty of time to rectify that once you tell them, whether you want to or not." She sat up suddenly and turned her light back on. "Is there any chance they might have found out about Sean and want some kind of joint custody?"

Nora shuddered. "I hadn't put that into words, but I guess that's been at the heart of my fear since I heard from the solicitor."

Val patted her and turned the light out a second time. In the dark, her voice was grim. "If they do, they'll have one hell of a fight on their hands."

Chapter Twenty-Seven

"You know that's the kind of observation that shocks people."
Ruth: Act 1, Scene 1

Friday, 13th April

9:25 AM

Declan watched Nora fuss over Sean at breakfast. Her nervousness showed in her over-attentiveness and chatter; that would be due to a combination of Sean's impending departure and her first rehearsal with the cast. The long table had adjourned to their rooms to prepare for a run-through that would now include Nora. He still wasn't happy about the idea, but at least it seemed everyone stayed put last night and there had been no further incidents. They'd eaten quickly and quietly this morning, leaving Simon and Maeve to clear the table in their wake. Agnes had surprised them by showing up in wellies and a mac after getting a lift from her neighbor. They'd enjoyed a full English breakfast. She'd taken the news of Gemma's death with a firm set to her lips but refrained from any comment other than "poor lassie."

Last night, Declan had dozed lightly, one ear peeled for footsteps or noises, until finally he fell into a deep sleep just after dawn for a solid two hours. On his way down to breakfast, he met Poppy Braeburn at the head of the stairs, coming out of her own room. Insinuating herself with Grayson, but not quite there yet. It was early days, and perhaps even the director had a sense of propriety. Declan wondered, as he finished his toast, how long it would take Grayson to tire of the young woman and hoped she wasn't another Maggie Denton in the making. Poppy didn't appear worldly to Declan, and if she was as besotted as Nora claimed, it could turn ugly quickly. He'd keep an eye on her as things progressed.

" ... and don't forget his favorite bunny when you put him down for a nap. I've written out a few things for you, Val." Nora turned to the baby. "You'll have such a good time with Auntie Val, right?"

Sean hit his keys on the tray of his high chair several times in response.

Val laughed. "Nora, you don't really think he understands what you're saying?" She smirked at Declan.

Nora narrowed her eyes. "Of course he does."

"Watch." Val leaned into the baby and said in the same sing-song voice: "And you'll adore eating beetroot and spinach, won't you, Sean?"

The baby banged his plastic keys even more enthusiastically. Everyone laughed.

"You're incorrigible." Nora turned back to the baby. "Don't forget, Auntie Val adores being up in the middle of the night."

Declan softened his heart, knowing that sending Sean away was rough on Nora. "Are you two always like this?" He moved his glance between the two women. His mobile rang before either could answer. When he saw who was calling, he excused himself and left the dining room.

"Morning, Higgins." Declan walked out the front door. The sun was shining off glistening puddles on the road, and there was thick mud in places around the bases of shrubs and trees.

"Trust there were no further incidents last night or I would have heard from you."

"All quiet. Let's hope it's not the calm before another storm."

"Should have those statements ready to be signed later today or early tomorrow. Fancy attending the postmortem? I could send someone around to fetch you."

"Not necessary. I have my own car." Declan hesitated. Nora would be busy getting Sean and Val off and then involved in those dratted rehearsals all day. He'd ask Burt Marsh to keep an eye on her. At the postmortem, he might glean some small information to point him in the right direction. Afterwards, he would debrief Nora, too. He grinned. He had to admit, he liked having her on his side. "What time and where?"

9:45 AM

Fiona Church checked her makeup and then her watch. Plenty of time before the first rehearsal with Nora. This would be an interesting and long day. She had no idea how much acting experience Nora had and how she would fit in. They had worked out their cues and entrances, too, and now they had to incorporate a last-minute newcomer. Only one long day to do that, yet Grayson had pushed back their start time to 10:30. He seemed to be in slow motion today.

She thought she'd go crazy if she didn't get out of here soon. When they came to Bowness on their recce trip, she'd found the area lovely. The idea of spending time at the lakeside had been appealing. Those three days with Gray and Gemma in tow had convinced her she could work with her former lover. That tart was exactly whom he deserved, and despite Gemma's overt jealousy, Fiona didn't have any personal animus against the woman; she just enjoyed getting her worked up. Not that it mattered anymore.

But it had all turned sour quickly, hadn't it? As much as she had tried to play the good sport, Gemma had stamped on her nerves in close quarters. Fiona needed to get away from here, and soon. She'd thought the play would be cancelled. According to her contract, they'd all receive some small compensation, and she certainly didn't owe Gray a damn thing. But there was no point in getting a reputation for being difficult to work with, so she kept quiet during last night's argument until bloody Nora Tierney had stepped up.

9:56 AM

Lydia Denton smoothed her hair and sprayed a stray curl into place. It was thinning on top, more than she liked to admit, but that was one of the things about aging: You couldn't control all of its effects on you. She consoled herself with the thought that at least her sweet Maggie would never know about the ravages of age, frozen as she was at the height of her youth and beauty.

She snapped the cap back on the can and she returned to the bedroom, watching Rupert. She saw his profile, still so strong and handsome, and her heart flipped. They'd had their heartache but had wisely turned to each other, and their love had seen them through. She'd tucked her pain away in a corner of her heart and tried to go on. Perhaps now Rupert would, too, after his outburst at Grayson Lange.

He stood staring out of one of the large windows in their room that overlooked the front of the lodge. She put an arm around his waist, and he tucked her under his shoulder. Across the road, she could see a handful of walkers venturing along the quay. One stout woman walked a Scottie dog sporting a tartan vest. She wished she and Rupert could be among them in the fresh air.

"Once we're released, we should take a walk, don't you think, dear?" She leaned into him. "I was watching Burt Marsh gobble up breakfast. He's our age, and I don't know how he manages on his own. I worry about that, Rupert. What if I go first and you're alone? How would you manage?"

"Hush. All this mess has given you morbid thoughts." Rupert kissed the top of her head. "We're doing the right thing, aren't we Lydie, letting this travesty continue?"

"I checked our contracts. Fiona was right; we have no real choice. We'll get through it." She turned to face her husband and made him look at her. "Just promise me one thing."

"Anything, dear."

"Once we leave Ramsey Lodge, I never want to see or be in the same room with Grayson Lange again."

9:59 AM

With breakfast cleaned up, Simon grabbed Agnes and hugged her. "Thanks for showing up this morning." Her arrival just as he and Maeve struggled into the kitchen early this morning had given him a momentary sense of relief. Agnes was filled with news of the flood.

"BBC Weather says some roads up to Carlisle are still closed, and the trains north are cancelled until tomorrow."

"I'm just glad to have you back." It was more than her cooking he'd missed; it was the sense of normalcy her presence brought.

Agnes smiled her delight. "Put fruit, milk and butter on that, dear." Maeve had started a shopping list. "We don't know yet if the food truck can get through for the big provisions. Have you heard from Callie?"

"She called to say Darby was fine and being spoiled by her entire family," Simon said. "Their road should reopen tomorrow."

"Good thing, 'cause those sheets need changing." Agnes' grey curls bobbed with her pronouncement. "I don't even want to know who slept where."

She gave Maeve a meaningful look, and Simon knew she'd be updated the minute he left the room.

Agnes pointed a finger at him. "I told Nora and now I'm telling you: Those theatre folks are manky, ye ken?"

"Then stay out of their way today, Agnes. Nora needs all the support she can get." Simon left the women sorting out menu ideas to tackle his list of phone calls, including someone to repair the generator. Nora and her list-making had certainly rubbed off on him. He had to admit, he'd felt a sense of relief that the play was going on. Maybe all was not lost. He smiled, thinking of Provence. He and Maeve had certainly earned time away.

CHAPTER TWENTY-EIGHT

"This situation is absolutely impossible, and you know it."
Ruth: Act II, Scene 2

10:02 AM

Grayson Lange rattled his painkillers around the bottle and shook two out, then put one back. He poured a glass of water and downed it quickly. The arm ached despite the rain passing. He'd have to start tapering off on the pills. They fogged his mind too much, and he'd rather have a drink at night. Mixing the two wasn't good. You might not remember your actions the next morning, and who knew what he could get up to in that state? He'd find himself married one of these days if he wasn't careful.

It was really amazing how much he could accomplish, despite the cast on his arm. Having it above his elbow would have hampered his movements, but having it only on his lower arm made him feel more clumsy than helpless.

He took care not to bump it, and he used the sling and didn't wave the bloody thing around—no sense letting people see how much mobility he had. It certainly hadn't hurt to have Gemma fuss over him, and Poppy seemed willing to take her place.

Poppy didn't simper too much; he couldn't abide a woman who played at being coy. A few pounds to fill out her figure and a bit of coaching. Yes, Poppy might work out, at least for a while.

He checked the bedside clock and wandered out onto the balcony. The water glistened in the weak sunlight, and if he didn't look down at the muddy roadway, it was difficult to tell there had been such heavy rains. It was a pretty area, he'd give it that much. No wonder Wordsworth and Coleridge and that lot had been drawn here.

But he was already itching to get back to town. The lights and frenetic activity of bigger towns appealed to him. He almost missed the bustle and traffic of London and his riverside house west of town in Chiswick, down the road from Hugh Grant's family home and in the same neighborhood where Colin Firth walked his dog. Who knew he'd miss home so much?

As he felt the first tendril of a buzz kick in from the pill, Grayson flexed his fingers the way the emergency doctor had instructed. He looked forward to this rehearsal. Thank God Nora Tierney had volunteered. He'd soon see if she could act or would ruin the play; Elvira was the pivotal role. People liked to make issues more difficult than they were, but with a firm plan and dogged determination, you could make things happen. And he considered himself a man of action.

10:12 AM

Nora opened the French doors of her room onto the small garden. Blooms from a cherry tree were strewn around the wet slates and stuck to the glass-topped table. Val pulled up in the van, and Declan carried out Sean's portable cot-playpen. He went back for the buggy base, dumped the changing bag and clothing sack inside it and then rolled it out. Val helped him stow that, too, while Nora carried Sean out and buckled him into his car seat. If Val got on the road now, Sean would take a nap, giving Val an easier ride for part of the way.

"Did you get the cooler with his formula?" Nora bent back into the car as Declan dashed back inside. She handed Sean his stuffed bunny and tied his plastic keys with a ribbon to his car seat. She kissed him one last time. Best not to make a big deal out of this for his sake.

"You know they sell baby food in Oxford." Val took the cooler from Declan.

"This way you won't have to run to the shops right away." Nora looked at the backseat, where Sean banged his feet on this car seat.

Val laughed. "I think we're being told off, dithering here. You've already kissed him, hugged him, checked his luggage twice—we're good, Yankee." She gave Nora a hug.

Nora tried to keep her chin from wobbling. Today was Friday; she'd be in Oxford Tuesday afternoon. "All set." Declan put an arm around her shoulder as Val buckled herself in and tooted as she drove away.

"He'll be fine. Val's a safe driver." Declan turned her toward her room. "You have a rehearsal in a few minutes, and I have a postmortem to attend."

Nora closed the doors and locked them. "Thanks for your faith in me, Declan."

"I'm just worried about you." He kissed her lightly. "Don't get me started again. Just do your job and be safe. Keep your wits about you and your eyes open. I'll be back as soon as I can."

10:33 AM

Nora clutched her copy of the play. Everyone else was off book, but for this first rehearsal she was allowed to consult hers. Declan winked and gave her a thumbs up as he went upstairs. Grayson Lange discussed the day's schedule.

"We'll do a full run-through before lunch so Nora gets her entrances and exits down. Nora, you come in and out of those French doors to the patio quite a bit. Keep your copy out there tomorrow night. I know we're expecting a lot of you to step in with only two rehearsals. If you feel you need more, we'll work with you again tomorrow after breakfast."

Nora nodded, feeling a flush start up her neck. Her eyes roamed the gathering before her, and she took in all the attitudes and emotions she could feel coming at her: reluctance from the Dentons, indifference from Fiona, annoyance from Poppy.

She gave them a brittle smile. Elvira didn't appear until page 26. That would give her time to calm down and study her lines again. Poppy had brought down the dove-grey gown she would wear. She didn't fill it out as well as Gemma had, but its flowing looseness fitted her well enough. It helped that Gemma hadn't been tall, and with the right shoes, Poppy could leave the hemline alone.

Grayson continued. "After lunch, we'll do full dress rehearsal for Poppy to make any costume adjustments, and with props, Burt."

Hearing his name, Burt turned from the fireplace where he was fiddling with a vase. It crashed to the hearth in pieces.

"Burt—" Grayson's tone was one of tolerant exasperation.

The older man bent down and scooped up the pieces. "Meant to do that for the climax." He slotted the pieces together, and in a moment, the vase stood whole again, its Chinoiserie pattern covering the faux cracks.

"It's Friday the 13th, you know." Helen's pronouncement had heads swiveling in her direction.

"Mum!" Grayson exploded.

The reaction was immediate.

"Mum?"

"She's your mother?"

"Helen's your mum? What gives?"

Poppy stalked off the stage and sat down in a chair, arms folded.

Fiona looked at Grayson, head on one side. "You bring your current lover, your former lover, your dead lover's parents all together, and now we find out you have your mum in the cast? I'd say you were a man of hidden depths, Grayson, if I didn't know better." She joined Poppy in a chair.

"Well played, Fiona." Helen rose from her perch on the sofa and smoothed out her skirt. "That's the first time my son has been cleverly put in his place, and it's about time someone did."

11:27 AM

Declan paused at the bottom of the stairs, listening to the voices from the drawing room. The doors were pulled together, but an opening of about six inches let him hear the rehearsal in progress.

"Let her have a nice cry. It'll do her good."

Was that Nora? She sounded so blasé. Grayson had the next line.

"You're utterly heartless!"

"Heartless!" Fiona sputtered.

Grayson broke character. "Fiona, I thought I told you it works better if you spring up from the sofa on that line. Take it again from Elvira's line."

Declan peeked through the gap. Nora's haughty expression shocked him. In less than an hour she'd taken on the cloak of Elvira, the selfish and petulant first wife of Grayson's character. She might just pull this off. He felt a thrill of pride and great admiration that she'd put her distress in parting from Sean aside and thrown herself into the role.

Sneaking across the hall to the door, Declan retrieved his car and set off for Westmorland General Hospital in Kendal to meet

DS Higgins for the postmortem. His GPS sent him southeast to Kendal, onto Burton Road.

He followed signs for the mortuary and drove around the main building to the rear entrance on the ground floor, where he found Higgins waiting for him. At least it wasn't in the basement. As they walked together, Higgins brought him up to date.

"We've done checks on the major players." Higgins smiled at his pun. "Nothing on Fiona Church or the Dentons—just the death of their daughter, classified as 'accidental overdose.' Two endorsements for Grayson Lange for speeding in his fancy car. Poppy Braeburn's parents have a history of camping in unauthorized areas plus a few hits for cannabis possession, but she seems clean." He rang the morgue bell and a buzzer let them in. They stopped inside the door. "A shoplifting hit as a teen on Gemma Hartwell, her stage name, you know. She was born Bernice Sipling, known as Bunny. We've traced her mother down in Bristol, and the locals went to notify her this morning."

Declan curled his fists. What had he hoped for? A cast member to have a history of sociopathic behavior or a previous arrest on suspicion of murder? Hardly likely. He thought of parents calling their little girl "Bunny" and winced for the mother.

"Won't have those statements till tomorrow; skeleton staff." Higgins guided Declan down the hall. "But then I hardly think your lot are going anywhere."

"No, they've decided to go on with the play." Declan explained about Nora stepping in and watched the sergeant's eyebrows rise.

"Oh. I expect they'd like this wrapped up so they can leave Ramsey Lodge right after the last performance."

"I expect the innocent ones would." Declan steeled himself for the postmortem, searching his blazer pocket for the strong peppermints he used to combat the scent of death during the procedure. None. He'd hardly expected to be involved in a murder investigation on holiday. He'd been lucky he'd even brought this jacket and smarter trousers, hoping for that candlelit dinner with Nora. So much for romance. He'd have to get through it today and hope the odors from Gemma's corpse didn't turn his stomach after that large breakfast he'd wolfed down.

Instead, as they approached the active room, the scent that reached him was of something else entirely: garlic, oregano, tomatoes—wine? Higgins inhaled deeply.

"Milo's Crock-Pot; smells like spag bol today."

Declan stopped short. "He cooks here?"

Higgins smiled. "Oh, yes, he'll feed his entire department later on, once the autopsies are done. Quite the cook."

The two detectives donned paper gowns and masks. Higgins pushed the swinging door into the postmortem suite. Another body awaited Milo on a trolley against the wall, its toe tag identifier swaying in the strong ventilation. Declan stepped around it and followed Higgins into the heart of the room. The room smelled of frequent washings with chemical disinfectants.

Milo Foreman stood at the side of the metal table, talking quietly into the voice recorder hanging over the well lit, brutally corrupted body of Gemma Hartwell. She was spread out over a body block, and a Y-incision had been completed under her breasts and down to her pubis, the reds, blues, grays and yellows of the interior of her body a stark contrast to her pale, mottled skin and curly, blonde hair.

Declan noted the skin around her mouth and nose had darkened. Milo's diener weighed a block of slimy sausage-like intestines and called out the number to the pathologist.

"Detectives, welcome. I took the liberty of starting without you." Milo's eyes crinkled over his mask; he wiped his gloved hands on the apron covering his scrubs. "The hands didn't show any tissue under her nails. The rest of the external exam was unremarkable barring the darker areas on her face. No evidence of serious drug use. There's a tattoo of a tiny rabbit on her back, just below her waist."

"Her childhood nickname was Bunny," Higgins said.

"Poor thing." Milo looked down in respect for a moment and carried on. "The hyoid bone was intact, no evidence of any crush injury." He put a hand out, and in a well-choreographed dance, the diener handed him a clipboard. "Blood levels show a fair amount of alcohol and a large dose of zolpidem tartrate—that's a sleeping pill to you gents—so she was in a deep sleep at the time of her death." He flipped a page. "Also, low oxygen but high carbon dioxide levels support asphyxia."

"Anything else?" Declan was itching to get back to watch over Nora.

"Ah, yes. The pillow showed traces of lipstick which match the victim's in color. I found a small cotton fiber in her nose; expect it to be a match to the pillowcase. There were two greyish-white hairs on the obverse of the pillow." He looked up at Declan. "I've rushed a lot of this for you, but the analysis of those will take a while."

Declan felt his pulse quicken. "White hairs that might be the killer's?"

Milo shrugged. "Or of anyone who leaned over the bed around that day or night. You know what the psych boys would say?"

Higgins shrugged; Declan answered. "Smothering instead of strangulation is less hands on, may indicate the killer didn't want to see her face as she died."

"Very good." Milo beamed. "Now, can I interest you gents in staying for lunch? Only one more to go today." He gestured to the body on the hall trolley.

Higgins demurred. "Thanks, but I have to get back to the station."

Declan added: "And I have to return to Ramsey Lodge and catch a murderer."

12:15 PM

Helen stood by the patio railing waiting for the others to gather for lunch. Simon had explained the stockist lorry wouldn't arrive in time and had made arrangements for them at The Scarlet Wench Pub. A glass of something with alcohol in it might do her good. Across the road, a handful of hearty yachties braved the roads to check their boats. A few took advantage of the winds, gamboling about the edge of the lake, and she envied the freedom they must feel on the water. Bowness was still cleaning up from the storm but things were returning to normal. But could they ever again be normal after Gemma's death?

The first run-through had had the usual stumbles from Nora, with Grayson moving her around a bit, but by Act II, she'd hit her stride and lifted her chin and it had gone more smoothly after that. They'd see how she'd hold up in dress rehearsal this afternoon. This whole thing was taking its toll on Helen. She was finding it more and more difficult to stay in character, something she'd always found easy to maintain.

Helen felt movement beside her. Burt Marsh stepped up to the railing and took in the view, nodding to her but not initiating conversation. She wasn't comfortable with long silences; after a moment, Helen rushed to fill the void. "Finally the weather clears, Mr. Marsh."

"Burt." More silence. Then briskly: "Must be difficult for you."

She pretended not to know what he meant. "Having a murder here?"

Burt snorted. "Having a man like Lange for your son."

Helen opened her mouth to fire a retort, but nothing came out. In a moment of clarity, she saw the man had found her out. It was why she allowed her son to call her "Helen" and why she didn't rush to acknowledge she was his mother. She simply didn't like her only child.

CHAPTER TWENTY-NINE

"I can't bear this for another minute ... "
Charles: Act 1, Scene 2

1:30 PM

Nora stepped outside the pub to take Val's call. Val and Sean were in Woodstock, approaching Val's flat, just outside Oxford's city centre. He'd had a nice nap, and Val had stopped once to change his nappy and grab a snack. They'd be settled in her flat within half an hour. Nora thanked her friend again for taking him away from the danger at Ramsey Lodge.

"No worries, Yankee. How was rehearsal?"

"It helped that I knew the role. I slipped into Elvira pretty quickly and only looked at my script a few times. We do it again with costumes and props this afternoon."

"Only two rehearsals before the big night?"

"Grayson feels the actors need to rest the day of performance, but he said he'd work with me if I felt uncomfortable, or maybe we'd do another run-through without costumes tomorrow."

"Not you; you'll be brilliant this afternoon, and then you can turn your nose to snooping properly all day. I'll call tonight after Sean's asleep, and you can tell me all about it."

Nora felt relieved and turned her attention to the play and the group inside finishing their lunch. The cast had split into factions when it came to seating: She'd sat with the Dentons and Burt at one small table; Helen and Fiona sat with Grayson and Poppy at a larger one. She thought of the reasons she was playing Elvira. It all seemed to revolve around Grayson Lange.

As if she'd conjured him up with her thoughts, Grayson strolled out to meet her.

"Here's Elvira." He slipped an arm around her shoulder. "You did a grand job this morning, and I've no doubt you'll be even better this afternoon."

Nora tried not to stiffen at the director's touch. "Thank you." This was an opportunity to get information from him. He saved her from finding a conversation opener when he dropped his arm to massage his fingers.

"How the mighty are fallen, eh, Nora?"

"I don't think the Old Testament has anything to do with this week's events, Grayson."

"That's where you're wrong, my dear. Everything man does can be traced to biblical times: war, jealousy, betrayal, revenge." He adjusted the sling on his arm. "We keep repeating the same themes over and over—in our literature and in our actions." He laughed. "You were the one who got away, Nora. Didn't fall for the Lange charm."

Nora ignored the personal turn. She noted that of all the themes he'd mentioned, he'd left out love. "So what's the motive behind your accident and Gemma's death?"

Grayson shook his head. "Don't know. I've been trying to work that one out myself."

Nora persisted. "You must know who has a grudge against you or a score to settle."

He blew out a breath. "There are far too many people here who fall into that category. Even my own mother." He turned to her. "Fancy a pudding?"

"No, you go ahead." She watched him walk back inside; he held the door open for Fiona. Here was another person to question.

"Needed a breath of air." The day had warmed a bit, and Fiona pushed up the sleeves of the cardigan she'd donned. "Lunch was better than I imagined." She paused. "So were you."

"Thanks." Nora consulted her watch, surprised by Fiona's thaw. "Still have half an hour. Buy you a beer?"

"Why not? Stella for me. I'm not the one Gray will be watching all afternoon."

They re-entered the cool, dim pub, redolent with the mixed odors of years of yeasty spilled brews, sweat and kitchen fat. Fiona wrinkled her nose. "I remember when the smoke from cigarettes covered all this."

A cheerful, plump woman wearing a damp apron waved to Nora. "Two Stellas please, Daisy." Nora withdrew money from her pocket and left it on the bar.

Daisy obliged, and Nora watched the foamy beer fill the glasses.

"Reminds me of the smell of baking," Fiona said.

"Smells more like grass and sweet corn to me, but that's my Connecticut background." Nora had to find a way to question the actress.

"That explains it." Fiona nodded her thanks to the barmaid as Daisy placed the glasses on beer mats in front of them. "Grayson wants me. Thanks, Nora." She picked up her beer.

Nora touched her arm before she could leave. "Fiona, you know this cast better than most of us. Can you think of any good reason—anything at all—that would prompt everything that's occurred?"

Fiona's face blanched. "Get off me—" She shook off Nora's hand. "All I know is I want *out* of this place, and I never want to come here again." She moved away.

"Tut—no fighting, ladies." Daisy wiped her hands on a bar towel and left Nora's change. "What else can I get you?"

Nora indicated the two tables. "You hear anything important from that lot before the accident the other night?"

"Big brooding man and that blonde jiggling her bits all over him? They sat with the brunette and a few others. You were with that nice-looking gent." She peered at Nora. "He the one you interested in?"

Did the woman have ESP, or was her relationship with Declan that obvious? "Just wondered if they said anything out of order." Nora took a sip of her beer.

Daisy thought for a moment. "Not a good tipper. Same thing the first time he was in."

Nora shook her head. "When was that?

Daisy put her head on one side. "Last autumn, just the three of them. The bad tipper, the blonde and that brunette you just bought the Stella. He had too much to drink that night, too."

"Keep the change, Daisy."

2:55 PM

Declan drove along the A591 past Staveley on his way back to Ramsey Lodge. He left Higgins sorting postmortem reports and supervising the civilian transcribing the witness statements into Kendal's system. The detective had promised to notify him if anything else turned up. Higgins seemed like a person to follow procedure, and Declan had agreed. Obviously, one of the people he'd interviewed had been lying, but which one?

He thought of what he'd learned. Gemma Hartwell had been in a deep, drugged sleep when someone entered her room, thrust a pillow over her face and held it in place until she stopped breathing. After being pressed, Milo Foreman admitted that once her oxygen levels dropped, there was a slight chance the young woman might have regained consciousness briefly to struggle weakly against her assailant, but more likely she had tried to get the pillow off her face, as there was no tissue under her nails. "Pure speculation," Milo insisted but was firm on one point. "The murder could just as easily have been accomplished by a woman as a man."

Declan grimaced at the thought of Gemma waking, frightened and gasping for her last breaths, and hoped that wasn't the case. They would never know. The method indicated the killer didn't want to see Gemma's face as she died. To Declan, that signaled he or she felt sorry but was compelled to commit murder. The grey-white hairs were the only positive gleaning. He thought of his suspects. Rupert, Lydia and Helen all had white hair. For that matter, so did Burt Marsh, and Grayson had silver-grey at the sides of his head. Thank goodness Agnes hadn't been on the premises, and so he could at least rule her out.

Declan examined them one by one as he drove along the curving road, his thoughts straying to Nora and her rehearsal. He'd been struck by how she'd transformed herself into the character of Elvira. And she wasn't a trained actress. He smiled. Of course, she did have a way of stepping into a role when it suited her, as he well knew.

Burt was on the premises, so Declan couldn't automatically rule him out, but neither did he have a motive. Could Helen, in some twisted way, have thought killing Gemma would be a slap in the face to Grayson and ruin his play? It seemed there was little parental feeling between mother and son. That left the car accident. Somehow, he didn't see Helen scooting under a car to tamper with brake lines.

And what of the Dentons? They had a motive to harm the director, and Rupert could easily have caused the accidents. Up until Gemma died, Rupert had been his prime suspect, but murdering Gemma would only indirectly hurt Grayson. The same could be said for Lydia, unless they were in it together. But blaming Grayson for their daughter's depression was one thing. Killing his current lover only to see her quickly replaced by yet another young woman under his spell seemed pointless.

It would take too long for DNA results on the hairs if he had to wait for that. He didn't have time to waste. There had to be another way to catch this killer, and he had to hope Nora would see or hear evidence that would lead to a solution.

4:45 PM

Fiona and Nora had their last lines and exited through the French doors, three pages before the end of the play. Fiona saw Nora shiver in her thin, gauzy costume as they stood on the patio, listening for the climax. She wore her own filmy dress for the last scene, and the breeze was cold.

Burt Marsh stood with them, following the play, holding a monitor in one hand. "You should leave coats out here tomorrow night for the wait before curtain calls." He wore a thick woolen jumper.

Nora rubbed her arms briskly. "Good idea." She checked her watch. "Two hours forty, right on schedule."

"Gray will be pleased, and you did well. I admit I'm impressed." Fiona yawned. "Look, I'm sorry I was rude when you bought me that beer today. My nerves are frazzled."

"I understand."

"I wonder if you really can."

The two women locked eyes. Burt hit a switch, and Fiona turned at the noise of the vase breaking on the hearth. "Let's watch."

Nora opened one of the doors, and they peeked in. Burt worked his computer. The painting that hung above the mantel crashed to the ground. The clock below it started to strike with increasing speed, causing Grayson to talk louder over it.

The lid on the phonograph slammed open and shut; a figure

from a table fell over to the floor. Grayson delivered his last line, left the stage and joined them on the patio. He opened the door wide, and the three looked in. The curtains opened and closed erratically, and just as the phonograph played "Always" with increasing speed, Burt raised a remote in his hand. With one push of a button, the chandelier prisms hanging over the table fell with a spectacular crash all over the table and ground.

Everyone broke into spontaneous clapping.

"Well done, all!" Grayson pushed Fiona and Nora onto the stage before him. "Now line up for curtain calls." The rest of the cast came in from where they'd been leaning against one of the doors into the lodge kitchen. "Tomorrow night, you'll be in the kitchen, so come out after the crash when the waves of applause start. And mind the bits and pieces lying around, come nearer the front."

He had them line up and hold hands to practice how to bow from the waist. Then he had Nora and Fiona take a separate bow with him. He hugged Fiona and then each of the others in turn. At that moment, Fiona wished she were able to unfreeze her heart.

5:12 PM

Declan looked over Nora's shoulder as her fingers flew over the laptop keys.

"I'm glad dress rehearsal went so well." He'd returned to watch Acts II and III and was impressed with the cast, and with Nora in particular. "You really became Elvira. And that dress clings in all the right places." He leaned forward and nuzzled her neck. She ignored him. "What are you looking up again that's so important?"

"I'd forgotten Grayson was here with Gemma and Fiona on a scouting trip in the autumn." She brought up the website for *Cumbrian Chatter.*

It was obvious he didn't have Nora's attention, and the feeling rankled him. This must have been what Anne had felt when he had been on a case. He moved a pile of clean sheets from the chair by Nora's desk and pulled up next to her. When had she found time to change the sheets? "And this is important why?"

"I was in the hospital that weekend. Sean was born Friday, October 29th—" She scrolled through the news archives. "—so I didn't see them then."

"This has significance because he didn't tip Daisy enough? I'm all ears, Miss Christie."

Nora gave him a withering glance. "Don't be impertinent." She paged down through the weekend news.

"Sorry, it's just that your ideas often get you into trouble." He had to admit he enjoyed teasing her. The truth is he was proud to see her in action.

"Do you want to hear this or not?" Nora stopped on the Sunday listings. "Here it is—" Her face glowed with excitement. She read the article aloud:

> In a hit-and-run accident, 69-year-old Bowness resident Estelle Marsh was killed Saturday night outside the Community Theatre. Mrs. Marsh, a retired teacher, was hit a glancing blow to the hip and thrown to the kerb. She died a few hours later of a head injury. Any witnesses are asked to contact the local police in Kendal.

"My God—Grayson killed Gemma because she knew he was driving that night." Nora sat back.

"You have no proof of that, Nora." Declan considered the scenario. "How do you know he was involved? And why would he cut his own brakes or have Fiona fall or any of the other silly pranks that happened here?"

"Fiona was with them, too." Nora's lips were set in a straight line. "It needs looking into, Mr. Detective Inspector. It points to Grayson as a potential killer, and you need to take this seriously. What if Gemma threatened to tell on him?"

"It's a theory." He watched her attitude change. She leaned forward, and her robe fell away. He couldn't keep his eyes off her cleavage.

"Declan, it wouldn't hurt to ask DS Higgins to pull out the accident report."

"You vixen. Are you trying to use sex to get me to listen to your theory?" He pulled her closer. He had his own question to ask Higgins. "Because it's definitely working."

CHAPTER THIRTY

"I seem to remember ... telling you that your views of female psychology were rather didactic."
Ruth: Act II, Scene I

8:50 PM

Maeve sat back down after last refills of coffee and tea at the long table. Burt thanked Simon for dinner and rose to leave for home. Simon accompanied him to the door as Declan drained his mug.

"All set?" Grayson Lange stood and led the way to the library. Poppy had found a movie on the shelves for the evening's entertainment that had generated great enthusiasm during dinner. "Good distraction for us, keep our minds occupied tonight." Poppy and Fiona filed out to the library after him. Lydia and Rupert waited a beat, talked in low tones with Helen and then followed the others out.

Nora excused herself for the loo.

"She's a great mum." Maeve nodded toward Nora's empty seat. "And not a bad actress." She poured herself a hot cup of tea.

"Did you think she wouldn't be?" Declan raised an eyebrow.

"I knew she'd rise to the occasion on all fronts." Maeve slipped off her shoes. "My feet hurt tonight."

Simon joined them. "With good reason. You've been brilliant, Maeve." He poured his own tea. "Who would have thought *Rear Window* would hold such fascination for that crew?"

"One of Hitchcock's masterpieces." Declan stated this as if it brooked no question. "Jimmy Stewart stuck in a wheelchair and Grace Kelly never lovelier."

"Don't tell me you're a Hitch fan, too?" Maeve shook her head. Simon laughed at her reaction.

"Isn't everyone?" Declan's retort was accompanied by a wry smile.

Maeve shuddered in exaggeration. "I think he was a dirty old man who had a thing for frosty blondes. No wonder you and Nora get on so well. She adores Hitchcock."

Declan smiled and looked down at his cup.

"Memories bringing a blush to the detective's face?" Maeve's teasing brought another question to her mind. She lowered her voice. "Seems they've split into two factions: the Dentons with Helen and the two younger women with Grayson."

"Yet they're all sitting in that library together," Declan pointed out.

Maeve considered this. "Better to keep an eye out for a killer if he's right in front of you."

"You'd make a good detective yourself, Miss Addams." Declan laughed. "Nora must be rubbing off on you."

"What am I doing?" They hadn't noticed Nora's return to the dining room.

Maeve explained. "Declan told me I've learned my detective skills from you."

Nora sat down and touched the teapot to see if it was still warm, then poured herself a second cup. "I didn't think you liked my snooping."

"I don't," Declan agreed. "But I'm learning to give your instincts some respect, too."

"That's a change." Simon rose. "Maeve, let's start clearing. Nora, we'll take care of this. You have lines to run."

Maeve threw her napkin on the table and put her shoes back on. "It will be good when things get back to normal around here."

Simon gathered their plates, then leaned over and kissed Nora on the cheek.

"What's that for?" Nora's puzzlement was genuine.

"For trying to salvage the play. I know part of the reason you're doing this is for me."

9:10 PM

Declan slipped out to the terrace and dialed Higgins' mobile. "Sorry to bother you so late, Higgins. I need two things from you. Do you have a contact in Chiswick nick?"

He explained what he needed and why. "Yes, ones that specialize in body work on Jaguars. That should narrow it down. And I need the accident report from last 31st October on Estelle Marsh."

Declan clicked off. Good man, Higgins. First thing in the morning, he'd organize enquiries through the Metropolitan Police. The Met's Hounslow borough had a station right on Chiswick High Road, and with any luck, Declan might have the information he sought by tomorrow night.

Now, he had to hope the killer wouldn't make any moves tonight. He thought of how to be with Nora and still have one ear open for movement upstairs. An idea occurred to him that seemed perfect.

Declan watched the bevy of boats docked in Bowness Bay Marina sway with the water's movement. The clang of sailboat halyards reached him with a change in the wind direction. To his right, north along the shore, a wildlife refuge housed the varieties of birds that frequented the lakeside. On his walks, he'd seen coots, cormorants and the migrating goldeneyes, but tonight they'd be bedded down in reed beds, and only a few squawking gulls moved through the night sky. They'd sleep better than he would.

He felt sluggish, tired from a lack of proper sleep and the building tension of the past week. This holiday had turned out vastly different from what he'd hoped when he'd packed in Oxford, especially when it came to Nora Tierney.

If he were a smoker, he'd be lighting up right now. No one could press his buttons like Nora, but he had to admit her instincts had been valuable. Not that he'd encourage her too much in her sleuthing.

He turned back to the lodge and Nora to hatch his plan and salvage just a bit of the reason he'd come to Ramsey Lodge. With Sean away, he could keep his ear tuned for a murderer, but he'd be sleeping in Miss Tierney's bed tonight.

11:15 PM

Declan closed Nora's copy of the play. "Almost perfect." He threw her script on her desk. "Same as you." He liked the simple nightdress she wore with her long hair hanging loose down her back. She'd acted out her moves in the bedroom as he'd stretched out on her bed in his robe and read out the other parts.

Nora smiled. "It helps that Elvira doesn't have many long speeches." She resisted the pull to enter Sean's alcove and miss him even more. "Val called earlier when you were out on the patio. Sean fell asleep right around his normal bedtime."

Declan rose and drew her into an embrace. "You sound disappointed."

"Not really. I want him to adjust well and not give Val a hard time."

"But you want him to miss you." He rubbed her back. "And maybe give Val a teeny bit of a hard time?"

She yawned. "See, not perfect at all."

"But plenty good for me." He kissed her passionately. "With no early riser around, we can both catch up on our sleep tonight."

He enjoyed seeing the mischievous gleam that came into Nora's eye.

"And then some … I'll light that scented candle you liked."

"Hold that thought." Declan grabbed the baby monitor from her desk and turned it on.

"What are you doing with that?"

"Bringing it upstairs to leave in my doorway on the floor. That way I'll hear any midnight walkers."

Nora nodded. "And Fiona is in the most danger right now, so that's closest to her doorway."

He kissed her again. "See, almost perfect."

The movie had ended, the cast already upstairs, although Declan noted lights shone from under several doors as he went upstairs and entered his room. He grabbed clean clothes for the next day and looked around to see if he was forgetting anything. Closing the door, he propped the monitor against the doorframe in a shadow and made certain it was turned on.

He'd just started to creep downstairs when Poppy's door opened. She stood in the doorway.

"I heard footsteps." She held a toothbrush and looked pointedly at his armful of clothes.

"Sorry to disturb you." He kept his tone even to avoid the sheepishness he felt. It was his business where he slept, and everyone at the lodge knew he and Nora were in a relationship. "Poppy, are you frightened?"

"Not really. I was just … checking."

"Good idea. Good night." He turned to start down again. Poppy closed her door and he heard the turn of the key.

As he passed Simon's door, he heard a low chuckle from

Maeve. His tiredness fell away, and he entered Nora's room with all the enthusiasm that had brought him to the Lake District in the first place.

By candlelight, Nora's nightgown looked almost sheer. She lay in bed in the flickering light, snoring gently.

Chapter Thirty-One

"It's most awfully difficult to explain."
Ruth: Act II, Scene 2

Saturday, 14th April

8:15 AM

Nora woke to the sounds of Declan showering. That sleep was the best she'd had in ages. She looked at the bedside clock. 8:15! She hadn't slept this late since before Sean's birth.

She fell back into the cozy pillows. It was awful she'd fallen asleep on Declan last night, but she reasoned he could have woken her. Did he let her sleep out of annoyance or consideration?

Grayson had decided on one last walk-through of their lines, not in costume and without props, just to reinforce stage movements, entrances and exits. It would give them all an added sense of ease. He had originally said he wanted them to have the day off before opening night, so was this run-through down to her inexperience?

Nora shook off a wave of nerves. Today and tonight she needed all of her concentration to keep her eyes and ears open while still inhabiting the character of Elvira. That meant reducing her stress level today, and her thoughts turned to the Pembrokes and to the call hanging over her head before the lawyer's visit on Monday.

What if Val's thoughts were right? She'd based her whole knowledge of them on one grief-stricken meeting. She hadn't taken into consideration that they must be reeling, lost in their sadness. And she hadn't been able to explain that she'd wanted to meet them before that horrid day.

It had been Paul who'd ignored her questions about his parents, always using work for an excuse not to drive down to Cornwall. Dull, he'd called them, stuck in the past. Could they have been abusive toward him? Not likely. That kind of anger would have expressed itself. So what had Paul wanted to hide about his parents? Perhaps they kept chickens or sheep, and they embarrassed him. But then Paul had been secretive about his job, too. Maybe that had just been his nature.

Her own emotional scars had built up walls that Nora knew kept her, at times, from reaching for trust and openness. The courage to see the truth of a situation went beyond her individual point of view; she needed to develop the ability to see a situation the way others might, and that extended to the Pembrokes.

How easily her protective mask fell off when she was with Sean. Even when he fussed or didn't sleep, she felt unequivocal, deep love. It was what she hoped to find in a partner, and yet by keeping her from his family, Paul had sown seeds of doubt that had kept Nora from completely trusting him. She wouldn't entertain her worst fears about Sean's custody. If it came to that, she'd borrow money from her mother and hire her own solicitor. But what if she was jumping the gun?

She heard Declan give a gentle whistle as he showered, a low tune she didn't recognize. Not annoyance, then, but consideration. He'd probably been exhausted, too.

Before her courage failed her, Nora unplugged her mobile from its charger and pulled on her robe and slippers. She opened the French doors and shivered as she went out into the garden. The signal was strong here, and Nora took a deep breath and dialed the number she'd loaded into her phone months before. It was early, yes, but country people rose early.

"Hello, Mrs. Pembroke—Muriel? This is Nora Tierney. We need to talk."

10:15 AM

Simon went over the potential menu for the weekend with Agnes and Maeve. "I'm so bloody tired of working out what to feed these people, knowing one is a murderer." The generator repairman hadn't been able to fix the current unit. A new part was on order and would be installed next week at great expense. Simon rubbed the back of his neck, where tension had given him a crick Maeve hadn't been able to massage away.

"The delivery lorry came through in the afternoon, and the market should be in full force." Agnes took the list from him. "This is fine."

Maeve pushed him. "We've got this covered. Go and do something artsy."

Simon moved into the main hall. The drawing room doors were closed, but he could hear the start of the play's last run-through. He cracked them open and watched for a moment. True to her word, Nora was off book and moved easily on the set. He'd seen her acting abilities firsthand in Oxford. Burt Marsh ignored the actors and set up rows of folding chairs, while others waited for their cues.

It was a sunny day, and Simon closed the drawing room doors and propped open the front lodge door, then immediately wished he hadn't. With dismay, he watched a broadcast van pull into the driveway and stop right in front, blocking the entrance. A reporter and a cameraman exited. Simon went down the walkway and stood his ground. He didn't have to admit them to the lodge, but he knew anything he said would be captured on film for the evening news and posterity.

"I'm afraid you can't leave that van there." He kept his tone casual.

The reporter nodded to the driver. "Pull around and wait in the car park, Bob."

Bob did as instructed while the light from the camera hit Simon's eyes. Simon recognized the reporter from the crowd that had rushed Ramsey Lodge after Keith Clarendon's body washed up on the shore across the road last autumn. He decided to keep his approach pleasant but firm.

"I'm sorry but the lodge is closed to the public for a play." That settled it neatly. He turned to go back inside.

"Oi! You're Simon Ramsey, the bloke suspected of murder last year. Another suspicious death, this time inside your lodge?"

Simon ground his teeth. Word of the death had leaked out, and soon newsmen would be crawling all over the place. "No comment." He reached the doorway.

The reporter was relentless. "A veritable hotbed of murder, Ramsey Lodge, eh?"

Simon clenched his fists. "Please allow the victim her privacy." The second the words escaped his lips, the reporter's face lit up, and Simon knew he'd made a glaring error.

"So it's a woman, Mr. Ramsey? Right in her bed here?" He thrust his microphone in Simon's face.

"Sod off!" Simon slammed the door behind him and leaned his back against it. This was only the start, and he'd handled it poorly. What would Kate say when that sound bite hit the news?

12:30 PM

The drawing room doors slid open after a smattering of applause. Declan hovered in the hallway, watching the cast adjourn for lunch. At breakfast, Nora had apologized for falling asleep on him and told him she had finally called the Pembrokes, but not the details, as Grayson had risen then to give a list of notes before the final rehearsal.

The cast chatted around Nora as they exited, exclaiming over her grasp of the part.

"Well done, Nora," Rupert said, shaking her hand. Lydia beamed her agreement as they strolled past into the dining room with Burt.

"Let's hope I do as well tonight." Nora's face flushed with excitement.

"Brilliant!" Grayson Lange kissed the top of Nora's head as he filed past, and even Fiona flashed Nora a thumbs-up.

"Dear child, you embody the very essence of Elvira." Helen, back in character, drew a silent Poppy with her. "Come along, Poppy." Helen shepherded Poppy into the dining room.

Nora threw her arms around Declan for a hug. "Went better than I could have imagined. I've got Elvira down pat again."

"More rehearsing this afternoon?" Declan took in the glow on Nora's face.

"Nope. Rest and relax." She arched an eyebrow. "I might need some distraction so I don't get nervous."

"I might be able of help with that." He directed her back into the drawing room to the seats set up for the audience. "Only Poppy seemed unhappy. Jealous she wasn't chosen, I expect." Declan turned to face her and took her hand. "We didn't get to talk much at breakfast in front of everyone. How did your call to the Pembrokes work out? I know it was a difficult decision, but I'm proud of you for choosing to tell them."

He was rewarded with her grateful smile. "Better than expected, once I got past the initial frost." Nora traced the veins on the back of his hand with a finger. "'A piece of Paul,' Muriel said; then she called for Harvey, and things got a bit emotional after that."

"Does that bother you?"

"It's who Sean is; I'm actually relieved they know. She seemed so different from the day we met, especially after I explained it was Paul who'd kept us away." She tucked a loose strand of hair behind her ear. "Once the thaw set in, she even apologized for her behavior at Paul's memorial."

"Which you gracefully accepted?"

"I told her I was sure no one was themselves that day. And then Harvey took the phone and said he had been quite horrified. 'Very out of character for Muriel,' he insisted. I did make it clear I wasn't looking for any kind of financial support from them."

"She was in shock, then." Declan pulled Nora close to his side. "Maybe not her best showing."

"Val pointed out the same thing. We'll figure out a meeting soon, but she said it could wait until I'd seen the solicitor Monday. It made it easier to not have to explain why Sean's not here."

Declan kissed the top of her head, inhaling the lemony scent of her shampoo. "Maybe she didn't want to overwhelm you."

"I suppose." At least her worst fears could be put to rest. The Pembrokes were surprised to hear about Sean. The solicitor must just be bringing a release to sign on Paul's estate.

He smoothed away the lines on Nora's forehead with his finger. "I admit my interest is piqued by this visit Monday. Until then, we have a play to get through this weekend." He didn't mention the reports he was waiting on from Higgins, but Nora seemed to read his mind.

"And a murderer to catch." He saw the gleam in her eyes and knew that despite opening-night jitters, Nora hadn't forgotten her goal.

Chapter Thirty-Two

"I believe she is completely sincere."
Charles: Act 1, Scene 2

4:30 PM

It had been an uneventful lie-down from Declan's point of view, with Nora too keyed up to do more than cuddle, although that was nice, too. There was always tonight to look forward to, with Sean away and the first performance of the play behind her. Val had texted Nora: `Break a leg. Sean lovely; keeping him 4ever, LOL xoxo V`

Nora insisted Grayson was a killer, that the cut brake lines and falls echoed events in the play itself. "You have to understand how theater people think. Everything's symbolic. They always have the play and the stage on their minds. Grayson hadn't meant to crash that wall so hard in the accident. He probably didn't realize the drive sloped down outside the pub and would pick up speed."

Declan decided to let her get her thoughts out. It was a distraction from her nervous energy toward the play. "And Gemma's death?"

"Gemma threatened to tell he'd been driving when Estelle Marsh had been hit, and she had to go." She gave him a wide-eyed look that meant she'd figured it all out.

He managed to talk with her without it escalating to an argument. In the rehearsal Declan had watched, Grayson had been left alone on the stage at the end of the play, so the detective knew the director wouldn't have an opportunity to harm Nora, just in case she was right.

Declan was almost relieved when Poppy knocked on Nora's door to bring her upstairs to do her hair and makeup with Fiona's help. He wouldn't see her again until the play started. She'd be fussed over by the women and would dress up there. At her bedroom door, he pulled Nora into an embrace and whispered in her ear: "Break a leg."

Her radiant smile was tempered with a wave of anxiety, and he gave her an extra hug before Poppy led her away. He hoped saying the traditional theatre wish to actors didn't mean it would come true. Then he gave a little shake. Helen's character had definitely infected him. He'd never been superstitious and wasn't about to start now.

Declan went into the lodge kitchen in search of a snack. Maeve and Agnes were putting on their coats. "I'm taking Agnes home for a quick change of clothes, and I'll pick her up on the way back from my flat." Maeve waved and left to bring her car to the kitchen door.

"You keep an eye on our Nora." Agnes pointed a finger at him, then brought him over to the refrigerator. "I've sent up a tray of sandwiches and cookies for the cast to snack on before they dress in their costumes. There's some for you and Simon in the fridge." Agnes opened the fridge door, pointing out covered dishes. "And fruit, and—just help yourself, Declan." There was an air of nervous excitement at Ramsey Lodge that had nothing to do with killings or accidents. Agnes waved and left in Maeve's wake.

Declan looked for Simon and found him onstage by the phonograph that would be used several times during the play, in discussion with Burt Marsh. For Simon's sake, Declan hoped there wouldn't be technical difficulties.

He stepped out onto the drive and strolled to its end. His mobile rang. Finally—DS Higgins calling, and precisely when Declan's mobile had good reception.

"Since I'm coming to the play tonight with the missus, I'll bring the statements," the Kendal detective explained. "You can get them signed tomorrow at breakfast."

"Anything else?"

"Gemma's mother arrived with her second husband and formally identified the body."

Declan had the distinct feeling Higgins was playing him. "Nothing else?"

Higgins laughed. "Impatient bugger, aren't you?" As Higgins proceeded with the rest of his report, Declan withdrew his notebook, and a wide smile spread over his face.

5:55 PM

Seated in Fiona's bathroom on a vanity stool, wearing her undergarments and her robe, Nora tamped down her burgeoning jitters and closed her eyes. Fiona brushed pale powder over the equally pale, silvery-grey face paint she'd applied with a foundation brush over Nora's entire face and down her neck. Fiona drew a smaller, dampened brush through black eye shadow and gently created ghostly hollows under Nora's cheekbones and in the creases of her eyes, adding a bit of brown on the eyelids to keep her from looking like a skeleton.

"We usually make everything a bit brighter, exaggerated for the theatre, but here the venue is small, and you're supposed to be a ghost." Fiona had done her own makeup and pinned her bobbed hair into classic 1940s victory rolls.

"Don't forget her hands." Poppy looked over Fiona's shoulder. She would add a maid's cap over her short hair after Fiona did her makeup.

"Already done." Nora held her hands up for inspection.

"Maybe a touch of eyebrow color above that eye shadow though, just so your features don't entirely disappear." Fiona used a small, slanted brush to darken Nora's eyebrows.

"Lips, Fi," Poppy urged.

Fiona rummaged through one of several makeup cases. "A nice scarlet, I think." She outlined Nora's lips with a pencil, then filled them in with the lipstick she'd chosen.

"For the wench I'm supposed to be?" Nora smiled, but a shiver ran through her as she remembered the legend of the Scarlet Wench and the reason she was being made up as Elvira.

"There, take a look." Fiona spun Nora around toward the mirror.

Nora didn't recognize herself. Her wavy hair, parted on the side and rolled into a chignon, had been sprayed with dry shampoo until it glistened a whitish grey. Her lips and eyes, the only spots of color in the pallor of her skin, kept her from looking insipid.

"I look—very ghostly." Nora couldn't stop looking at the reflection in the mirror. It was so far from her normal look. She remembered getting made up in college for this role, with white pancake that left her looking clownish and talcum powder in her hair. Fiona's touch was infinitely more professional and believable. "It's brilliant, Fiona, thanks."

"You know the title of the play comes from a Shelley poem." Poppy thrust herself back into the conversation. "'To a Skylark.'"

"And with your grey dress, the effect will be perfect, Poppy." Nora picked up on the young woman's insecurity. "I knew Coward wrote it on vacation at Portmeirion in Wales, but not where he got the title." She smiled at Poppy, who seemed guileless. Nora felt a moment of acceptance into this closed community.

She'd enjoyed this time getting ready with the women but

hadn't learned a thing toward her investigation. She'd decided to keep an open mind, even though she thought Grayson was to blame for all of the happenings and she could see him being callous enough to murder Gemma. But it seemed lame to bring up Gemma's name now when everyone was keyed up about the performance. Without Gemma, Fiona's prickly attitude had dropped, and Nora could see she had a softer side. Poppy seemed anxious that the play would succeed. Whether that was for Grayson or for her own involvement didn't matter. Nora didn't see Poppy as a killer. She'd keep her eyes and ears open as she and Declan had discussed. "The others do their own makeup?"

Poppy nodded. "Fiona helped Gray already. He usually does his own, but not with the plaster cast. Helen and the Dentons do theirs, although I expect Lydia helps Rupert."

"I think I'll just say 'break a leg' before I put my costume on." Nora stood up. "Thanks again, both of you.

Nora left Poppy taking her seat and knocked on the Dentons' door. Lydia had on the dress she wore in Act 1, and her makeup was complete. Rupert had toilet paper tucked around the collar of his shirt to protect it from the face paint. "Just popping in to say break a leg before I dress. Do either of you need anything?" Nora felt baffled. Despite being angry with Grayson, the couple had rallied together to save Simon's investment. She couldn't see them behind any of the week's events, including murder.

"Nora, you make a wonderful Elvira." Lydia opened the door wider. "Rupert, look how Fiona's worked her magic."

Rupert came to the door and inspected Nora. "Damn good job. You'll be the star tonight, Nora."

She felt her color rise. "Nonsense. But thanks for staying to see this through for Simon. It's important to him and to the lodge."

Lydia smiled. "We'll soon be able to go home. And thanks for checking, dear, but we're fine. Just finishing a sandwich before I put my lipstick on. Not long to your debut."

Lydia closed the door, and Nora walked to Grayson's room but hesitated. She couldn't think of a good excuse to knock on his door and didn't want to incur his wrath if he was getting into character just before the play started.

Nora felt butterflies in her stomach kick in hard. In minutes she was really going to be Elvira again but had no evidence yet firmly establishing Gemma's killer. Was it vanity that had pushed her into this role? She knew her desire to help Simon was real. Then she realized she also felt a need to show Declan she could be a good partner to his work. She just hoped it didn't backfire in some horrible way, because she didn't feel one step closer to actually proving who was responsible for Gemma's death. She needed a plan to get Grayson to confess.

Then she remembered her last full line before her final exit: "There's something I want to say before I go." And Nora decided in that instant to add: "I know you killed Gemma" and watch while Grayson Lange lost it in front of everyone.

6:10 PM

Declan had to find Grayson Lange before the play began. To his surprise, the man appeared at the bottom of the stairs when Declan started to look for him. He was made up for the play and wore a dressing gown, his cast hanging out of one sleeve.

"Saved me a trip upstairs. We need to talk." Declan pointed to the empty library.

"Can't it wait? Those cackling women have given me a headache, and I've come down to see if Simon has any paracetamol."

Declan guided him into the library. "No stronger painkillers for you?"

Grayson sat down in a wing chair. "Too much going on. Can't take the chance of spacing out." He rested his cast on the arm of a chair. "But you can jolly well believe I'll take some the minute the punters leave."

"I'll get you some paracetamol after we talk." Declan plunged in. "I've had a report after enquiries around Chiswick. Are you familiar with The Jag Workshop on the Mall in Ealing?" He watched the man's reaction.

"What if I am? Surely it isn't illegal to have repairs made to my car." The director's bluster came accompanied by rolling eyes and a shake of the head.

Declan consulted his notebook. "Last November, you had the Jag in for bodywork on the front, left bumper a few days after your visit to Bowness. Care to tell me what happened?"

CHAPTER THIRTY-THREE

"It was all a mistake, a horrible mistake."
Charles: Act 1, Scene 2

7:25 PM

Nora paced the patio, waiting for her entrance cue. She'd thrown her coat over her shoulders and tried to tamp down her racing heartbeat. She could do this. The air crackled with excitement from the audience and nervous energy from the actors. Only the Dentons appeared composed and regal as the play commenced.

Nora had watched from the patio as the audience filled with people she recognized, carrying programs and chatting with anticipation as they took their seats. Callie sat with her brother and parents; Agnes wore a stylish spectator hat with a feather and took a seat next to Simon and Maeve. She could see Daisy in a row near the back with the large man who cooked at The Scarlet Wench. The pathologist, Dr. Foreman, was accompanied by a delicate woman Nora took to be his wife. Declan took his seat, followed by Higgins and a woman she assumed was the sergeant's wife. There were no empty seats by the time Grayson started his welcome. He made a brief announcement that the role of Elvira would be played by Nora Tierney, to the rustling of programs and many surprised faces. When he noted the performance was dedicated to the memory of Gemma Hartwell, Nora watched people flip through their programs, but for many, the news wasn't that an actress they'd never heard of wasn't available but that someone they knew from town was taking part in the play. Nora thought Simon would be grateful that the report of Gemma's murder must not have hit the evening news before this crowd arrived.

At the far end of the patio, Burt Marsh had set up a laptop on a table next to the winch to follow the action. He must have a camera mounted on the back wall, as the scene on his screen matched the audiences' view when she looked over his shoulder. Other equipment allowed him to follow the script and work his magic on cue.

Nora could hear Act I progress through his laptop, even with its volume turned low. She tried to stay focused, but her thoughts kept wandering to how closely the events of the past week were tied to this play. The fall, the cut brakes lines, the death of Condomine's second wife when it should have been Condomine himself—there were too many incidents related to the play for it not to be the focus.

Nora kept one eye on Burt's monitor as her mind raced. The man was focused on his work, one finger following the script, the other hand readying different controls. She'd been so certain it was Grayson who was responsible, but suddenly she saw that if Estelle Marsh's hit-and-run accident was the center of everything, no one had suffered a greater loss than the man sitting in front of her. She recalled his prostrate form in St Martin's graveyard, his howls of grief.

The Dentons, Grayson and Fiona sat at the table during the first séance scene as Helen ran across the room to the light switch. The lights were to dim slightly, and Nora watched Burt slide a dimmer switch to match Helen's actions perfectly. Helen took her seat and intoned: "Is there anyone there?"

In the play, Grayson and Poppy would be victims of a fall. And Fiona would die by taking the car with the cut brake lines and would join Nora's ghost in Act III. Nora thought of Daisy talking to her at The Scarlet Wench about Grayson's first visit to Bowness: "He had too much to drink that night, too."

The realization hit Nora like a thunderbolt. Grayson hadn't

been driving the night Estelle Marsh died. Gemma had. And Burt had been asleep upstairs the night she'd died.

Nora shivered, despite her warm coat. Could Burt be responsible for everything that had happened? She'd have to get to Declan if she could and tell him her new theory.

Fiona, as Ruth, was admonishing Grayson for his flippancy as the séance progressed. "Charles, how can you be so idiotic? You'll spoil everything."

"Won't be long now," Burt muttered.

Nora thought Burt referred to her entrance, still two pages away. Burt's hand was shaking the monitor; then Nora realized that what she was seeing was the chandelier shaking as his hand gripped the line by the winch. She tiptoed away from Burt to the French doors and cracked them slightly. The director would hit the roof if he noticed her peeking, but he and Fiona faced the audience, and his back was to her.

Her pulse hammered in her throat. The chandelier hung suspended directly over the table where Grayson sat with Fiona, Helen and the Dentons. The sharp glass prisms swayed slightly, reflected in the light. Then Nora noticed something that made the hair stand up on the back of her neck, and she knew her suspicion was accurate. The table's position had been moved, not enough to be noticeable at first, but just enough so that Grayson and Fiona sat directly under the weight of the large chandelier. If the crystals came down early, everyone seated at that table might be hurt. But if the chandelier itself came down, Grayson and Fiona could die. What better way for Burt to be certain he'd evened the score with Grayson Lange? Nora's skin crawled, and she broke out in a cold sweat. Could she be mistaken? Could this gentle old man have coordinated everything that had happened in revenge for his wife's death?

Nora kept her eye on the crack, trying to direct her thoughts to Declan. Please look up, she prayed. She tried to remain calm and couldn't look at Burt. She knew if she did, her face would betray her thinking. How could she warn the others and get them away from the table in time?

Lydia was speaking: "How disappointing; just as we were getting on so nicely."

How ironic, Nora thought fleetingly. This line was Helen's cue to stand and move away toward the phonograph. In a moment it should start to play the song "Always."

Across the patio, instead of pulling the props board toward him to ready the start of the recording, Burt reached for the line to the winch. He seemed to have forgotten her presence, and she knew she was too slight to overpower him.

Nora made her decision. Time slowed to a crawl.

Heart ready to burst out of her throat, she pulled the French doors open two pages before her entrance was due and stood in the doorway.

The audience gasped at her appearance. The Dentons and Helen frowned at her early entrance, as she frantically looked at Declan, who stared back at her. Even *he* knew she shouldn't be there yet. Nora quickly pointed up to the ceiling and out to the patio. "*Please, get there in time. I can't tackle the man alone*," she telegraphed to him.

Nora saw him lean over and whisper to Higgins. The two men stood to work their way down the row of seats. She turned to see Burt getting ready to release the dog on the winch, a glazed expression on his face.

Too late, not enough time for Higgins or Declan to stop Burt.

Nora rushed onto the stage, yelling "Get away!" Everyone at the table stood as she launched herself at the table, pushing Grayson and Fiona off to each side. The Dentons jumped back as Nora's momentum knocked the table over and the chandelier came crashing down, sending its prisms scattering like daggers.

7:45 PM

Declan reached the end of the row when Nora hurled herself at the table and the fixture crashed down. Pandemonium broke out, the audience standing, some yelling, others rushing to leave. Simon took a post at the door to calm them and started to shepherd people into the empty library with Maeve's assistance.

Declan ran to Nora, lying awkwardly under the overturned table. It had protected her head and back, but one of her legs was pinned between two arms of the chandelier. He knelt beside her and lifted the table but stopped her from getting up. One of the prisms had cut her calf, and he used his handkerchief to stop the blood flow. "You all right?"

"It's Burt," Nora said, tears streaming down her face. Whether she cried in pain or relief, he couldn't tell, but at least she was conscious and talking to him.

"Want me to take a look at that?" It was Milo Foreman.

Declan nodded, and the large man knelt and helped him gently lift the heavy chandelier off Nora's leg.

Milo inspected Nora's wound while asking her a few questions about her head. "Just sit here a moment."

The cast stood around the stage in shock. Fiona roused herself, and Poppy helped Grayson to his feet.

There was a crash from the patio, and a moment later Higgins frog-marched Burt Marsh into the room, hands cuffed behind his back. "Got him trying to run from the patio." He stooped in front of a chair, thrust Burt into it and stood guard over him. "I've called for back up."

Agnes appeared onstage with a broom and shovel, still wearing her feathery spectator. "I'll sweep these shards to one side so no one else gets hurt."

Rupert had his arm around Lydia and assured Declan they were both all right. "That was very brave of Nora."

"I agree." Declan turned to the others. "Everyone take a seat, please."

Helen and Poppy sat on the sofa with Fiona between them. Declan righted the overturned chairs, and the others took seats onstage.

Agnes closed the doors to the drawing room just as Simon slipped inside. "Maeve is having everyone leave names and addresses before they leave. No one else was hurt by the flying glass." He looked relieved. "Maeve will stay with Mrs. Foreman and Mrs. Higgins."

"Good thinking, Simon." Declan turned to Nora and Milo.

"No stitches required, more of a minor puncture wound." The pathologist looked to Simon. "If you have a first-aid kit, I'll clean and dress it. With a bit of ice for the bruising on either side of her leg, too."

Agnes left to get what Milo had asked for, and Declan helped Nora stand and limp to a chair. Declan strode over to Burt and stood looking down at him. "Just what the hell were you trying to do?"

Burt looked around in confusion. "It wasn't supposed to go this way." The man looked at Nora, his eyes wild.

"I saw your grief in the graveyard, Burt. I thought it was Grayson, but Gemma was driving when Estelle was hit, wasn't she?" Nora shook her head. "That's why she had to die."

"I never wanted to hurt anyone." Burt moaned. "I missed Estelle so much." He glared at Grayson. "You drove over my beautiful wife and left her to die. I didn't know who was driving. I wanted them all to die." His voice rose in hysteria. "You're a bunch of bloody murderers!" Tears streamed down his face. "If it wasn't Lange, it was that whore of his. I couldn't let either of them get away with it."

Fiona suddenly jerked upright to her feet. She screeched: "You killed the wrong driver! *I drove that night*—" She looked around at the shocked faces and seemed to deflate. "But it was an accident." She sank back down to the sofa, her voice reduced to a whisper. "I'm sorry, so sorry."

Helen looked shocked, and Poppy sucked in a breath and moved away from Fiona.

"What?" Burt's confusion increased. He looked wildly about him at the others.

Grayson Lange dropped his head in his hands. "Oh, Fi … "

Chapter Thirty-Four

"I'm beginning to understand."
Madame Arcati: Act III, Scene 2

8:23 PM

Nora sat in the dining room at one end of the long table with the remaining cast members. She was enveloped in a blanket with her leg propped up on a chair and an ice pack wrapped around her calf. If she weren't feeling the pain in her leg, she might be in a dream. Her eyes were heavy, and her limbs felt shaky. Maeve brought in the tea and cookies that were to be for after the performance and left the tray on the sideboard. They were untouched by the cast members, who sat in silence.

Maeve had helped Nora out of her costume and into a loose pair of yoga pants and a soft top. Nora had tried to scrub off the sticky face paint and had run a brush through her hair with hands that trembled. Hopeless. A shower would have to wait until she gave her statement to DS Higgins.

"You're probably in shock." Maeve touched Nora's shoulder. "Have a few sips of this." She brought Nora a mug of hot, sugary tea.

The audience had been allowed to leave, and the Foremans offered Mrs. Higgins a lift home. Callie drove Agnes home after she'd hugged Nora and promised to make her a special breakfast. Kendal police swarmed the drawing room and patio, taking photographs of the crime scene.

It was Helen who spoke first. "I'm stunned." Her admission gave everyone permission to talk.

"I still can't believe it." Poppy's makeup was rubbed off in places. "Gemma dead by that horrid man, and she wasn't the one who killed his wife."

Helen shook her head. "Fiona should have stopped the car the minute she knew she hit something."

"It was dark, and she thought it was a dog." Poppy's eyes were huge as she stood up for Fiona. "I heard her tell Declan and that other detective. Gray told her not to stop, so he's just as much to blame." She glared at Helen, daring her to disagree.

Lydia sighed. "I'll be happy to leave here."

Rupert pushed his chair back and poured his wife a cup of tea. "We can leave in the morning." He stopped by Nora's chair. "I told Declan and I'll tell you: You were very brave. You saved Fiona and Grayson."

"I had to do something when I saw Burt was going to release that lever." Nora gave him a wan smile. "Honestly, I was terrified." He patted her shoulder and sat back down. "Still, I found the sight of Burt Marsh being carted off in handcuffs painful."

Simon entered and heard her remark. "You're soft, Nora. Higgins had no compunctions about bundling a handcuffed Fiona with Grayson into the back of a police car."

"It was like a circus for a while." Maeve stood by Simon, and he put his arm around her shoulder.

Nora couldn't help but wonder what this would do to business at Ramsey Lodge. Everyone's ticket money for both performances would have to be refunded, a tedious process at best. She hoped Grayson wouldn't try to wrangle out of his share of the mess.

Declan arrived in the doorway. "Ready to give your statement?"

Nora nodded and carried her ice bag.

"Higgins is out with the CSIs, be here in a moment. No need for you to go to Kendal." He helped her limp into the library where Higgins would take her statement. "Very painful?"

"Just by the cut and sore along the sides." She sat down and propped her leg on an ottoman.

"Milo said you'll have bruises on the leg, and it will feel stiff tomorrow, so be prepared for that." Lights outside bounced off the ceiling, and Declan moved to the window and pulled the curtain aside. "Crime scene van arriving. Higgins has a uniformed guard by a barricade blocking entry to the driveway." News vans pulled up along the quay, and cameramen rushed toward the new arrivals, trying to get a picture of the occupants.

"Vultures." Nora yawned. As the adrenaline rush had left, so had her energy, but at least the trembling had stopped. "And yes, I know I used to be one of them." Now that they were alone, she waited for him to tell her how stupid she'd been.

"Sorry you were hurt." Declan stayed by the window.

Nora was learning from Declan that sometimes silence was best.

He finally turned to look at her; she saw him swallow hard before he spoke again. "You could have been killed."

"I had to do something." She tried lightness and diversion. "Mental telepathy to you didn't work. What will happen to Fiona?"

"If she sticks to her story, it's still reckless endangerment, a death by dangerous driving. She didn't stop to report it as she should have, and that's its own offence. Under the Road Traffic Act, even if she hit a dog she should have reported that within twenty-four hours. She insists she wasn't drunk, that she stayed sober to let Gemma and Grayson get hammered, and there aren't blood alcohol levels to contradict her." He twisted his mouth. "That's what she did the night we saw them at The Scarlet Wench, so she might be telling the truth." Declan exhaled. "She's facing six months to two years, but her clean record and a good solicitor will help. A minimum of a heavy fine, and she'll lose her license for quite a while. Don't expect they'll keep her on remand; she's being cooperative."

"And Grayson? Will he walk away from this?"

"I expect he'll say he was too out of it to remember anything. The car's been repaired so there's little for forensics to find, but they'll impound it anyway and give it a look. If either of them did know she'd hit a person, it's a wonder they would come here again. That may actually work in their favor—at least if I were a solicitor, that's the tack I'd take."

Nora thought of Fiona's behavior all week. "She became more and more upset about staying here, but I thought that was due to Gemma's death. Maybe talk of Burt's wife made her realize what she'd done. I'm not the only one who could Google Estelle's accident."

"And she'd have seen that her little bump knocked a woman to the kerb, where the brain injury caused her death. We may never know the truth of what happened that night." Declan moved from the window to sit on the arm of Nora's chair. "Once you've given your statement, I'm going to have to go to Kendal for a while with Higgins."

"I know. All part of the job." Nora allowed herself a wry smile. "Some acting debut."

"I doubt many people who saw it will forget it any time soon." He smiled down at her. "You were right. Your knowledge of the theatre and this play led to the killer. And if you hadn't been backstage to see Burt—I can't imagine the carnage."

Nora shook her head. "I can't imagine what's going through Burt's mind tonight, knowing he killed the wrong person."

"He said he couldn't tell who was driving when he saw the car drive away after Estelle was hit. That's what made him cut the brake cables on the Jaguar when he saw it parked in the lot here and recognized it. He assumed Grayson was driving. Then he thought he'd sussed out it was Gemma behind the wheel when he heard her say she'd driven his car before." Declan looked at her hard when she moved her leg and winced. "Hurting more?"

"The ice helps." She pointed to the bag lying in her lap.

"I've found it works better if you apply it directly to the affected part." He kept his face neutral.

"Smart-ass. I knew there was a reason I liked having you around." Nora reapplied the ice pack. "It's your common sense."

"I don't think I've ever been called a smart ass before."

"You have to say it all in one word: smart-ass."

"I'll keep that in mind the next time I want to use it." Declan's hand reached out and stroked her cheek.

Nora leaned into his touch. "I'm glad you were there tonight."

She saw the hint of a smile play around his lips. "Someone has to protect you from yourself."

11:25 PM

Simon left the hall light on for Declan's return. He paused in the doorway to the drawing room. Crime scene tape spread across the opening, and he could see more flutter in the breeze on the patio. In the daylight, it would be visible to anyone on the quay, a stark reminder of all that had gone on this week at Ramsey Lodge.

His hopes had been so high at the beginning of the week. He felt as if he'd been on a roller coaster these past weeks: the rush up to Kate's wedding, the troupe arriving soon after, hiding their financial straits from Kate at what was supposed to be the happiest time of her life. It wasn't an irretrievable situation—yet. But the play would have shored up their reserves and taken off the pressure.

Tomorrow, when he could think straight, he'd pull out the contract with Grayson Lange. There was a clause he'd insisted on in case the play had to be cancelled. The fees for the rooms would be paid. The ticket money would be refunded, and he had to see the language for handling that. His half of the prop rental was lost, but he had to hope Grayson would be in a position to pay up his half—unless the man was sitting in jail. Once the drawing room was released, he'd have to repack the props and arrange for them to be taken away early.

"Here you are." Maeve joined him in the doorway and took his hand. "Sad scene, isn't it?"

"What a mess." He shook his head. "I was just thinking of all the things I need to attend to in the next few days"

She put a finger to his lips. "Don't think of that tonight. Get some rest, and we'll tackle a list tomorrow when we're fresh."

"I'll need help getting all this stuff packed up—"

"And we'll get it done. We can have Callie's brother down for a day to help once you get a schedule." She put her arm around his waist. "I saw the cordon the police put up at the end of the drive."

"Should keep the news vans at bay for the moment." He wrapped an arm over her shoulder. "This may be the end of Ramsey Lodge."

"You can't know that, Simon. You have to see how it all shakes out. The notoriety may bring people out."

"Still, I'm closing the lodge until Kate gets home."

Maeve stood away from the circle of his arms. "That's fine. Let the dust settle. But you'll bounce back, Si."

"Right now, I'm not sure I want that to happen." He meant it, too. This week, he'd had his fill of Ramsey Lodge.

Maeve tilted her head to one side. "Look, you've had a lot of changes in the last six months: Nora moving toward Declan, us getting together, Kate getting married and now this mess—" She gestured toward the darkened drawing room.

"My point exactly."

She waved him off. "*My* point is that change can be good, but change takes getting used to—you need to find your new normal. You can use this notoriety to bring people into the lodge. Nora said a choral group is already booked for June. I can see classy evening concerts with string quartets next."

Simon drew her into a brief hug. "You're right. I'm unsettled tonight. Things will feel better when these people leave tomorrow." He turned her toward his room. "But I'm still not looking forward to explaining it all to Kate."

11:58 PM

Declan swung his car into the head of the lodge's driveway, and Grayson got out to move the barricade, easily done with one hand. The guard and news vans had dispersed, but just the same, Declan told him to replace the barrier once he'd driven through. He stopped at the front door, and Grayson got out and pushed his seat forward. Fiona struggled out of the narrow backseat and walked stiffly ahead of him into the lodge.

Grayson hesitated and bent down. "Thanks, old man. You've been better than either of us probably deserve."

"The law's the law for everyone; I just enforce it. But you'd both better find damn good solicitors."

Grayson nodded and moved off into the lodge. Declan continued up the drive and parked.

At the station, he'd reviewed the medical file on Estelle Marsh's accident. If she hadn't hit her head on the stone kerb, she might have survived with a badly bruised hip, and none of the events of this last week would have been put in motion. Burt

Marsh had withdrawn into himself after admitting to being behind all the accidents and pranks except the generator. He sat curled into a corner of the cell at the station while the others were interviewed. Declan didn't envy Higgins trying to get his statement in the morning.

He stopped at the garden trellis. The lights were out, and he hoped Nora had taken a good, hot shower. He stood for a moment and drew in a deep breath of the cool night air, filled with hints of sweet spring fragrances. Springtime spoke of renewal and rebirth, yet these past days his thoughts had centered around death once again. His optimism for the future just a few days ago felt very far away tonight.

Declan walked into the lodge, closed the door quietly behind him and bolted it. When he turned around, Nora stood in the doorway of the dining room. She wore her blue robe, and her damp hair fell across her shoulders. In the light from the desk, he saw her hold her arms out to him. He rushed to her and wrapped her up in an embrace as she laid her head against his chest. All of the anxiety he'd felt left him. She sighed deeply, then looked up at him, and he bent down and kissed her with a fierceness that surprised them both. Suddenly the future opened up before him again, bright and beckoning.

Chapter Thirty-Five

"Love is a strong psychic force, Mr. Condomine.
It can work untold miracles."
Madame Arcati: Act III, Scene 2

Sunday, 15th April

11:55 AM

Nora opened the lodge door and peeked out. The news vans had not returned. Declan had left for Kendal to sit in on the interview with Burt Marsh. By 9 AM, the police had taken the cordon away and released the drawing room.

She inhaled a deep, cleansing breath and mentally crossed her fingers for Ramsey Lodge's survival. Val had been shocked when she called to hear how Nora's acting debut had turned out. She reassured Nora that Sean was fine and commiserated with her over her minor injury. More than ever, Nora knew she was fortunate to have friends who loved her and cared for her.

"How did Declan take the whole thing?"

"Remarkably well, considering." His voice echoed in her mind: *You could have been killed*. She was doing her best to ignore her sore leg. "He even admitted I was useful and saved more people from being hurt."

"Proves my point, though, Yankee."

"Which point would that be?"

"That you're cut out to be a partner to someone like Declan more than you ever were for Paul."

Bringing up Paul's name had Nora describing her conversation with the Pembrokes.

"Muriel actually apologized?" Val sounded incredulous.

"And Harvey agreed it was far from her usual behavior."

"So you're on a first-name basis now?"

"It was one call, Val. Let's see what this solicitor has up his sleeve tomorrow."

As Val rang off, laughter from the drawing room brought a sense of normalcy to the pretty spring day. Callie and her brother were starting to wrap the props, and their gaiety was a start at crowding out the recent horrors.

Two taxis drew up and honked. The first driver rolled down his window and called out: "Lange?"

"You can turn around there." Nora pointed to the parking lot, and the driver moved off, the second taxi following.

Simon rolled two large suitcases down the pathway, followed by Fiona dragging another and carrying her huge leather bag. The actress hadn't bothered to hide the dark circles under eyes that spoke of a sleepless night. Nora almost felt sorry for her. Almost. She watched Fiona struggle under the weight of her makeup case before turning to go into the lodge to assist the others checking out.

"I'll help," Maeve volunteered. She and Nora walked to the stack of luggage at the bottom of the stairs. Piled on top was Poppy's sewing machine. Several trips later, piles of luggage stood at the end of the path, and the taxis were lined up and waiting. Fiona sat slumped in the backseat of the first one, eyes closed.

Helen came downstairs, trailed by Poppy. Grayson followed Poppy, arguing all the way. "But Poppet, you said you'd take care of me."

Poppy reached the bottom of the stairs and turned to him. "Grow up and get over it. I've changed my mind." She waved a finger in his face. "And don't call me Poppet again. My name is Poppy."

Helen waved goodbye to Nora and Maeve and wiggled her

fingers to Simon. "Come along, Grayson." She swept out of the lodge in a cloud of musky perfume.

Grayson moved off and passed Nora. "I can't say it's been much fun, Nora."

"As Judy Holliday said in *Born Yesterday*, 'Likewise, I'm sure.'" Beside her, Maeve giggled.

Grayson threw them a dirty look and moved off stiffly. At the taxi, his mother pointed to the front seat. He sat with the driver, and Helen slid into the back beside Fiona. The first taxi roared off.

The Dentons arrived, and shook hands with Simon. Lydia stuffed a handful of Ramsey Lodge brochures into her purse. "For our friends, Simon. You run a wonderful place when it's not inhabited by the likes of us." She stopped to give Nora a hug. "Enjoy that baby; he's precious."

"I know, Lydia," Nora assured her. She was surprised when Rupert turned to Poppy, waiting at the door.

"All right, Poppy?" He ushered the two women to the second taxi, helped Lydia in and then Poppy, who sat wedged between them, a huge smile on her face.

"I'm relieved to see them go." Simon stood beside the two women. "Looks like Poppy's been adopted."

"A rat deserts a sinking ship, and Grayson's has already sunk." Maeve was in rare form.

Nora had another view. "The Dentons are a much better alliance for her than Grayson Lange could ever be."

"End of a chapter. Props to wrap." Simon moved off with Maeve.

Nora lingered in the doorway. Sunny daffodils that had braved the flood waved in a faint breeze. She felt a trill of excitement mixed with nervousness for the future.

She felt closer to Declan than ever, but what if she drove him crazy? There were so many unknowns when what she most wanted to feel was—serene, yes, that's the word she searched for. Joyful, too, was part of what she longed for when she thought of being with Declan. She'd seen flashes of that joy already in their intimacy, in his acceptance of Sean. But she knew she couldn't control all the events of her life. Real life was raw and gritty, sometimes filled with indecision, hurt and pain that balanced its sweetness.

She walked a few steps down the drive and looked at the lake and at the host of white sails that tacked back and forth across it. The steamer left on its ride to Ambleside. The white and green shops along the quay were open and drew a brisk business on this sunny spring weekend after the flooding.

Nora felt surrounded by nature. A ring of mauve around the edges of cottony clouds tempered the clear blue of the water and the sky. She knew with certainty that her stay at this lovely place would soon draw to its close.

In the distance, the horizon shimmered, an antique-penny-postcard kind of view. As Nora turned back to the lodge to help the others pack up the props, she remembered a line from Thomas Gray's poem: "And all the air a solemn stillness holds … "

The poem was "Elegy Written in a Country Churchyard," and Nora had a sudden vision of Burt Marsh lying grief stricken under the ancient yew tree. His loneliness had driven him to horrendous acts. To thrive in this life, we need to feel connected, whether it is to a partner or a child, a relative or even a good friend. We need others to share our journey, to enrich our lives. It kept the loneliness at bay. It kept us from committing unspeakable acts.

5:15 PM

Nora emptied the dishwasher in the lodge kitchen and ruminated on her meeting tomorrow with the solicitor while Simon drew on graph paper. Agnes had gone home after lunch and would have a few days off. Maeve had left to take Callie and her brother home after a productive day. Best of all, Declan was on his way back from Kendal.

The rental company would arrive in the morning. All of the props were packed against the walls, except the chandelier and its parts that were in police custody. The risers were undone, and the chairs stacked. With the younger helpers gone, the lodge seemed quiet and almost peaceful.

"Nora, take a look at this." Simon pushed his pad toward her, and she dried her hands on a towel. "It's a new seating plan for the drawing room, incorporating a few pieces Kate found and is shipping back."

Nora scrutinized the plan that had conversational groupings and allowed for the inclusion of a new sideboard and several new chairs. She knew Kate had phoned, and Simon had spent a long time out on the patio, talking to her. She'd seen his arms gesticulating while he'd explained the events of the previous week. "It looks great. More seating with a lakeside view now." She folded her towel. "How did Kate take the news?"

Simon pulled the pad back toward him. "Amazingly well. Agreed with me about closing until she gets back, didn't blink an eye. She said the drawing room needed remodeling, and we'd wipe out any traces in people's memory of the aborted performance." He shook his head. "She seemed almost excited to have a decorating project."

Nora laughed. "It's what she does best. Good for her and good for you, too."

He brushed his hair off his forehead. “Last night, I almost wanted this damn place to stay closed, but now, with a break and a new look—”

The back door opened, and Darby scampered in, followed by Maeve carrying a loaded basket. The terrier leapt at Nora and Simon until he tired of their petting and trotted to his bed by the stove to plunk himself down with a satisfied sigh.

“He’s happy to be home.” Nora smiled but at the same time felt a pang, missing Sean. Would he have noticed she wasn’t around? She couldn’t wait until Tuesday to drive to Oxford with Declan to pick him up. They’d stay in Oxford for a few days, and Val would drive her back at the weekend. She could handle a few days away herself, and with Declan in Oxford, it would be interesting to see the town from his perspective.

Maeve unpacked loaves of crusty bread, cheeses and mixed olives. “There’s plenty for four, so forage later, Nora. Simon and I are having a picnic in his room.” She held up several bottles of pinot noir. “I’ll leave you one of these, too.”

Simon looked up. “We are?”

Maeve had a mischievous glint to her smile. “We most certainly are.”

Nora laughed at Maeve’s expression. “Thanks, but Declan said something about dining alfresco on the heated roof terrace of Porto Restaurant.”

“Suit yourselves.” Maeve beckoned Simon. “Show me your plans.” She gathered half the supplies, and Simon picked up the wine and his pad and followed her out.

Minutes later, Nora luxuriated in the shower, taking her time. She primped and dried the moistness out of her hair, then piled it on top of her head, curls spilling down. She scrutinized her reflection. She hoped it looked artfully messy.

The bathroom mirror kept steaming up, and she cracked her

bedroom door to clear it faster. Wrapped in her robe, she opened the armoire that held her clothes, brought out the teal silk dress she'd been saving and hung it on the door. The salesgirl had promised it brought out the green in her eyes. Now which shoes … ?

"I like what you're wearing better." Declan leaned against the doorjamb.

Nora whirled around. "I didn't hear you come in."

In an instant, he was next to her and gathered her up in his arms. He kissed her neck, and she reached up to pull his head down for a real kiss. The ring of her mobile sang, and she sagged against him and groaned.

"Better answer it." Declan's voice was husky. He closed the bedroom door with his foot.

Nora picked up her phone from the night table. Val. She croaked a hello.

"Just wanted you to know my godson is an absolute delight and there's no need for you to rush here on Tuesday. We're having friends in tonight … "

Nora listened to Val's plans and how everyone fussed over Sean. Declan slid the robe from her shoulders; it fell in a puddle at her feet. He left a trail of kisses up and down her exposed neck. She shivered and pressed back into him.

"Have fun, then, tonight." Nora bit back a gasp as Declan's hands encircled her breasts. "I'll call you after the solicitor leaves, all right?"

"Sure. Tell Declan I said hello and he's welcome." Val rang off with a throaty laugh.

"She's a witch, I swear." Nora turned to face him. "Are we going to make that dinner reservation?"

"I certainly hope not." He grinned and lifted her onto the bed. "There's always tomorrow."

CHAPTER THIRTY-SIX

"Think kindly of me, and send out good thoughts."
Charles: Act III, Scene 2

Monday, 16th April

11:42 AM

Declan roared off to Kendal for the last time, watching his speed but letting the MGB out when he could, enjoying the throaty purr of the engine. Today the sky was an impossible shade of blue he'd never noticed before. And those clouds had to be the whitest and puffiest he'd ever seen. A few reports to look over and sign off on, and he would be back with Nora by this afternoon. Depending on the length of her meeting with the solicitor, they might have time to drive to Brantwood, Ruskin's house by Coniston Water. There was that silk dress and the dinner he'd promised her they'd never made it to last night—and after that, they still had another night alone ahead of them.

Last night, his muscles had felt as tight as piano wire. His blood had sung in his veins as he and Nora had explored each other and given of themselves, all reticence gone as they became more comfortable together. It had felt like a huge wave engulfed them, sucking them down into the undertow, only to throw them up high against the sand, gasping for breath.

They'd dozed and then surfaced after midnight when they couldn't ignore their empty stomachs any longer. Nora had gathered a tray of Maeve's olives and cheeses while he'd taken bread, two glasses and a bottle of wine back to her room.

He shook his head as he slowed for a lorry to turn off. Talk about nights to remember. He turned on the radio, and when

Joe Cocker came on singing "You Can Leave Your Hat On," he turned the radio up loud and opened the windows to feel the wind in his face.

1:48 PM

Nora waved to Maeve and Simon, who were heading for a walk around the bay with Darby on leash. They'd used the sunny day as an excuse, but she suspected they'd timed their stroll to give her privacy with the solicitor. As she paced the length of the patio, she wished Declan were with her. The furniture was back in place, and she could almost make herself believe Saturday night was a fantasy. She sat down and traced the condensation on the pitcher of lemonade she'd brought out.

She'd looked up "Declan" online after he'd left for Kendal and found it meant "full of goodness." Nora would tease him about that tonight, but it suited him. Her writer's nature tried to put words to last night. Certainly she'd felt adored, and the world they'd created between them felt fresh. There had been laughter, too, and a sense of easiness. She'd woken this morning feeling peaceful and—dare she think it—serene.

Her mood contrasted sharply with how things had been with Paul, when there had been flashes of happiness that weren't sustained. She wouldn't dwell on that now. If she hadn't been with Paul, there would be no Sean, and she knew if Paul were here, she would tell him she would always be grateful to him for her son.

A sleek, grey sedan turned into the drive. Sunlight glinted off the winged **B** on its bonnet as the majestic Bentley drove into the parking lot. A pricey solicitor, then. Nora walked through the drawing room and stood at the door, her stomach roiling.

A middle-aged man came around the corner, carrying a black briefcase in the same soft leather as his shoes. Wire-rimmed glasses gave him a studious look. Despite the long drive, Kemp's bespoke, navy-pinstripe suit looked fresh. A deep-blue shirt with crisp white collar and cuffs brought out the light-blue eyes Nora could distinguish as he approached her and held out his hand. She'd bet anything his cuffs were monogrammed.

"Daniel Kemp, Miss Tierney. Good to meet you." His handshake was firm and businesslike. He stepped into the lodge and took a moment to admire the original wainscoting and period details.

"I thought we'd sit outside if that's all right." Nora led him through the drawing room and onto the patio. If he wondered about the haphazard furniture piled into corners and the stacks of chairs and packed boxes, he kept silent as he followed her outside.

"Can I get you something to drink?" Nora pointed to the lemonade as they took their seats.

"No, thanks. Mrs. Kemp and I started early and had an excellent lunch at Morecambe on the bay." He placed his briefcase on the glass-topped table and snapped it open. "I dropped her off at the Belsfield, as you suggested, and will meet her for tea. Lovely place, thank you for suggesting it." He looked out at the lake vista. "Quite a view here, too. What a beautiful day."

"Yes, it is." She felt her stomach flipping. He must have no idea what had happened at the lodge recently, and she wasn't about to inform him. She watched him pull out a file and a silver fountain pen, which he laid across the folder.

"I had a call from Muriel yesterday, very excited to hear she has a grandson."

Nora nodded woodenly. Would he ever get to the point? She saw his thoughtful expression and waited for him to rebuke her for not getting in touch with the Pembrokes sooner.

"Of course, that changes things on a certain level, but I'm certain Muriel and Harvey will rise to the occasion as needed." He pulled a square cloth from his pocket and removed his glasses, giving them a thorough cleaning and Nora a cheerful smile.

"It does?" Nora found her voice. "Mr. Kemp, perhaps you could explain. I have no idea why you're here."

Kemp replaced his glasses and gave her a look over the rims. "Muriel didn't tell you?"

"Tell me what?"

Kemp opened his folder. "Just like Muriel, making me earn my fee." He chuckled.

Nora's mouth dried up while Kemp ordered his papers to his satisfaction. He finally turned to her.

"I did tell you on the phone that the Pembrokes are settling Paul's estate?"

"Yes, but how does that apply to me?" Nora had the sudden desire to throttle the man.

Kemp pursed his mouth. "You really have no idea, Miss Tierney? Paul never mentioned anything to you?"

Nora shook her head. "I'm lost."

The solicitor slapped the folder closed and explained. "Muriel and Harvey Pembroke own Port Enys, a Grade 1-listed estate on the Cornish coast. As Paul was their only child, your son is his heir, and at some future time will inherit the house and grounds."

Nora's mouth gaped open. And here she'd thought the Pembrokes were sheep farmers. She snapped it shut and sat back in her chair.

"Still, Harvey and Muriel are in rather good shape, so that's far down the road, I expect." He reopened the folder. "In the meantime, my original purpose in coming here is because Paul made you beneficiary of his life insurance policy."

Nora sat forward, eyes widening. "He never told me any of this."

Kemp pulled out a document. "Let's see. The face amount is for one and a half, but taking into account the manner of Paul's tragic death, the double indemnity clause kicks in, so that brings the value to a nice round three."

"Three thousand?" She'd start a college fund for Sean right away.

"Three million." He looked up, and Nora saw him register the shock on her face.

"That's British pounds sterling, not euros, of course."

"But—but that's—" Nora sputtered. "—that has to be over four million U.S. dollars!"

Kemp consulted his notes. "$4,966,890 in dollars, to be exact. At today's rate."

Nora's head swam as her heart hammered in her ears.

He peered at her over his glasses. "Modest, but enough to allow you to set up a trust for your son's school fees and such and still have a nice, tidy sum to live on." He shuffled his papers. "I understand Paul didn't know of your pregnancy at the time of his death."

"Neither did I." The man seriously thought this sum modest? What kind of circles did he run in? It was all too much to take in. Nora took several deep breaths, afraid of passing out.

"Too bad. He might have included a rider for any progeny." Kemp shrugged. "Still, if you put a portion aside for your son in trust and it's properly invested now, you'll find it helpful. But I'm quite sure Harvey and Muriel will be prepared to cover any slack when he comes of university age."

"Mr. Kemp, I'm overwhelmed." Nora wiped nervous sweat from her brow. Her hands were clammy, and her lips tingled. "I wasn't prepared for anything like this."

Kemp jumped up. "Oh dear, sorry to have shocked you." He grabbed a glass and poured her a lemonade. "Sip this. I'm not very good with fainting women." He handed her the glass with a wide smile and patted her back. "You'll adjust, Miss Tierney."

2:35 PM

The papers were signed with Mr. Kemp's silver fountain pen. He left Nora his card and told her he'd be in touch when the funds were released. In the meantime, he suggested she find herself a competent financial planner. She heard words like "Swiss accounts," and he dropped several names, but she couldn't take it all in, and he said he'd put the information in an email for her to review.

Nora sat alone on the patio and contemplated how her life had changed yet again, this time with the flash of a pricey pen.

She wouldn't have to rush out and find work and leave Sean any time soon if she invested correctly. That meant she could raise him and keep working on her children's books. Kate and Ian might want to expand their rooms and use her suite in the near future. She had funds to use for where she wanted to be planted, and she could choose now where that would be.

But it went beyond her situation. There was Sean's future to consider, although as Kemp had said, that was for "down the road." She had legal issues to explore, too. If she decided to move back to America, how would that affect things? Could she use this money to give her security without letting it change her? She couldn't wrap her mind around the fact that in a few months' time, by most people's reckoning, she'd be wealthy.

The unreal feeling passed, but she had so many things to decide in the upcoming weeks and months. She didn't want this windfall to change how people viewed her, either. What would her friends think? How would her American family feel?

Declan's MGB roared up the driveway, and Nora stood, relieved to have him back. Then she had a different thought: How would he react to this news? Would he view her differently? She'd best wait to digest this all for herself, take time to let it sink in and see how she was going to handle it.

Nora met Declan in the hallway, and he swooped her into his arms and raised her off her feet, just the way Grayson Lange had done a week earlier.

"How's my girl?" His face lit with his smile creasing the corner of his eyes.

Nora liked being called his girl. She hugged him tightly.

He put her down. "How was the solicitor?"

"Interesting. Very nice." The next words just fell from her mouth. "Apparently I'm to have money from Paul's estate."

"Wonderful! That should take the pressure off you." Declan drew her to him. "How about that drive I promised you?"

"Let me get a jacket and my phone." Nora escaped down the hall before he could see her reddened face.

Why did she lie? All right, she hadn't straight-out lied, but she'd not been honest. She needed to know where this relationship with Declan would lead. She wanted him to love her for herself, not an inheritance. She chided herself for even thinking that. But what if her money became an issue between them? A detective inspector's salary might be livable, but it wouldn't come near her new funds. She argued with herself all the way to her bedroom and back.

Nora felt like a tornado had run over her and flattened her out. Her leg stung and reminded her of the past week; she reeled from Daniel Kemp's news. And she offered a silent prayer to Paul, who had not only left her his child but the means to care for him. He must have loved her more than she'd known. How sad. But how wonderful, too.

It was reasonable to absorb this news before she shared it with anyone else. Nora pushed Daniel Kemp and his shiny pen into a neat compartment. Tonight was for Declan.

"All set?" Declan held her hand as they walked in the sunshine to his car. "Maybe over dinner if you wear that slinky dress I'll convince you to think about moving back to Oxford down the road." He winked at her as he opened her door.

"Maybe." She tried to match his mood. "You never know what I may have up my sleeve."

ACKNOWLEDGMENTS

Ramsey Lodge and The Scarlet Wench Pub as well as all of my characters are pure fiction, but they live in a real and glorious part of Cumbria, on the west coast of England's largest lake, Windermere. The entire county forms the Lake District National Park, and for centuries its beauty has engaged nature lovers, writers, artists, fishermen and boaters. I have tried to describe the lakeside and St Martin's Church in the village of Bowness-on-Windermere, and even Westmorland General Hospital, as accurately as possible. And yes, The World of Beatrix Potter does exist. Just ask Bowness resident Evelyn Blatchley, who told me which flowers would bloom in April. There is a real Helen Mochrie, but she lives in Australia and is a wonderful mum and gran. Any errors are entirely my own.

Despite my familiarity with the area, along with copious notes and photographs, setting a novel in a different country represents a distinct challenge. To that end, I wish to sincerely thank the following:

In the United Kingdom:

Steve Sharpe, retired Cumbrian South Lakes police officer, was my resource for all things Cumbrian, from the weather to policing and where the mortuary is located in Kendal. His help has been invaluable, and I owe him more than a few pints at a real pub one day.

Averil Freeth and Helen Hood read the manuscript in draft and helped plump up all things British, from customs to language. They pointed out which of my Golden Age colloquial expressions were outmoded and gave me correct slang or "Britspeak" to bring me into modern times. Enormous thanks to both sterling ladies.

My mentor, P. D. James, and Joyce McLennan offered me advice, friendship and a lovely afternoon tea.

In the United States:

When a writer lives with a story in her head for almost two years, sometimes explanations don't always make it to the page. Readers with keen eyes and gracious hearts contributed valuable time to read and edit the manuscript. Each also provided thoughtful questions when something didn't make sense, so that (hopefully) everything now does: Jennifer Brecht; Kimberly Graff, MSLIS; Matthew Graff, MSLIS; Arthur Graff; and Lauren Small.

Lisa Reiner gave me crucial information on what Sean would be doing at his age, based on her own young son. Thank you, Lisa. I'll be in touch again soon.

I've been working with four wonderful women in the Screw Iowa! Writing Group for ten years. Our workshops are filled with suggestions, advice and encouragement that keep me engaged and writing: Mariana Damon, Nina Romano, Lauren Small and Melissa Westemeier. Thanks again to Lauren Small for her vision in creating Bridle Path Press and for keeping me in print.

Giordana Segneri shapes each book with her design and is responsible for the wonderful covers and interior art as well expert copyediting and layout. We're a great team, and I'd be lost without her input, especially when we work together on the final product. This is your year, G &J …

Thanks, too, to the readers who give me great feedback on the series and look forward to the next book. You make all the hard work and sleepless nights worthwhile. And I'm grateful to those who help me when I'm on a book tour by feeding me and letting me sleep in their guest rooms: Elissa and George Longo, Dana and Steve Beenstock, Kimberly and Matthew Graff, Barbara and Mike Jancovic, Toni Amato and Michela Croke, Paul Hoffmann, Anne and Rob Jacobs, Robin Casey and Charlie Teague, Gretta Keene and Bill Murray, Laura and Peter Hamilton, and Jeanne Petta.

My family—the Minnesota Graffs, the Schoharie Graffs, the Belhaven Burks and Barbara Jancovic—give me love and encouragement at all times, for which I'm very grateful. This series wouldn't be possible without the support and patience of my husband, Arthur, who takes our dog on long walks to give me time to write; reads my drafts and provides a man's point of view; and puts up with the rollercoaster of deadlines, travel and emotions that is a writer's life.

When I was a little girl, every afternoon my mother and I would sit in a green wing chair where she read from the Childcraft book *Poems of Early Childhood* over and over, until the words became familiar and I learned to read. By the time I started kindergarten, I had read *Storytelling and Other Poems* and was reading the *Folk and Fairy Tales* volume. After that, *Life in Many Lands* took me traveling, and on through fourteen volumes that formed the basis of my young reader's world. Thanks for instilling in me your love of books and reading, Mom. This one's for you.

About the Author

M. K. Graff is the author of the Nora Tierney mystery series, set in the United Kingdom. *The Blue Virgin* introduces Nora, an American writer living in Oxford, a setting inspired by Graff's literature studies at Exeter College. The novel won First Prize as Best British Cozy from Chanticleer Media in 2013. *The Green Remains* follows Nora's move to Cumbria, as does continued murderous activity. Graff has published poetry and creative nonfiction and is also co-author of *Writing in a Changing World*, a primer on writing groups and critique techniques written with the other members of the Screw Iowa! Writers Group. She writes crime book reviews at www.auntiemwrites.com and is managing editor of Bridle Path Press. A member of Sisters in Crime, Graff runs the North Carolina Writers Read program in Belhaven and teaches writing workshops. *The Scarlet Wench* is Graff's third in a series of Nora Tierney mysteries.

CPSIA information can be obtained
at www.ICGtesting.com
Printed in the USA
FFOW05n0501090514